THE TWENTY-FIRST CENTURY ORGANIZATION

THE TWENTY-FIRST CENTURY ORGANIZATION

Analyzing Current Trends — Imagining the Future

Guy Benveniste

Jossey-Bass Publishers · San Francisco

Substantial discounts on bulk quantities of Jossey-Bass books are available to corporations, professional associations, and other organizations. For details and discount information, contact the special sales department at Jossey-Bass Inc., Publishers. (415) 433-1740; Fax (415) 433-0499.

For sales outside the United States, contact Maxwell Macmillan International Publishing Group, 866 Third Avenue, New York, New York 10022.

Manufactured in the United States of America. Nearly all Jossey-Bass books, jackets, and periodicals are printed on recycled paper that contains at least 50 percent recycled waste, including 10 percent postconsumer waste. Many of our materials are also printed with vegetable-based ink; during the printing process these inks emit fewer volatile organic compounds (VOCs) than petroleum-based inks. VOCs contribute to the formation of smog.

Library of Congress Cataloging-in-Publication Data

Benveniste, Guy, date.
    The twenty-first century organization : analyzing current trends. imagining the future / Guy Benveniste.—1st ed.
        p.   cm.—(A joint publication in the Jossey-Bass public administration series and the Jossey-Bass management series)
    Includes bibliographical references and index.
    ISBN 1-55542-626-3 (alk. paper)
    1. Organizational change—Forecasting.   2. Twenty-first century —Forecasts.   I. Title.   II. Series: Jossey-Bass public administration series.   III. Series: Jossey-Bass management series.
    HD58.8.B464   1994
    658—dc20   93-35549
                                                              CIP

FIRST EDITION
HB Printing   10 9 8 7 6 5 4 3 2 1   *Code 9424*

For Karen

*"If Sages Are To Be Heedful Of Their Words,
How Much The More Should Those Who Are Not Sages?"*

TALMUD

Contents

ix

Preface

Imagine the organization of the future: picture The Firm, a large American enterprise in the year 2050. . . .

Every morning, entire families go to The Firm—the children to the nursery or to school; the parents, to work. At lunch they all eat together at one of the many dining facilities provided by The Firm. The CEO of The Firm is a woman who delegates, yet guides, her staff. What matters to her is The Firm's ability to meet client needs, which are ever changing in the global economy of the age. She knows that the success of the organization lies in reducing the queuing time needed to translate ideas into action, so this is one of her primary goals. In The Firm, work spaces can be moved around by instructing a robot, and work teams self-initiate their own activities. Coordination and cooperation exist within The Firm because novel incentives encourage everyone to help one another. Government regulations have been replaced by totally new professional institutions that protect the public or the workers. These institutions are part of The Firm, and the professionals who head them are members of the CEO's own senior staff. When plant closings take place, these professionals help ease the transition. Routine work, such as typing, no longer exists. Instead, personal services, such as massage therapy and gourmet cooking classes, are offered.

This scenario is not a utopian dream; it is drawn from careful analysis of future trends. This book examines the implications of trends that are shaping the way organizations may evolve in the long-term future. Three main issues drive the analysis: the ability of organizations to radically decentralize and still maintain continuity and purpose, the need for organizations to internalize what is now the work of external governmental regulatory agencies, and the creation of new societal arrangements to reduce the cost and pain associated with rapid social and technological transformations.

For discussion purposes, I present fictional accounts of some of the institutions and practices that might be found in a large organization circa 2050. I lean into the distant future to better understand the present and to ask questions about changes we should think about now. The image of the future offered here is based on six major transformations that are already taking place within and around the social invention we call "the organization." Obviously, organizations in 2050 will be affected by far more than these trends, and a reader in 2050 might only be amused by the evident deficiencies of this analysis. But my aim is not to be comprehensive, but rather to present a plausible snapshot of specific future possibilities. My purpose is to challenge the reader to think about the future: to incite policy makers both in the public and private sector to think how America might begin to shape the future of the organization.

Preface

Scope and Treatment

The Twenty-First Century Organization is an unconventional analysis. It is not based on cases that illustrate practices and innovations I have observed in a variety of environments. I deliberately say little about current state-of-the-art management experiments. This book neither forecasts nor prophesies. It explores tangible issues facing the future of the organization: What does it mean to radically decentralize? How do the organization and the overall society handle accelerated rates of change? How do we organize so that we can adapt rapidly? What new social institutions might be needed?

My arguments are mainly sociological, although the sociology of organization does not usually venture into futuristic analysis. This is unfortunate because the sociology of organization has developed a set of concepts—power, authority, rules, positions, roles, and so on—that, taken into the context of future conditions, can be used quite profitably to explore how management may evolve. Social scientists generally write about the known past rather than the future because historical facts allow for rigorous analysis. But well-wrought speculations can lend form to theory. Thus there are good heuristic reasons to engage in this work, as long as its limitations are made clear from the outset.

Background

I know from personal experience that predictions about social change are always precarious. In 1959 I undertook a major futuristic study of the potential impact of nonmilitary scientific developments on U.S. foreign policy. This study was undertaken for the United States Senate Committee on Foreign Relations (Stanford Research Institute, 1959).

At that time we already had much to say about technological advances in food production, energy, materials, synthetics, and communications. We also urged the Senate and the Executive Branch to focus on arms control, the problems of developing countries, and the fostering of international scientific exchanges. The study caused quite a stir at the time, as it suggested that synthetics—including synthetic coffee—could greatly alter world trade. It alluded to the widespread use of poll taking in shaping future political debates, and mentioned the potential use of drugs, such as LSD, in affecting the human mind (p. 76). But the study never mentioned the Organization of Petroleum Exporting Countries (OPEC) nor its impact on world trade and investment, nor did it mention the drug trade and its impact on both producers and consumers of drugs. At the time, the communist totalitarian threat was very much on the minds of many of the individuals we interviewed in preparing the report. We certainly did not foresee the transformation of Eastern Europe or of what was then the USSR.

In short, that study is interesting in the context of 1959, but if rereading it today, we are quickly aware of its limitations. It bears out Schnaar's conclusion in his 1989 study of forecasting: most forecasting is inaccurate. Consequently, this book makes no claims about what will actually happen in 2050. What matters is the here and now. The image of the future that I offer here is designed only to help shape our thinking about the present.

Preface

Six Trends

The six trends that follow form the basis of the image of the future presented here; they are clearly powerful in the present and seem to carry significance for the future.

1. *Worldwide competition for new ideas.* American management practices are already blending with practices emerging from different cultures. As capital, raw materials, and products flow freely across the world, organizations and ideas will matter more than discrete cultural identities. To be sure, cultural differences will remain, and will probably be encouraged, but an overarching management culture will be shared as successful experiences are adopted, whatever their origins. Today we may be impressed by Japanese management or by the ways the Japanese culture has fostered successful economic enterprises bridging government and private sectors. In the future, we Americans will be far more attentive to the ways we organize so that we can reduce the time it takes to convert ideas into action, so that we can continue to be competitive—not by reducing our standard of living, but by having the best ideas, organizations, and social institutions that will permit us to quickly adapt, innovate, and maintain our advantage.

2. *Education of the work force.* As levels of education rise, professionalism and quality of work life become dominant considerations. In fifty years, we will all be "professionals," whether we are doctors, lawyers, engineers, or file clerks—a position that may then be labeled "techno-information retriever." This does not mean everyone will be well educated or that all work will be professional work. On the contrary, much personalized (person-to-person), rou-

tine, low-discretion work will still prevail. But the work force will be different, and people's aspirations will have evolved. Unionization will probably change in important ways as much of the work force finds new sources of power in expertise, differentiated talent, and knowledge, instead of in the massing of sheer numbers. Managing an "expert" work force will require recognition of different human aspirations within a new work culture of professionalism.

3. *Feminization of organizational culture.* As women achieve more equal levels of participation in the workplace, their presence will permanently alter some of our concepts of the organization—not only because women may have different values or styles of doing things than men but also because full participation of women in the workplace will entail a rethinking of the boundaries of family and of work life. As a result, our concepts of careers and personal success will change. The narrow definitions that prevail today will be replaced by a more holistic appreciation of what the "good life" is.

4. *New technologies—particularly in communication and information.* As recently as 1955, there were only ten or fifteen computers used as management tools in the United States (Myers, 1967, p. 1). The current transformation of inter- and intraorganizational communication is bound to accelerate as media richness increases and the need for faster decision making modifies managerial tasks. Moreover, greater use of information technology and programmed robotics could have repercussions for the work force—namely the possibility of far fewer routinized jobs (except for in-person services, which will expand greatly) and the increasing sophistication of technology operation and analytical

white-collar jobs. It is not the new technology that will dictate the characteristics and quality of work life; the technology will be neutral, as it is today. Decisions to centralize or decentralize, to delegate or not, to control or not, will be determined by the need for innovation, the pressure of competition, the impetus of new cultural values, and the need to accommodate the aspirations of an increasingly credentialed and educated work force (Carrier, 1990).

5. *Institutionalization of rapid change.* We are already well aware of the increasingly high costs of rapid economic changes such as the loss of jobs or plant closings. In the future, we may see increased protection of organizations' human assets through systematic retraining, and the protection of group assets, such as cities, revitalized by rapid, systematic programs of reinvestment. The institutionalization of rapid change may well result in greater managerial and professional preoccupation with the externalities of the organization. As change accelerates, the regulatory process will increasingly have to take place within the organization. Therefore, the concept of organizational boundaries will be altered as organizations are integrated into their environment, and as management and the professions take a more holistic view of their roles and responsibilities.

6. *New understanding of organizations.* The theoretical concepts of organizations are showing signs of shifting from hierarchical to somewhat more egalitarian models as the culture of world politics shifts away from totalitarian to more democratic ideals. The values of a cross-cultural, educated population will eventually span the world as new technologies are used to achieve a better life at work and at play. In such a climate, the organization per se becomes an asset and the design of organizations takes on new importance. As

competition shifts to quality issues, organizations will need to be designed to facilitate innovation. The organization will have to be concerned with real creativity and effectiveness, far less with their trappings—and will need to be far more concerned with clients and far less with corporate protection and survival strategies.

Who Should Read This Book?

The Twenty-First Century Organization is designed for all educated managers and professionals who enjoy some theory, who think ahead, who attempt to focus on issues as they emerge, and who solve problems. This book aims to meet the needs of policy makers both in government and in the private sector who are concerned about American competitiveness and want to see beyond the nitty-gritty details of the present. Students of organization will find it useful because I pay close attention to organizational design issues. The book is also intended for those who like an element of fantasy, of invention.

Overview of the Contents

Part One comprises Chapters One through Four. It provides the analytical basis for the fictional narrative in Part Two. Chapter One presents the following six trends shaping the organizations of the future:

- The international competition for ideas increasingly obliges firms and government to become internationally competitive.
- The persistent demand for access to education to better oneself can imbue the work force with professional ideas.

- The feminization of the culture of organizations enhances organizations' ability to cope with rapid change.
- New technologies facilitate decentralization.
- The consequences of rapid change can increasingly result in societal remedies.
- The successful organization of the future is the one that can reduce the queuing time needed to transform ideas into action.

Chapter Two asks whether the organization of the future can become flexible, adaptive, and able to learn, or whether it will evolve defensive and manipulative strategies to control clients and the public. A *typology of errors* explains why organizations adopt dysfunctional defensive strategies. Organizations of the future may be inclined to handle these errors by decentralizing and professionalizing their work force, by internalizing regulatory processes, and by having society find ways to correct some of the unforeseen consequences of rapid change after they happen. The chapter considers why organizations of the future would do well to look outward rather than inward.

Chapter Three describes *meta rules,* that is, rules that allow us to change rules. It stresses the importance of meta rules in permitting innovation as structures are altered to meet changing needs. It also shows the utility of shared understandings and of "future myths" to provide a framework for collective action. It analyzes both the controls and the governance structure of the new organization.

Chapter Four examines how lateral linkages are facilitated by membership in entrepreneurial self-funded informal groups and networks, how networks become the source of continuity as they acquire importance, and how risk management, coordination, and conflict resolution are achieved by a new emphasis on shared goals.

Part Two provides fictional narratives of future organizations, based on the analysis in Part One. Chapter Five posits a new set of professional institutions that have two major functions: (1) they allow selected external governmental regulatory functions to be taken over inside the organization by professional bodies, thus providing much more rapid, low-cost, and well-informed protection to staff, client, and public; and (2) they provide joint insurance schemes to handle major disruptions created by rapid technological and economic changes.

Chapter Six takes us on a visit to "The Firm," an organization of the future. The chapter provides an insight into the advantages and disadvantages of an organization expanding its discretion and monitoring controls to meet the needs of a new work force. It illustrates the requirements of an adaptive learning mode of action.

The Conclusion explains why (1) the large organization is likely to live on and not be replaced by an electronic cottage industry; (2) the organization of the future will probably be adaptive; (3) education and training will become more critical in future economic competition; (4) discretion is likely to become decentralized, which will require high levels of trust; (5) some ways must be found to correct errors after they happen, partly to reduce resistance to change; (6) the internalization of selected regulatory practices can increase competitiveness; (7) our thinking about the organization will evolve; and lastly, (8) why the culture of the organization of the future will truly be international.

The Appendix reviews the various methodologies applicable to future research work and explains how this study was undertaken.

How to Read This Book

Because we are analyzing the future, there is no data. Of necessity, the scenarios in Part Two follow and derive from the analysis presented in Part One.

The logical arrangement of the chapters follows this sequence: we begin with an assumption, discuss the implications of a number of trends, analyze the consequences of these trends on the structure of the organization, and present scenarios that show the consequences "in action." Readers who prefer to work from the construct to the analysis, however, may want to read the book backward, beginning with the Appendix and the scenarios, then reading the Conclusion, and then back up through the analysis. The message in both sequences will be the same.

Acknowledgments

Many individuals have helped me, at one time or another, to write this book—although some of them are unaware of their contributions. I thank Bo Anderson, Frederick Balderston, Charles Benson, Ladislav Cerych, Steven Cohen, James Guthrie, Peter Hall, Judith Innes, Richard Meier, Paul Mussen, Karen Nelson, W. Richard Scott, Eugene Staley, David Stern, and Aaron Wildavsky. Many students at the Graduate School of Education have helped me clarify my ideas and have provided important insights. Manuel Castells encouraged me to write this book, and he, Dennis Jaffe, Hal Rainey, one anonymous reader, and the editorial staff made extensive and useful comments on earlier drafts. As usual, the author is the only one responsible for what is still wrong with this book. I also thank Vanessa True, who produced the manuscript with dispatch, accuracy, and great good humor.

Berkeley, California   Guy Benveniste
December 1993

The Author

Guy Benveniste is professor emeritus of policy planning in the Graduate School of Education at the University of California, Berkeley.

He was born in France and received both his B.S. degree (1948) in engineering science and applied physics and his M.S. degree (1950) in mechanical engineering from Harvard University. Between 1950 and 1960, he worked with the Mexican Light and Power Company (Mexlight) in Mexico City and the Stanford Research Institute in Menlo Park, California. In 1959, he coauthored with Eugene Staley a futuristic study for the U.S. Senate Foreign Relations Committee. This was a study of long-term possible scientific developments and their potential impact on American foreign policy. In 1960, during the Kennedy administration, he joined the Department of State in Washington, D.C. Starting in 1962, he worked for the International Bank for Reconstruction and Development, also in Washington, D.C., and then for UNESCO in Paris. He was instrumental in the creation of the International Institute for Educational Planning, which is located in Paris.

In 1965, he obtained a major fellowship and returned from France to the United States for further study. He took the first Stanford University doctorate in the sociology of planning in 1968. His dissertation was subsequently published under the title *Bureaucracy and National Planning* (1970). Also in 1968, he was appointed to the faculty of the Graduate School of Education at the University of California, Berkeley.

Benveniste teaches courses in organization theory, planning, and management in the Graduate School of Education. He has edited and authored several books dealing with professions, education, and bureaucracy. He coedited *Agents of Change: Professionals in Developing Countries* (1969, with W. Ilchman). He authored *From Mass to Universal Education* (1976, with C. Benson), *The Politics of Expertise* (1977), *Regulation and Planning: The Case of Environmental Politics* (1981), *Bureaucracy* (1983), *Professionalizing the Organization* (1987), and *Mastering the Politics of Planning* (1989). He is also the author of several dozen articles dealing with organizations, professionals, and planning. Benveniste has traveled widely and consulted and lectured in the United States and abroad.

Benveniste lives with his wife, Karen Nelson, in Berkeley and Carmel-by-the-Sea, California.

THE TWENTY-FIRST
CENTURY
ORGANIZATION

PART ONE

Current Trends and Factors

Part One presents a theoretical argument to explain why and how the organization of the future will differ from that of today. This argument is based on a set of trends that are relatively well understood today. The analysis leads to a description of the way change takes place in organizations, and the mechanisms that permit some organizations to reduce the queuing time needed to convert ideas into new programs, products, or services. Obviously, organizations differ. There exist wide varieties of problems, tasks, and functions. Therefore, there are many ways to organize. This book does not attempt to take such variety into account. It focuses instead on an "ideal type," namely an organization in a very uncertain environment, faced with the imperative to rapidly adapt and learn.

CHAPTER ONE

Six Trends Shaping the Twenty-First Century Organization

I have picked six fairly self-evident trends shaping the future organization that are often discussed in the current management literature (Drucker, 1992; Peters, 1992). I want to delineate some of the forms these trends are likely to take as they continue and possibly accelerate in the coming decades. My underlying assumption is that current processes will lead to vastly decentralized and innovative organizations, informal networks that will effect innovation and change, the possible removal of the responsibility for regulation from government and the placement of it within the organization proper, and new social institutions that will facilitate rapid changes that do not cause excessive damage and pain as jobs are lost and created anew.

The first trend I discuss is the international competition for new ideas in the world economy. Today, we see the major impact of internationalization in the private manufacturing sector, but this is only the beginning. If we look at the generation of ideas, we find dramatic internationalization of research and development, with impacts on both private and public organizations.

The second trend discussed here is the continued upgrading of the educational and training qualifications of part of the work force. The third is the growing numbers of women in the workplace. The fourth is advances in new technologies, particularly in communication and information.

These four trends underlie and give rise to the last two: an accelerated rate of change that results in change itself being institutionalized, and, finally, a new concept of the organization, growing partly out of the tendency of government and the private sector to work together in vastly expanded networks.

The International Competition for Ideas

Investors have always looked for profits at home and abroad, but since the middle of the twentieth century, world financial resources have moved on an international scale to take advantage of the location of markets, the availability of trained manpower and technology, the availability of raw materials and energy resources, the incentives other governments may bestow, the proximity of local entrepreneurs, and the flexibility provided by multicountry siting. There is no doubt this trend will persist and accelerate in coming decades (Scott and Storper, 1986; Castells, 1985, 1989). As a consequence, we are likely to witness the "bureaucratization of the world" (Jacoby, 1973).

Today capital moves easily almost anywhere in the world. Tomorrow, it will become increasingly easier to move raw materials or manufactured products. Energy, particularly from nuclear sources, can also be generated in varied locations. Therefore, in the future, the most important factors in economic competition become (1) the availability of ideas, namely sophisticated research and development; (2) the availability of a trained and capable work force; (3) a stable government that encourages and protects productive enterprise; and (4) organizations that are designed to adapt.

Internationalization of Research and Development

Awareness of the importance of research and development (R&D) in world economic competition has changed. In the past, many countries have thought it was sufficient to copy or adapt innovations from the more advanced nations, but no longer. The example of Japan as well as other economically successful countries has completely altered these earlier perceptions. At the same time (as I will discuss at greater length in the next section), the demand for access to higher education has risen and will continue to rise, thus providing the countries that can meet that demand with trained people who can further development of R&D capabilities. It is not always universities that provide the institutional roof for the new R&D complexes. In many countries, specialized R&D centers are attached to universities or to large government-sponsored organizations, as in France and Russia. Such centers may be funded by government, philanthropies, and private donors. But the importance of R&D and the status attached to the international recognition of R&D are evidenced worldwide, in Eastern Europe, Asia, Latin America, and increasingly in Africa.

In the coming decades, this trend is likely to accelerate. More resources will be directed to economic R&D as investments in military R&D become less significant. In fact, in the future, economic competition is likely to serve to legitimize government investments in R&D, much as military security did in the last decades. A number of current trends will probably become stronger:

1. *Increasing cooperation between government and the private sector.* Government assistance in private sector efforts is likely to increase, in part because of the new legitimacy of funding them and also because of the need to share the burden of increased costs of R&D. Many R&D fields require investments too large to be undertaken by single firms or agencies. Today, government partnership with the private sector dominates R&D planning in a number of countries. As the costs of research and development increase, collaborative efforts will become the norm in the United States and elsewhere. Government and private sector collaboration permits the massing of resources and allows for the sharing of risks in difficult ventures. In such fields as high-energy particle research, biotechnology or fusion energy, and high-temperature plasma research we already see international funding and cooperation in the development of research facilities.

Government partnership with the private sector may appear to run against the ideology of the free enterprise market. But as economic competition intensifies, investments in ideas, like investments in education, are likely to be increasingly perceived as providing collective benefits and will therefore be seen as a state responsibility.

2. *Growing cooperation among researchers in many parts of the world.* Science has always bridged national boundaries, but international cooperation is likely to increase markedly in the future. It will be necessary, partly because of the complexities of many fields of research

6

—where talent, equipment, and developments are so specialized that unique capabilities tend to be located in very diverse and distant locations. This is increasingly evident today in medical research, biotechnology, agricultural research, and many other fields.

3. *Accelerating geographical concentrations of talent and capabilities.* In the United States we are already familiar with the Silicon Valley in California, where the proximity of important research universities, government laboratories, and autonomous think tanks has led to the creation of a vast R&D zone. Indeed, the combination of intellectual resources, research opportunities, venture capital, and skilled labor has attracted even more R&D talent and clients. Similar concentrations already exist elsewhere in the United States, Europe, Japan, and increasingly in the rest of the world. This is the pattern that we can expect to see accelerate, but in specialized areas, as local governments, philanthropies, and private sector interests seek to support specialized R&D capabilities suited to their intellectual, cultural, and economic assets.

4. *Tightening of the linkages between research and development.* Economic competition places a high premium on the implementation of innovations. This has important consequences both for institutions of research and for the design of the new organization. In the United States, research will continue to take place in the research universities, so that future generations of researchers can be trained. But the separation of research and teaching functions will also increase markedly. More and more, research will be located in specialized centers with full-time research staffs whose links to development will take them outside ordinary academic preoccupations. In countries where research is

already taking place outside the universities, closer links with universities will be established to ensure the training of future researchers.

5. *Intensification of difficulty defining intellectual property.* As more and more laboratories cooperate in joint research endeavors, as collective private-government-philanthropic financing increases, as the links between research and development tighten, problems associated with the ownership of intellectual properties are bound to become far more complex and difficult to resolve. This will be an area where important new institutional arrangements will have to be established to allow for effective international cooperation. Means of providing for collective rewards will need to be invented to reinforce individual or organizational motivations.

6. *Growing importance of long-term strategy.* Most R&D innovations require long-term strategies. The development of new economic sectors is often a matter of many years or of several decades. Government and private sector cooperation in developing R&D investment strategies will require far more attention to flexible planning than is practiced at present (Benveniste, 1989).

Impact on Private and Public Organizations

The internationalization of the search for ideas and innovations will not be limited to the private sector. In fact, what will make the next century so different from this one will be the increasing competition of governments for the allegiance of their citizens. Public organizations and services will become as concerned with development abroad as private firms.

We underestimate how insular American organizations have become. In 1950, American technology and managerial practices were copied everywhere. We had little to learn abroad. But by 2050, the reverse will very likely be true. We will need to keep up with developments everywhere else. The worldwide economic competition of the future will be a competition for the perceptions of citizens—namely, both clients and voters. With vastly increasing worldwide channels of information—world television, computer communication networks, increased travel opportunities, and the like—larger numbers of citizens will be able to see for themselves what is accomplished elsewhere: not only what new product or services are available but how life is organized and government is operated.

Today, we still think of international economic competition very much in terms of commerce or manufacturing. Tomorrow, economic competition will have a much wider scope, encompassing all aspects of the political economy. For example, how governments organize public services, the relative safety of citizens in cities, the availability of health care, the quality of education, the availability of mass transit systems, the quality of the environment will all be constantly compared, and successful innovations will often be adopted or adapted across the borders of nation states. Thus the political economies of public institutions will begin to look much more like those of the private sector. Comparisons across national borders will greatly increase the need for information contact and intelligence in public organizations. Government organizations that, until now, have hardly paid any attention to what was happening in other parts of the world will be scanning the world environment.

Regional Economic and Trade Groups

The total number of nation states will probably increase in coming decades as many more cultural minorities seek self identity and, at a minimum, seek educational and cultural independence. This proliferation of nation states will also result in larger regional political, economic, or trade blocs displaying varying degrees of political, social, and economic integration. These regional arrangements will tend to foster much greater intra integration, thus facilitating the flows of capital, ideas, and other human and physical resources within regions. At the same time, the very existence of regional entities such as the European Economic Community (EEC) will also increase flows of capital, ideas, and other resources across regional economic blocs, as private sector economic organizations seek to establish access to ideas, labor resources, and markets.

During the next century, Asia, and China in particular, will play a dominant economic role. In Europe, by 2050, it is probable that a vast economic market may exist, spreading far beyond the current EEC to include Eastern Europe and many of the states composing the old Soviet Union. South and Central America may be linked to the North American trade area. Other blocs may be formed. These regional blocs will result in greater flows of financial, human, and physical resources across regional economic boundaries as R&D is internationalized. The flows of international financial resources will move wherever combinations of R&D capabilities, skilled and trained labor, local entrepreneurial talent, and a supportive governmental environment—including a solid educational infrastructure—prevail.

Given the complexities of such worldwide transfers, pri-

10

vate sector involvement in this new international economy will require much closer long-term private-public sector cooperation. The current cultural barriers and mutual suspicions between the American private sector and the government, particularly with the government in Washington but also with state and local governments, will simply no longer be. To succeed in world markets, American enterprise will have to rely far more on governmental cooperation. Attracting foreign investments to the United States will also require far more sophisticated involvement and awareness on the part of local and state governments. In other words, change will not be confined to large corporations, but will also occur in the smaller enterprises and, more importantly, in the public sector, whose potential role will suddenly loom very important. The principal question, then, will be what kind of collective incentives will help transform public organizations—mainly government agencies that have until now played only a minor role in a complex endeavor? How will dull bureaucrats be transformed into active Schumpeterian entrepreneurs (Schumpeter, 1947, p. 132)? Obviously our concepts of public service will have to change. New incentives will have to be invented to reorient the public sector and convert it into an effective partner of the private sector. Similarly, new controls will have to be invented to ensure that government serves all the people, not just the narrow private interests of dominating corporations.

Levels of Economic and Social Development

While ideas, capital, financing, skills, production, and consumption move worldwide, levels of growth and prosperity will remain highly differentiated.

As recently as the 1960s it was thought that capital and technologic transfers—along with a proper mix of technical assistance and the combined efforts of local entrepreneurs, governments, and people—would be sufficient to transform the developing nations of the world. W. W. Rostow (1963) argued that with proper help, "transitional" societies could lift themselves into a "takeoff," which would allow them to invest 10 to 20 percent of their national income in sustained economic growth. This sustained economic growth would then regularly outstrip increases in the population as these nations caught up with the rest (p. 9). The laggards were expected to catch up since comparable levels of prosperity were expected when each nation state developed an industrial and manufacturing base and modernized agriculture, fisheries, and the exploitation of local natural resources.

The experiences of the last thirty years have completely shattered these myths. Instead, the internationalization of the world economy has produced very differentiated growth and retrenchment patterns. Areas of the world with an industrious population that could easily be organized into a skilled work force, with an entrepreneurial merchant class that could organize it, and a sophisticated financial elite that could generate and attract capital, saw a complete transformation of their economy. Such areas—for example, Singapore, South Korea, and Taiwan—occupied a new niche in the world economy, providing highly competitive assembly and manufacturing capabilities in a wide range of industries and in many new trade and service facilities. At the same time other areas stagnated or even lost out as facilities were closed and capital moved to better, more promising sites.

In other words, the problems of world economic development in the coming years are completely different than they have been in the past. It is no longer a matter of helping those who are behind so they "catch up" with the front-runners. It is instead the much more complex problem of adjusting to rapid changes as centers of prosperity surge forward in many parts of the planet, while other areas remain stagnant or, worse still, slip downward.

These problems affect both rich and poor nations equally, as industries and other economic activities move from old areas to new ones in response to the opportunities inherent in technological innovations, resource availability (including skilled labor), organizing capability, capital mobilization, and market expansion. The world economy thus becomes a process of "flows," simultaneously expanding economic areas as new wealth is invented and stripping others as plants close and old practices are abandoned (Castells, 1989).

As new labor forces emerge in countries with lower standards of living, it will become increasingly difficult for organizations in wealthier areas to compete solely on the basis of price. All other factors being the same, jobs tend to move where skills are both available and less expensive. Therefore, quality becomes far more important. This is already well understood today. Private firms focus on the needs of clients; they anticipate client needs and strive to meet them. Moreover, in the current literature, common topics include such ways of meeting client needs as flexibility, networking, on-time production, and so on (Coriat, 1990; Kilmann, Kilmann, and Associates, 1990).

New ideas and the ability to translate them into tangible products and services will matter more in the future. Therefore, the designers of the new organization will have to address these issues; and to do so they will have to ask more complex and profound questions: specifically, they will have to take into account why individuals and groups resist change.

The Education of the Work Force

The modern organization is increasingly based on the idea of merit. In the past, family ties and wealth mattered, but the modern organization dates from the nineteenth century, when a new concept emerged: individuals were no longer to hold jobs in organizations only because they could buy a position or because they inherited privilege through their family or clan. Instead, they were to be selected and appointed on their merit, because they were qualified, and because they had the necessary training or skills to undertake the specific tasks associated with the position. This was an important departure from the old order, wherein wealth and prestige emanated from the ownership of land or commerce and class distinctions were reflected in organizational arrangements.

The nineteenth century saw the birth of a new elite, the professional men and women—mostly men at first—who acquired their status not from the land they owned or the commerce they practiced, but from the expertise they acquired by spending time in apprenticeships and, increasingly, by attending institutions of higher learning. In the nineteenth century, the concept of a "career" emerged. One's life was no longer necessarily determined only by one's family wealth and by the opportunities offered in serving one's king or church. Choices were open: it was also possible to become a lawyer, a journalist, an engineer, even a college president, and while the new elites were often unsure which career to choose or how to achieve something significant, the possibility of social mobility outside of one's inherited status was greatly enhanced. New colleges were created; Americans went to study in Europe, and careers began to matter more because they offered the key to social mobility. Burton Bledstein (1976) points out that the 1803 *Oxford English Dictionary* was the first to include the following definition for the word *career:* "A person's course or progress through life." He also indicates that by the end of the century the word *career* was used to mean personal success, the achievement of some fame. By the end of the twentieth century, the meaning was broadening to include any course of employment, as everyone, or nearly everyone, claimed to be pursuing a career (Benveniste, 1987).

Today career, social mobility, and employment are closely related to a person's level of education. Parents throughout the world are concerned about educating their children so that they might have good life chances, or possibly better ones than the parents had. During the second half of the twentieth century, systems of higher education were vastly expanded (Coombs, 1968; Hanson and Brembeck, 1966). College graduates did not always find employment commensurate with their training or preparation, but demand for access continued unabated. I recall vividly a poor and *humilde* peasant in the state of Puebla in Mexico telling me he was doing all he could to send a son to school "because I do not want him to work in the sun." The schools, colleges, and universities have largely replaced the old apprenticeships and have become the credentialing institutions, the places to obtain the necessary knowledge and skills to begin or continue one's life work.

Thus our educational institutions are the new social mobility valves, replacing, at least to some extent, inherited wealth as the important determinant of one's career opportunities. To be sure, inherited wealth can buy and furnish education, but education is nearly always a prerequisite to achievement in the world of work—except, of course, for those endowed with unique talents.

We do not always think of education as a social mobility valve, but this is exactly one of the functions it performs in modern society. A detailed look at how education fulfills this function is worthwhile. Let us take a case of education not being generally available, for example, Afghanistan in the early 1960s.

I visited schools in Afghanistan at that time with a World Bank mission. We were accompanied by local dignitaries. We would visit primary schools, say in Herat or in Kabul, and we would go through the classrooms and meet the children. The local dignitaries would point them out: "Here is the daughter of General X, and this is the son of the governor, and here is my own child, and these young ladies are daughters of [a prominent land owner]" and so on. The primary public schools of Afghanistan were the social mobility valve, because at that time the vast majority of the peasant or nomadic populations had no access to these schools. It was sufficient to enter the primary stream to sharply differentiate one's life chances from those of children who had no access to the government schools or who had access only to a few religious schools run by the Mullahs, where one could learn to recite the Koran by heart but not have access to secondary or higher education.

As systems of education were expanded and access to schools became generalized, the social valve function of education moved upward within these educational systems.

In many countries, primary and secondary education became universal during the first half of the century, meaning that practically every child had access to a primary and even to a secondary education. Therefore, when I was a child in France in the thirties, the French social valve function of education was in the secondary system. If one was in the lycée stream within secondary education and if one completed the terminal secondary examination for the *bachot,* one had good life chances, either for immediate employment or for continuing one's studies in the system of higher education. In other words, at that time, finishing the secondary examinations was perceived as sufficient to ensure social mobility, even if one went on to attend institutions of higher education.

As a higher percentage of the age cohort completed the *bachot,* the social valve function moved upward to higher levels within the system of education. One had to attend the university, or the *grandes écoles,* or at least take specialized courses or do something more than what was being achieved by most of the other secondary school graduates.

Conventional wisdom tells us that the demand for education is related to the increasing complexity of the world of work. In a modern technological world, education is necessary to be able to function. To use a computer, you need some minimal level of computer literacy. Thus a *technical* imperative exists driving the demand for education. Economists argue that more highly educated workers command higher salaries because they are also more productive. They are more productive because they have the skills needed to use more sophisticated machinery and processes or to network and manage complex activities. But the link between higher education and productivity does not hold across occupations. To be sure, as new scientific and techno-logical innovations take place, more advanced education and training are required for some occupations, but many others remain as they were or may even require less education or less skill. Therefore the technical imperative is not sufficient to explain the growth in demand for access to education, whereas the social valve function is.

The new economy requires trained workers, and firms and governments need more and more employees who have mastered sophisticated economic and social skills. But, at the same time, another transformation is taking place: there is social demand for credentialing, driven by social mobility considerations, which grows faster than the needs of the economy and, as a result, has a dysfunctional impact on the education system.

I am going into considerable detail here, because there is an important transformation under way that has not received sufficient attention. Everyone is aware today that the United States faces stiff international economic competition. Most everyone is also aware the American public schools are not on a par with most European or Japanese public schools. But few realize that another fundamental process is at work: the overall levels of credentialing of the work force keep rising independently of the technical imperative. This has consequences for attitudes, expectations, roles, and manage-ment structures.

Since education is a very significant mobility valve, indi-viduals seek more education because they perceive that cre-dentials may open opportunities for advancement. If and when overall productivity increases are achieved, higher wages are paid to workers, many of whom may have higher levels of credentialing than are strictly required for their jobs. One does not need a college degree to work in a fast food chain, yet many college graduates work in such occupations, even though they may ultimately find employment elsewhere. It has been amply demonstrated that modern economies generate many more low-skill jobs than they generate high-skill jobs (Ginzberg, 1977; Kutscher and Personick, 1986; Attewell, 1987).

The consequences of continued demand for credentials to achieve social mobility are many:

• *Greater importance is given to credentialing than to actual learning and training.* When we say that the overall levels of education keep rising independently of the technical imperative, we mean that credentials are wanted although the quality of the learning and training may be quite unsuited to the needs of the work force. The education system responds to demands for credentials, not necessarily to demands for know-how.

• *The primary and secondary educational systems become differentiated.* This is particularly true in countries where a substantial private educational sector exists. If the state has a partial monopoly on education and elites send their children to private schools, the tendency is to allow the public schools to deteriorate. This is exacerbated when the public system is decentralized and is allowed to lose its monopoly on high-quality schools. In the United States the state's partial monopoly affords neither the advantages of privatization nor the benefits of a state monopoly on quality education, as is the case in centralized educational systems of Europe and Japan.

• *The deterioration of the quality of education with the corresponding rise in credentialing tends to result in a potentially alienated work force with very high expectations*

19

for social mobility but few means of achieving it. To put it simply, many people have high aspirations because they have credentials, but they are poorly trained and do not know what they can or cannot accomplish. Therefore in work settings there is less trust as to abilities, more suspicions and doubts. While more highly educated individuals increasingly aspire to discretionary professionalized work roles, suspicions and doubts about their ability still result in increased bureaucratization and control.

Similarly, the deteriorating educational sector is increasingly bureaucratized as top-down controls are imposed in an effort to arrest deterioration and to provide the political appearance of reform.

• *As levels of education and training in labor markets rise, employers tend to prefer better educated employees because they have been thoroughly socialized into bureaucratic practices.* Employers tend to raise educational requirements on job descriptions in response to the qualifications of available candidates rather than in response to a technical imperative.

Looking to the future, we have to assume that economic competition will result in a new awareness in the United States of the importance of rebuilding the public schools. How this will be done is another matter. It will also be as important to maintain the quality of the higher education system. Interestingly, while the partial privatization of the American public primary and secondary systems has resulted in the deterioration of the public schools, the partial privatization of higher education has not yet resulted in the abandonment of high-quality public universities.

While the American system of higher education is still the best in the world, there are several factors at work. The principal one is probably the significance of research in the American university. As long as the American university can adapt to its changing world environment and maintain a dominant role in research and development, it will be able to maintain high-quality standards in its leading institutions—both public and private. But if wrong policy choices are made, if the American public university is not able to adapt, the rapid growth of research and development outside the United States and outside our public universities may result in the deterioration of these valued institutions.

These trends are likely to accelerate in the twenty-first century for several reasons:

• *The internationalization of organizations will be likely to result in the internationalization of the social mobility valve.* Individuals pursuing careers in the public or private sector increasingly seek to differentiate themselves by acquiring an international education—namely, degrees from foreign universities or experience in international programs that qualify them for work abroad or that provide them with necessary insights into the institutions and mores of other cultures.

• *Heightened uncertainty about changing patterns of research, development, investment, and production, the "flows" alluded to above, will increase demands for access not only to education but to reeducation and retraining.* As major international economic shifts take place, as capital, as well as human and physical resources are redistributed across the globe, the demand is likely to grow for further preparation and repreparation as individuals have to adapt to change. But once again, demand may well exceed need as varied skills are perceived as necessary to compete and advance in a fast-changing job market.

• *The demand for access to higher education will continue.* The upward movement of the social mobility valve is limited by its cost—namely, the time and income involved in attending school, plus the costs of education or training. Nevertheless the demand will accelerate because better educated parents will seek more education and better credentials for their own children. Consequently, we can expect more people to be willing to pay for more higher education, even as the costs increase. This does not mean that the growth of the demand for access to higher education is linear. For example, in recent years the total numbers of advanced graduate degrees awarded in the United States have dropped somewhat and then risen again. People's willingness to invest in higher learning is limited by financial, social, and personal considerations, not to mention the limited number of places in institutions of higher education. But by and large, in the long term, the trend will persist.

Differentiation among institutions is likely to take place increasingly within the system of higher education, and individuals will seek access to programs and degrees in fields of expanding development and employment. Systems of higher education throughout the world are likely to become increasingly differentiated and stratified because they will be the principal path to social mobility.

• *A highly credentialed work force will develop new characteristics.* The aspirations and the culture of the work force of the twenty-first century will be radically different from those that prevailed in the nineteenth or early twentieth century. A far more credentialed work force—which is, we hope, better educated—will, in any case, aspire to the work life of the professional. Highly trained employees will expect to play a more discretionary role and have a more collaborative relationship with management. We can already perceive the trend toward the professionalization of the organization (Benveniste, 1987). This trend will become far more significant as professional education becomes the dominant zone of social differentiation and advancement. The future organization will need to take these aspirations into account, even if many or most of the new jobs of the future do not require extensive discretion or advanced degrees.

The Feminization of Organizational Culture

Starting in the 1960s, with Betty Friedan's *The Feminine Mystique,* a new awareness of women's roles in society has emerged. In the last thirty years our perceptions of women's roles in the workplace have changed, as well; for example, today one would not expect to hear the wife of a major candidate for the United States presidency describe herself or her work as "just a bit of fluff!" Yet that is exactly what Mrs. Wendell Wilkie answered nearly half a century ago when she was asked at a press conference what it was she did (Cleveland, 1989, p. 35). Her answer marks the time and changes under way. By the end of the century, the wife, husband, or significant other of a presidential candidate is expected to have his or her own career (even though some Americans still seem to prefer a family role for the first lady).

The feminist revolution swept the world of work, and today, it is not only poor women who hold jobs outside of the household. Most young women seek the same kind of education and training that men obtain so as to be given the same career opportunities (Higginson and Quick, 1980; Lee, 1980). Even within the churches, many women seek access to the ministry and are obtaining it in some, including the Church of England.

Why has this occurred, and why did it occur when it did? Several reasons may be advanced: Women were enticed to enter the work force during both world wars, when labor shortages developed while men fought on the battlefield. Subsequently, the mechanization of the household—the advent of the washing machine, nylons and polyesters that require no ironing, the frozen food industry—the growth of house maintenance services, and a new awareness of men's changing role in the household have allowed women more free time away from household chores and thus permitted them to enter or reenter the labor force.

Advances in health care have sharply reduced illness and infant mortality, greatly reducing the amount of time women have to devote to childbearing and still assure continuation of the species. The advent of social legislation and creation of retirement plans has reduced the need to have many children to ensure support in old age. Life expectancy well beyond childbearing years has greatly increased opportunities for women's participation in the work force.

Economic necessity, the advent of liberal divorce laws, and the dissolution of traditional family ties and support systems have obliged more and more women to enter the labor force, either to support themselves and their children or to help increase the earning capability of their family. Quite often employers have sought women out because they could be offered lower wages than men. More importantly still, women's entry into the labor force is related to the role of education and training in a society where status is based on merit.

The Search for Gender Equality

The entry of women in the work force and the pursuit of women's equality with men are not due to any one factor, and all those listed above are significant. Indeed, the pursuit of equality, or the balancing of women's and men's power, takes place in all societies. However, accommodation of that balancing process takes different forms at different historical times. Thus it is possible to interpret the feminist revolution of the sixties as a predictable reaction to the transformation of men's role and the disappearance (or sharp reduction) of the role of lineage in status differentiation. In other words, it is no coincidence that modern women of all classes demand equal economic opportunities with men.

As long as social status derived from the ownership of land and as long as women could acquire or inherit land in their own names, they had the same opportunities for status as men. Aristocratic women at the eve of the French Revolution played complex social roles. To be sure, men had much control over women's fate, but it was not only men who had control. Widows could also play dominant roles, and many aristocratic women were highly influential in family or court circles.

Lineage was more important than gender, so that in some countries the daughter of a king could become queen if there was no male issue, and even if a woman was married without meeting her husband prior to the marriage ceremony, if she was a young aristocrat, she could certainly reject a man on the grounds he did not have sufficient status, wealth, and lineage to marry her. The roles of women were differentiated from those of men particularly in matters of

25

warfare and religion. Yet their status was not differentiated. They were equals to the extent that they could inherit land from their parents or wealth upon the death of a husband. In that last respect, daughters fared better than younger sons, who did not inherit and had to join the military or take religious orders to make their fortunes.

In the nineteenth century, status increasingly came with one's performance in work, and the meritocracy replaced the aristocracy. If status is derived from career advancement instead of land ownership, the differentiated role of men results in a differentiated status for women. I stress this because it explains why the new emerging role of women in the work force is bound to have far more repercussions within the organization than a mere increase in work force participation.

In the nineteenth century, as men acquired new opportunities for social mobility, women had a much more restricted access both to education and professional careers. Role expectations from the past were enshrined. Men saw it as their duty to "protect" women, to keep them at home, and to be the breadwinners. A working woman was either poor—a woman of low status—or a woman engaged in family business activity. Even family businesses lost significance as corporate structures replaced family enterprise in the late nineteenth and early twentieth centuries.

The unbalanced power relations between men and women were therefore transitional and could not resist the changes and opportunities new technologies created. Wartime employment opportunities, mechanization of the household, decrease in time devoted to childrearing, and many other factors brought about status equalization between men and women. Women rejected the life roles they had been playing and began to enter the workplace in large numbers. By 1950 nearly 30 percent of all American women were in the work force. By 1970, the figure was more than 40 percent; by 1990 it was more than 50 percent. As the last decade of the century approached, women represented more than 50 percent of all enrollments in higher education and they were receiving as many degrees in business administration as men (Coates, Jarratt, and Mahaffie, 1990).

If this is right, if women's entry into the labor force is the historical correlation of the unbalanced status relations of men and women, we have to assume that this process is irreversible. Women will not leave the workplace once they find out that it is a costly life activity. More likely, they will transform it, adapt it to their needs, and contribute to its success. Looking to the future we not only have to assume that larger and larger percentages of women will enter the workplace. We have to assume that these women will achieve power parity with men and have a corresponding impact on the culture of the organization.

Women's search for equality in the workplace has been slow and painful (Kanter, 1977; Margolis, 1979). Let us focus on four aspects of the current transition: the issue of pay inequalities, the problems faced by working women who still maintain family responsibilities, the issues of sexual harassment, and the feminization of leadership styles.

Pay Inequities

Current gender-based wage differences reflect widespread discriminatory practices, historical antecedents, and, to a lesser extent, higher costs of employing some women (Blau, 1977; Halaby, 1979; Pfeffer and Ross, 1990; Schwartz, 1989).

But in a longer term context we have to assume that such differences will disappear as organizations adjust to the realities presented by large percentages of women workers at all levels of the hierarchy. In other words, as organizations adapt to women's needs, women will match men in terms of performance, if they do not already do so. Salary discrimination will necessarily be eliminated. In many ways, current salary differentials, when they are not discriminatory, still reflect accepted norms of responsibility. Women might be considered to be less reliable at work because they still maintain more responsibility for their households than men do. But working women strongly resent having more child-rearing and household responsibilities than men (Berg, 1986; Googins and Burden, 1987; Olson, Frieze, and Detlefsen, 1990; Hertz, 1986). We have to suppose that in due time, men will assume more of these duties, or will increasingly be socialized to want to assume them by their working mothers. More importantly, organizations will adapt to their work force. Many family needs will be provided within the organizational context as our concepts of what work is and what family is change.

Sexual Harassment

Sexual harassment in the workplace has attracted attention because it is indicative of the many ways power can be used in organizations (Gutek, 1985; Hearn and Parkin, 1987; Rubin and Borgers, 1990; Gutek, Cohen, and Konrad, 1990). In a world still dominated by men, formal grievance procedures are not always sufficient to ensure male compliance with rules against harassment. It is obvious that sex influences behavior and attitudes, but it is also a fact that in many

28

traditionally male-dominated work activities women have had a harder time gaining salary parity and acceptance—and avoiding being treated as sex objects. This is well documented in a recent study of the problems encountered by female blue-collar workers in the steel industry, where sexual harassment is clearly an exercise in power and dominance and not an expression of sexual interest (Deaux and Ullman, 1983).

Why do I predict that women will ultimately achieve salary parity, share household responsibilities, and extinguish sexual harassment in the workplace? Because the role of women in organizations of the twenty-first century will be too important to be handicapped by such impediments. As we shall see with greater clarity in coming chapters, women's contributions to organizational culture will be made more significant as informal dimensions of organizational life become more important than formal hierarchical dimensions and as trust, support, and participation become necessary to maintain organizational cohesion.

Gender Differences in Management Style

We can already discern gender differences in management style, and these will be increasingly valued in the future. Interestingly, as women first enter male-dominated work environments, they tend to adapt to masculine styles of performance. Male styles of leadership tend to be associated with the following descriptors: aggressive, assertive, autocratic, analytical, confident, competitive, forceful, and dominant. Feminine styles of leadership tend to be associated with others: affectionate, appreciative, caring, compassionate, gentle, emotional, understanding, and supportive (Cann and Siegfried, 1990). Of course, leadership requires both, but male-dominated work environments are often highly competitive. As women enter these male competitions, they rapidly find they have to swim if they are not to go under. They may initially play supportive roles, but they soon learn to mimic men and to hold their own, even if men dominate at first (Duerst-Lahti, 1990). As a result, at present, gender differences in leadership styles tend to be obliterated and gender differences in management are not consistent. It is generally recognized that men tend to be more oriented toward action and getting things done (an *initiating* style of leadership), while women are more oriented toward a supportive, sharing, and consulting approach (a *concerned* style of leadership) (Baird and Bradley, 1979; Denmark, 1977; Jurma and Wright, 1990). But while women have, for the moment at least, adapted to a man's world, and while it is often difficult to discern differences, the evidence shows that female-dominated organizations can be quite different from male-dominated organizations (Fenn, 1980; Brazelton, 1985).

Current feminine adaptation to masculine style has costs, but, more importantly, other factors are increasingly creating a need for a different management style—a style that turns out to be more "feminine" than "masculine." Suzanne Gordon (1991) describes the costs and resulting social dysfunctions of having women increasingly behave as competitive men, and she emphasizes how this change affects women. Some adapt easily and others do not. Yet, women's adaptation to male roles is a transitional phase in a much larger process of change.

It is not only that women will sooner or later achieve close-to-number parity with men in the labor force and thus be able to exert influence and revert to more caring and supportive styles of leadership. More importantly, the behaviors usually associated with feminine styles—caring, compassion, supportiveness, and understanding—are the ones that matter in an uncertain environment where organizational learning and adaptation require high degrees of trust and where highly professionalized workers seek a participatory role in management. Therefore, as we look to the future, we begin to perceive that women in organizations have important contributions to make. As they become the problem solvers, they will also acquire power, not by mimicking men, but by being themselves. As they acquire power, they will also achieve salary parity, share household responsibilities, or transform the organization to meet family needs and eliminate sexual harassment.

The New Technologies

Scientific and technological advances will undoubtedly continue over the next fifty years, but it is not possible to predict so far in the future what the great scientific or technological advances of the next century might be. What we do know is that change will continue because governments, philanthropies, and the private sector increasingly focus on research and development (R&D) investments as an instrument of economic competition.

A recent set of predictions by seventeen leading futurists serves as a general benchmark for this premise. When questioned about future breakthroughs, the seventeen futurists agreed that we could expect major advances in telematics (telecommunications, computers, electronics), biotechnology, areas related to the creation of new materials, efforts to find relatively inexhaustible sources of energy (such as fusion and thermal energy), and a few others (Coates and Jarratt, 1990). I mention this list because it illustrates quite clearly our inability to predict beyond what we already know. The seventeen thoughtful futurists are probably quite correct about what they do know, but it does not help much to understand how existing or future technologies will affect organizations.

Starting from the premise that change will accelerate as worldwide investments in R&D increase, let us pursue two themes: First, in very general terms, how will new technologies affect organizational structure? For example, how might advances in telematics directly affect managerial practices? Second, what will be the complexity and overall patterns of production and consumption?

Impact on Organizational Structures

Scientific and technological advances have considerable impact, but they are not the only driving force determining organizational arrangements. Characteristics of the work to be performed, environmental factors, preferences, and cultural traditions have more influence, although much will be possible in the future that can only be dreamed of today (Huber, 1990).

Advances in telematics, including information technology, are likely to prove particularly significant. They directly affect management practices. These advances may provide many new opportunities, particularly in areas of routinization and control, reduction of hierarchical levels, and centralization and decentralization. But we cannot and should not expect technology alone to radically transform managerial practice—if only because technologies merely provide means to ends.

New programmed technologies differ markedly from the more mechanical (cause and effect) technological processes developed during the last centuries. Artificial intelligence continually provides new opportunities to combine skilled human operators with programmed machines, but basic organizational principles appear to remain constrained by human values, purposes, and preferences. Some authors argue that totally new concepts of the organization might arise from the widespread introduction of programmed technologies together with an evolution both of procedures and of our procedural understanding (Goodman, Sproull, and Associates, 1990, p. 257). But neither they nor anyone else has yet been able to make that leap and describe what they predict. For the moment, we are obliged to proceed along the mechanistical cause and effect paradigm we are familiar with. The important conclusion I wish to stress and illustrate is that scientific and technological advances —while important—will not be as fundamentally significant as some of the other trends we have already described. Let me give you examples.

We are already in an informational economy (Rice, 1984; Truxal, 1990; Porat, 1977). We are therefore able to describe how our new scientific and technological advances are used. Let us take a step further and illustrate the argument by venturing briefly into a simplified futuristic scenario.

Let us assume that all current telematic technologies are far more advanced, common, dependable, and inexpensive than they actually are. Moreover, let us assume that some new ones have been invented. In the scenario in Chapter Six, workers talk to a machine called the "Informator" and it responds with facts and analysis. The "Informator" records, compiles, computes, analyzes, and even "speaks." Let us assume that everyone in the organization has access to these machines. They enable employees to communicate in three dimensions with anyone and everyone anywhere because all the telematic networks of the world are linked. The organization has vastly expanded monitoring and control systems that provide on-time information about all the corporation's processes and even new sensory monitors that record significant behaviors and attitudes. In short, we have a new managerial environment where we can know much more and where we can link clients, designers, providers, or sponsors (Bezold and Olson, 1986; Miles and others, 1988; Fulk and Steinfield, 1990).

Understanding the consequences requires a good grasp of the work itself and of the ways new technologies permit what could not be done before. But the fact that we *can,* does not imply that we *do.* We do not have to assume that all managerial practices will be altered. For example, one might imagine that in a future managerial environment, all managerial work will be done at home since production is robotized, programmed, controlled, and can be directed from a distance. But this scenario does not take into account the social context in which production takes place, the limits of routinization, the culture of professional workers, the fact that complex systems are not static but are learning systems that continually adapt—or the simple human equation that translates as people having to be with other people.

On the other hand, there is little doubt that advances in telematics will result in more work being done at a distance—hence the term *telework.* But the notion of telework has less to do with work at home, and more with the possibility of greatly enhanced linkages both inside and outside the organization (Korte and Robinson, 1988; Huws, Korte, and Robinson, 1989). Designers continents apart can already work together in real time on three-dimensional representations. Opportunities for worldwide networking across and within organizations will increase even more in the coming decades. But overall, at this point we can only be sure that the new technologies will facilitate the redesigning of organizations.

Media Richness

The term *media richness* is used to describe the characteristics of communication channels: for example, the number of senses a medium engages; that is, whether the audience can hear, see, touch, smell, or taste the message. Television involves two senses, radio one. The "feelies" in the novel *1984* were supposed to provide a third sensory access to the feelings of actors (Orwell, 1949).

The term *media richness* can also be used to indicate that there is feedback, that the technology allows two-way communication, the extent to which the message is personalized, and the ways the communication channel affects the psychology of the communication process. Low media richness is associated with low complexity and routinization. High media richness is associated with complexity and problem solving (Daft and Lengel, 1986). At lower levels of the hierarchy, where work is predictable and routinized, rules provide single channel one-way communication of low media richness. At the highest levels of the hierarchy, most important decisions are made in face-to-face meetings which, by definition, provide high levels of richness.

As higher media richness becomes easily available, we can assume that technologies will provide better communication than is possible even in face-to-face meetings, but their use will still be constrained, as was pointed out previously, by the nature of the work to be performed and other social and cultural factors. For example, if the function of face-to-face meetings is to provide a visible, tangible, felt evidence of the importance of management, if these meetings reinforce the symbols of authority, if they reaffirm the legitimacy of top management, it is not self-evident that new technologies replace meetings. On the other hand, if the decisions management makes require access to the information the new technology provides, these will be used. In other words, in the future, the organization is likely to be highly decentralized because innovation and adaptability will require it. To be sure, the new technologies greatly facilitate decentralization, but they do not bring it about.

Decentralization

Most writers on organizations have long realized that to be adaptive and able to respond rapidly, most organizations have to decentralize (Burns and Stalker, 1961; Thompson, 1967; Daft, 1983). This is not a new idea, but it is more possible than ever with new technologies.

Imagine a team of workers at a plant in the future that produces high-speed magnetic vehicles. These vehicles move people at very high speed in magnetic tunnels by spontaneously forming trains designed by computerized programming. One calls or punches in the destination, the computers take over, and the vehicle is channeled directly to its destination by joining trains composed of similar vehi-

36

cles. These vehicles achieve the advantages of private as well as mass transportation.

Imagine that manufacturing practices have changed almost as much as vehicles. Links between consumers and production are direct. Customers specify their own requirements directly to teams at the magnetic vehicle plant. Team members, in turn, program orders directly to part manufacturers and schedule robotic assemblies in real time. All routine assembly work has been automated. Customers specify modifications and the teams supervise computerized design solutions. Thus you may order a vehicle with advanced three-dimensional television, sleeping berths, a kitchen or a prepackaged food dispenser, and accommodation for your pet or your invalid aunt.

Direct on-time linkages between the production team and the customers greatly increase the team's autonomy and discretion. They use programmed analysis to make final decisions on choice of design, purchase of components, scheduling of batch manufacturing, and immediate cost accounting and pricing of scarce internal organizational resources. On the one hand, we have much more problem solving and decentralized decision making on the plant floor. On the other hand, new high-media monitors and controls give supervisors and managers direct overview of decision performance, productivity of designs, current validity of internal pricing and design rules, and even of workers' morale and attitudes toward work. At times, management still has to intervene when design rules have to be changed or when errors creep in. As pointed out, the new technologies facilitate decentralization, they do not bring it about. The competition for quality and the ability of the production team to design products tailored to the unique requirements of their clients make it necessary to decentralize. The aspirations of professional workers make management want to give them more discretion. The new technology only helps.

Changes in the Work Force

Let us assume that in fifty years' time, robots perform most complex programmed tasks that can be routinized, widespread monitoring and automation ensure control and compliance, and further, much discretion is left to workers to handle what is not routinized and these workers have become sophisticated technology operators.

One important consequence is that the work force is transformed. Since most or much routine work has been automated, the new work force breaks down into three distinct components, each requiring specialized training and education. First, there are symbolic analysts. There are the people who handle ideas and symbols: managers, designers, analysts, planners, bankers, lawyers, and so on. Second, there are sophisticated technology operators who build, maintain, and operate the robots. Third, there is a new and growing class of in-person service workers who perform important tasks such as child care, food preparation and service, massage, hairdressing, and the like, whose skills have also become far more sophisticated (Reich, 1991).

New advances in telematics enhance problem-solving capabilities, high media richness combined with vastly expanded information and programmatic technologies greatly increase the organization's ability to decentralize so that it can learn and adapt to its environment. It is not only the demand for credentialing that transforms the work force. Technology also transforms it. As machines eliminate certain kinds of routinized work, the labor force is also transformed and these changes alter the ways the organization is structured and operates.

Interdependent Organizations

Scientific and technological advances are likely to greatly facilitate and increase international exchanges for the following reasons: (1) Idea generation and exploitation increasingly take place in a world forum. (2) Innovations create new dependencies on raw material utilization —reducing some and creating new ones (fusion energy, if it is achieved, will reduce dependency on petroleum resources; low-cost solar energy will create new dependencies for the use of open desert spaces). (3) Innovation alters the comparative advantages of existing production or distribution centers, thus resulting in further geographical displacements of capital and both human and physical resources. Synthetics may replace existing materials, and, more importantly, totally new materials (for example, multilayered materials) may have completely different properties and displace existing patterns of use (Holusha, 1991). (4) These innovations will greatly facilitate communication and transportation over the entire globe—say new packaging and processes that permit long-distance movement of foods, new high-speed ground transport and communication systems that greatly expand the possibility of moving clients to markets or markets to clients, new telematic systems that erase linguistic barriers, new monetary linkages that provide for immediate transfer of credit to any regional economic location, and so on.

As a result, interdependent relations across organizations

can become far more important than they are now. Organizations will rarely work alone, but will increasingly form tightly linked multiorganizational arrangements designed to handle complexity and rapid change. Such patterns already exist in innovative and changing fields of activity. For example, they exist in the worldwide electronics industry, with R&D activities concentrated in selected geographical areas where venture capital, high-level scientific talent, research facilities, and skilled labor are present, and with production or assembly activities concentrated where a low-cost skilled work force, an entrepreneurial class, local capital, government support, and proximity of transport facilitate access to markets. Saxenian's current studies of electronic business organizations in the Silicon Valley of California clearly illustrate this pattern (Saxenian, 1989, 1991).

New scientific and technological advances are likely to generalize this pattern. It will become possible for other economic sectors to adopt the patterns that already exist in the electronics industry because technology reduces the significance of distance. Saxenian describes a complex inventive field wherein new products are constantly created and production and distribution patterns are internationalized. R&D may take place in the Silicon Valley, but important components, such as chips, are produced locally or abroad, assembly is mostly carried out in low-cost skilled labor areas—often abroad—and distribution is handled by diversified firms all over the world. In other words, it is increasingly evident that vertical integration in a single geographical area (namely, firms that handle everything from initial research to the finished product in one location) is going to be replaced by fragmentation and differentiation in many geographical areas.

As the work environment becomes too complex to allow centralization, small specialized firms are better able to move rapidly into new technical fields, to change course as new products are invented, to link with relevant producers and consumers, wherever they are. The advantages of smallness are rapidity, low overhead, and flexibility—but more importantly, the limitation of risk. Venture capital can be more easily attracted to specific single-purpose undertakings whose potential success and failure can be readily assessed. Computer assisted design can rapidly reduce lead time from innovation to prototype, and feasibility is then more easily evaluated. Small firms can be disbanded if they fail and new firms created in their stead. Meanwhile, these small firms can coexist with relatively larger and better established mass production firms that rely on the smaller firms to provide them with components or new products. At times smaller firms become better established and grow, but there is a constant flow in and out as some firms fail and others succeed.

Future scientific and technological advances will inevitably increase the numbers of economic sectors where production and consumption patterns are internationalized. What is true today of selected manufacturing industries, such as the electronics industry, will generalize to other industries and domains—transportation, agriculture, biotechnologies, many services (particularly tourism, banking, health, and education), and even certain extractive industries will increasingly adopt the differentiated patterns of the electronics industry. This will have immediate and long-term consequences. Even now, organizations cannot take their environment for granted. A long-term view will become essential as the environment becomes more diverse and changeable.

In other words, a main consequence of future scientific and technological advances will be to increase the international complexity of the environment in which organizations operate. It will make the ability to plan and deal with the long-term future a dominant factor of organizational life.

Institutionalization of Rapid Change

The reader should not be deceived: environmental complexity and accelerated changes will not necessarily always result in adaptive and learning behavior. On the contrary, there is much organizations can do to mitigate external calls for organizational adaptation and learning. Organizations do not always respond to their environment. Learning and adaptability or the introduction of innovations do not take place automatically (Van de Ven, Angle, and Poole, 1988; Von Hippel, 1988).

To some extent this state of affairs is desirable. Resistance to change reflects the costs of change. Organizations can handle just that much change. Any change involves changing ways of doing things, which means people have to play their roles differently. As you increase the rate of change, beyond a certain limit it becomes impossible to maintain sufficient cohesion and role continuity. Most large-scale historical transformations are actually slow processes that allow individuals enough time to learn to play new roles. Taking that perspective, one can argue that intensification of international economic research and development does not necessarily result in the intensification of change. Some organizations are better able to respond than others. These differences may be most important in a competitive setting.

Queuing Ideas into Action

A queue is a file of individuals or objects waiting in line in their order of arrival. Sometimes it is possible to jump the queue. Let us conceive of a queuing theory of change in the following way. If and when scientific and technological advances outpace organizational and societal ability to adapt, organizational constraints act as gate keepers. New ideas queue and are gradually adopted. Those ideas that are less threatening to existing interests, that require minor retooling and reeducation, that harmonize with existing practices, that fit with existing values and beliefs tend to be adopted sooner. This assumes, of course, that these innovations meet needs and preferences and result in higher levels of performance (Benveniste, 1989).

If the theory holds, the problem takes on a comparative aspect. We want to know whether organizations in different societies are better able to learn and adapt than organizations in other societies, whether queuing is facilitated or deterred in different organizational structures. We want to know what can be done to alter organizational ability to adapt and learn, whether new institutions and government action are needed.

Before we turn to these questions, we have to agree that there are transformational forces at work and that the most important is international competition.

Take the example of Third World countries. Earlier I mentioned Rostow's "takeoff" theory (1963). Rostow assumed that Third World countries had to maintain protective tariffs to achieve economic growth. In terms of a queuing theory of change, he assumed that ideas had to be imported and that once imported all would be well. Therefore, when

Third World countries began to industrialize, they often used raw material exports to finance finished equipment imports. They began by nurturing infant industries to serve their national markets. During the fifties and sixties many Third World countries adopted protective tariff policies to defend their infant industries from the intense competition of large world producers. But protective tariffs also resulted in inefficient local producers. Given the strength of labor unions and the interests of local entrepreneurs, high external tariffs were maintained long after the infants had grown up, resulting in the marginalization of the economy. In terms of a queuing theory of change, new ideas were not generated, or if they were, they just queued endlessly. Therefore, these nations had to continue to rely heavily on raw material exports because their own producers were not able to compete in the more efficient world competition. Moreover, they were also faced with the corresponding protective tariff policies of other nations, including those of more advanced countries. To break this impasse, it was necessary to radically alter protective tariff policies. This implied a major transformation of the local economy, yet in recent years quite a few governments have been able to obtain sufficient internal support to achieve such radical changes.

The United States faces similar problems today. Strong forces are urging protective policies against the international displacement of employment. But international competition makes it doubtful protectionism will prevail. In the long run what matters is competitiveness, not marginalization and mediocrity. I posit instead that much is being done and will continue to be done to facilitate organizational adaptation and learning, and that government and the private sector will seek to find ways to reduce the queuing—that is, to open the gates of innovation wider.

Current evidence suggests that organizations in other societies have shorter queuing times. They are quicker and better able to allow ideas to become action. Let us focus briefly on Japan. Recent polls already indicate that a majority of Americans and Japanese believe that by the next century, Japan will have completely overtaken the United States and will be the number one economic power in the world (Weisman, 1991, p. 5).

I will not attempt to account for all the important organizational and institutional differences between the United States and Japan, but it is illustrative to contrast a current change in American management culture with a set of Japanese cultural characteristics. This may suggest why Japanese organizations appear today to be better able to absorb change, or to have wider gates, allowing ideas shorter queuing time.

The Anxiety of American Middle and Top Management

In recent years there has been a radical transformation in one aspect of the culture of American management and technical leadership. American organizations were never paternalistic in the sense of employing people for their entire working lives and perhaps employing their children also. Social and geographical mobility in the United States results in career paths that are usually multiorganizational (Glazer, 1968). But until the eighties, it was generally expected that seniority rights of middle and high management would be protected. An employee who served for ten or more years with the same organization could expect that short of a major calamity, he or she would have the option of pursuing a career in the same firm. Employees might always find better opportunities elsewhere, but as the years went by, they knew they could count on their employer. For various reasons, this pattern of expectations has been shattered. In the eighties many factors came into play and new technologies provided opportunities to collapse hierarchical pyramids by expanding the span of top management's control.

American managers were impressed by Japanese management structures, which seemed comparatively leaner. Consolidations and mergers resulted in reorganizations and in an excess of managers, which resulted in the removal of management layers. It also seemed important to acquire greater flexibility. New production patterns and increased use of out-sourcing (purchasing components from specialized firms) reduced the need for vertical integration. "Mean and lean" seemed to suggest a greater ability to change and innovate; there was a sense of excessive bureaucratization, of individuals doing unnecessary work. In short, desire for increased flexibility and lower administrative overhead resulted in greater reliance on part-time employees and reduction of middle- and upper-level layers. As a result, higher levels of employment uncertainty now prevail among American managers then ever before (Leventman, 1981; Newman, 1988; Bennett, 1990). Managers' uncertainty about their long-term prospects is accentuated by the vagaries of economic downturns, which make the fear of being without employment very real. We will want to question whether these strategies can persist in the future, since high levels of internal uncertainty tend to reduce group cohesion and constrain risk-taking behaviors.

Japanese Cultural Artifacts

Slightly more than a hundred years ago, Japan was still a medieval feudal society. A large peasant class living in poverty supported an aristocracy of territorial lords (*daimyo*) and a warrior class (*samurai*). Many internal problems beset the country. There were also external threats, which, all together, led to major reforms. The restoration of the emperor in 1868 led to accelerated modernization and industrialization. Young Japanese students were sent to study abroad, public administration was reformed, a new constitution was adopted, and by the end of the century industrialization was well under way. Modern Japan had been created, but modern Japan kept many of its cultural traditions (Lockwood, 1963).

Ruth Benedict's classic study of Japan (1946) undertaken during World War II still provides valid insights into Japanese cultural traits that can help us understand the abilities of current Japanese organizations to learn and adapt:

• Benedict stresses the importance of performance and the fear of disgrace in Japanese culture. For example, during World War II, Japanese soldiers would fight to the end. Victorious Western armies were accustomed to a captured/dead ratio of 4 to 1 when fighting other Western armies. Benedict states that in the north Burma campaign the captured/dead ratio for the defeated Japanese army was 1 to 120, or 142 Japanese soldiers taken prisoner against 17,166 killed (p. 39).

• She mentions the importance of knowing one's place in life. Japanese social hierarchies are so precisely defined that there are different names for different relationships and different terms of address for superiors and inferiors (p. 47).

• The importance of social obligations looms large, particularly obligations to one's superiors, to one's inferiors, and to one's duty to work, or *nimmu* (p. 116). As a consequence the master of the house has obligations to his household, as they have to him. He has to consult and have high regard for group opinion (p. 55). In work situations, shame for not meeting one's obligations is a very important motivator; professional performance is an obligation (p. 150).

• Benedict refers to the importance of group cohesion. Western competitive practices do not work well in Japan, where cooperation is much more important (p. 154).

Benedict's study is useful because it clarifies how current Japanese organizational characteristics derive from traditional norms of behavior. The concept of long-term employment and the dedication of the employees and their families to the firm result directly from a system of social obligations that tie the society together. For example, quality circles are a natural Japanese invention since they provide strong channels of cooperation and communication within well-understood hierarchical levels. The lower classes have guarantees and autonomy within their trades. There is also low power distance between hierarchical levels (Hofstede, 1980). Namely the perceived power difference between bosses and subordinates is small. Many Japanese firms appear to have a very egalitarian culture. Bosses may have no special title or even any visible sign of differentiation. This characteristic fits a society where distinct obligations tie the subordinate to the boss and the boss to the subordinate, and visible power differences are not necessary to maintain the social order.

An account of the transformation of the Japanese electronic industry written by a leading Japanese physicist gives us further cues (Kikuchi, 1983). The author studied briefly in the United States at MIT in the late fifties. In his book he contrasts Japanese and American laboratories of that time. He points out that in the late fifties and early sixties, Japanese research laboratories were far more disorganized than their American counterparts. No one was punctual. Meetings never began on time, research offices were poorly maintained, piles of notes accumulated on desks, research data was organized and processed haphazardly, filing rarely took place, secretaries were little more than errand girls who bought cigarettes, poured tea, and or opened car doors for their bosses. Scientists were poor at presenting the results of their work, and overall R&D productivity in the electronics industry was low (pp. 43–58).

Yet in a short span of thirty years, the Japanese electronics industry has caught up. New Japanese electronics R&D is at a par with if not ahead of that of the United States. Many factors have influenced this development. For example, it is probably easier to catch up than to run ahead. The author differentiates between "independent" creativity—namely "individualistic" talent, the work of geniuses who break into new pathways of thought—and "adaptive" creativity—the ability, once a pathway has been mapped, to move ahead, to test, use, and apply the ideas. The author argues that Japan has its share of geniuses but is far better than the United States at adaptive creativity. He quotes a leading American scientist who points out that Americans are always coming up with good ideas, but they do not follow through, whereas there are always Japanese to take these ideas and move ahead with new products (p. 186).

Where does this adaptive creative ability come from? The author attributes it to characteristics of Japanese culture, namely to the fact that "adaptive" creativity fits a culture where norms of reciprocity tie the group closely together and allow the kind of teamwork and collective support necessary to translate ideas into action. In contrast, he observes, "independent" creativity fits a culture where individualism matters more than collective action.

I take a different view. I stress instead the facilitation of risk taking. A cohesive organization with long-term strategy is better able to support individuals who are willing to take risks. Moreover, when the organization rewards for long-term success instead of short-term achievement, long-term considerations become dominant.

It would appear that in the Japanese organization, intrinsic and extrinsic rewards are more closely tied to long-term collective concerns than to short-term individual interests. Japanese commitment to the organization provides for a long-term view—so that the group is better able to consciously adopt risk-taking policies, not only at the top but within the ranks. For example, the reason quality circles work well in that culture is that they are for real. They are taken seriously because they do not threaten a well-established hierarchical structure (Ouchi, 1981). In other words, the Japanese organization is better able to reduce the queuing time needed to transform ideas into action.

In contrast, the American organization is more fragmented. Individuals are motivated to pursue collective goals, but they are also watchful when collective interests may not benefit them. Social distancing is far more important in a society where social mobility is perceived to be dependent on merit, not social class. Japanese managers do not need fancy offices because their role is well understood. American managers think otherwise, lest someone ask who they are.

The lesson is that different cultures bring forth different management patterns. Some are perceived to be more successful, and these successful patterns are imported and adapted. The experience of Japanese firms in the United States indicates the trend. As I explain at greater length later on, it is feasible to create new reward systems that specifically encourage a long-term perspective. Similarly, it is possible to design organizations with less social distancing or to increase participation and empowerment. Cultural adaptations become more important in organizational design as economic competition increases.

Implications for Queuing Time

Ideas queue in organizations, and increased international competition is bound to result in deliberate efforts to transform organizations so that they can reduce queuing time. This does not mean that Japanese or other practices will become more important. It suggests that organizations will be designed to facilitate innovation within distinct cultural contexts. It suggests that in the American organization, empowerment, flexible informal arrangements, and new reward schemes will be used to reduce queuing time. It also suggests that much more attention will be given to the causes of resistance to change. In organizations of the future the pain and cost of change will be shared more equitably than they are now. This means that our concepts of what is government and what is private will evolve. Government and the private sector will inevitably have to cooperate closely to create new institutional arrangements that reduce the costs of change and therefore also reduce resistance to change.

New Understanding of Organizations

Our understanding and perception of the organization are changing, in part because organizations are changing as they respond to their environment, and in part because our thinking about organizations is also progressing (Perrow, 1986; Scott, 1992). In the next century, our understanding of the organization will continue to evolve. I believe that the following areas will prove to be of importance.

Long-Term Versus Short-Term Thinking

While the modern military campaign tends to be concluded in a matter of months, or at most a few years, economic competition is a matter of several decades. Vast economic transformations take fifty to seventy years, as in the cases of both Japan and Sweden. Yet our current organizational construct tends to orient behavior toward short-term considerations. Our awareness of the importance of long-term considerations is highly likely to increase dramatically in coming years. This will translate into new reward systems that encourage long-term strategic thinking.

Collective Versus Individual Advantage

The current organization is centrally preoccupied with its own survival and advantage. Moreover, reward systems today are mostly or entirely centered on achievements of single organizations, with little, if any, concern for collective or communitarian impacts. Yet successful economic competition is necessarily based on the collective action of groups of organizations, whether these be public or private. Our awareness of this aspect of our current organizational culture is bound to change in the coming decades. As we shall see later on, outcome-based rewards will tend to replace output-based rewards.

Trust

Innovation, change, and organizational learning all imply trust. But trust, as an organizational value, is not encouraged in a competitive setting. Moreover, trust requires multilevel or collective accountability, and while we have not yet invented ways to achieve this, it is likely we will be far more concerned with this issue in the future. Much of our discussion of rewards later in this book centers on the importance of participation, truthful communications, and professional ethos in maintaining trust.

Adaptability

The current organization tends to focus more on short-term efficiency, less on long-term adaptability. It is a problem related not only to short-term vision but also to three central factors: (1) opposition to change because it is not in our interest or does not fit our values, (2) lack of knowledge that we should change or of how to perform differently, and (3) lack of resources, such as the time or the capacity, to implement changes that we know we should make. Again, these problems tend to be related to insufficient collective orientation. It is more likely that in the future, change will become normative and expected. We will then directly address the resistances that impair it. In other words, we will tend to be far more conscious both of the reasons for resistance and of how to deal with it.

Informal Dimensions

Much that will be of significance in the twenty-first century organization will be informal. This important difference will derive from the fact that much innovation and change begins outside formal structures. A small group gets together, perceives a need, and innovates. But our current concepts of the linkages and transitions from informal to formal are not well developed. This will be an area of great importance in the future, as we become aware of the significance of informal structures in the change process.

Scanning of the Environment, Boundary Spanning, Networking, and Planning

The internationalization of the world economy greatly increases the importance of organizational scanning and boundary spanning: namely, organizational ability to keep in touch with and to act upon significant changes in its environment. Informal interorganizational networking is an important and fashionable boundary spanning activity, but networking is still a poorly understood process. Informal networking will become as important as formal processes and will transform planning. Strategic planning can no longer be bureaucratic, but will need to be action oriented.

It will have to rely increasingly on informal networks to create and maintain supportive coalitions.

Democratization and Professional Participation

As the credential and education level of the work force increases, as the organization becomes more adaptive, as organizational learning and change accelerate, the dominant organizational model will shift from a bureaucratic one (say a production line management model) to a professional model (say an R&D management model). But our current notions of organizational democracy, of worker or client participation, are not particularly useful to an understanding of how the twenty-first century organization will provide more professional discretion and participation to achieve greater levels of flexibility and adaptability.

Achieving Change, Maintaining Continuity

Economic competition results in beginnings and ends. New firms emerge, old ones disappear. Organizations are restructured; some departments are abolished, others expanded. Much resistance to change is related to the visible costs of these transformations: costs to individuals and to communities. The most important question for the future turns around this problem: how do we accelerate innovation and still maintain continuity? Much of the discussion so far in this book, and much in the coming chapters, centers around this theme. If ideas are to queue in less time, the perceived costs of change have to be altered. Or, put differently, organizations have to become better able to change internally so that the perceived threat of extinction is reduced. Otherwise, the fear of extinction compels the tendency to resist. Yet when there is no threat, there is no need to change.

Government and Private Sector Relations

Much resistance to change has to do with the costs of making errors. Our society has, over time, invented ways to adjust or mitigate the impact of errors. For example, government regulates so that we avoid doing environmental damage, or government provides for unemployment insurance to help laid-off workers.

Reducing the queuing time needed to translate ideas into action is tied directly to these arrangements. In some instances, government helps innovation, in others it does not. Government regulation and programs directly affect the innovative capabilities of individuals and organizations. This is an area where we should expect important changes.

CHAPTER TWO

Errors, Innovation, and the Ability to Compete

This chapter deals with an important question: will the organization of the future become flexible, adaptive, and innovative, as we seem to assume, or, in sharp contrast, will it actually become increasingly large, impersonal, defensive, bureaucratized, and able to control clients and public? Will it turn outward and respond or turn inward and resist? It is relatively pleasant to assume that rapid change translates into purposeful adaptive behavior; that a better-educated work force becomes professionalized, autonomous, and risk taking; that flexibility and problem solving become the dominant organizational ethos; that ideas queue in less time to become action.

My purpose is to explain why exhortations to adapt—to be innovative and flexible—too often fall on deaf ears. Many authors have examined the ways uncertainty affects organizations (Galbraith, 1977; Lawrence and Lorsch, 1967). But it is not uncertainty in itself that affects the way people behave, it is the way they perceive the possibility of making mistakes, of being involved in errors. The following discussion focuses on different types of errors—marginal, common, and

57

articulation errors—and how each of these is likely to evolve in the next century. Subsequently, my crucial concern is with a fourth type of error called organizational control errors—namely, how organizations attempt to impose their will on their clients or on the public while avoiding change and innovation.

Uncertainty

Without uncertainty life would be dull, but organizations are structured to reduce uncertainty. Bureaucracy reduces uncertainty by using rules and regulations to control much of the behavior of participants. Rules are statements about the future: "If a patient shows these symptoms, follow this procedure." Rules reduce the uncertainty and arbitrariness of behavior. We know what we should do if the patient's temperature reaches a certain level or if bleeding occurs. Rules are preparation for dealing with future eventualities.

In fact, much of social life depends on our ability to reduce uncertainty by providing guidelines on how to behave. But uncertainty is essential to that portion of our social environment in which we are able to apply our creativity. Without uncertainty life would be repetitive and predictable. Rules and procedures give us some certainty about the future; they reduce uncertainty, but they do not eliminate it.

Some years ago I interviewed a young woman still working in an old labor-intensive oyster packing factory. Her job consisted in opening oysters and removing the meat for packaging. It seemed a very repetitive and facile process. She had an oyster knife in her right hand, she sized the oyster with her left hand, applied the knife, pried open the shell, slid the knife along to slice the oyster muscle, and deposited the oyster meat in a container in what seemed to be a single five-second repetitive procedure. I asked how she liked her work after I watched her perform this same operation some thirty times. She picked up an oyster, pried, slid, sliced, dropped the meat, dropped the shell, picked up the next one, pried, slid, sliced, dropped, picked up the next one, and on and on she went. She said she liked it; one learned about oysters—they were so different, there were so many differences in how they were built, how one held them, how the knife could be pressed to pry and slice. I had thought her work to be a dull repetitive routine. She was explaining how complex her task was, how oysters differ, how she had to size each oyster, determine where the knife should be applied and how to give her thrust sufficient leverage to pry and slice the muscle. Yes, there was a routine, but there was much problem solving. What looked repetitive and predictable was only repetitive because she was able to suit her performance to a wide variety of angles, cornices, and shell projections.

The skills of her trade provided her with rules of procedure that allowed her to invent solutions to fit the variety of oysters that she handled. She was effective because she knew enough about oysters to be able to approach and solve each new problem as it came along.

Suppose the oyster worker is suddenly faced with oysters from a different ocean bed that cannot be easily handled. These oysters keep breaking, adding too many shell fragments to the meat. Uncertainty has increased, but that is not the worker's concern. Her problem, her concern, is the potential consequences: too many shell fragments might be noticed and result in her being reprimanded. Maybe clients will complain. She is fearful she will be found inadequate and lose her job. For her, for her firm, for the client, too many shell fragments in the oyster meat is an error. The error needs correction, the organization needs to innovate, but will the worker facilitate the process?

Individuals fear sanctions and they protect themselves. The oyster worker knows that if too many shell fragments get into the oyster meat, she might be reprimanded. She has a new problem: the shells keep breaking although she has tried every different method she knows to pry open the oysters. She has been working under a set of techniques and rules that provided her with sufficient discretion to handle many varieties of oysters, but those techniques and rules no longer work. Will she obtain help to solve the new problem? Should she hide the problem, or will she tell her supervisor? Will the supervisor tell management? Will management bring in experts? Will these experts suggest that using a knife with a slightly broader blade will provide sufficient leverage to reduce shell fragmentation? Or will they urge management to automate and get rid of the worker?

At this point, it is too early to know the answer. I will leave the oyster worker with the fragments of shell and her doubts. Instead, I will turn to a discussion of different types of errors. A typology of errors may provide a theory that can help explain why individuals and organizations do not always solve problems.

Errors

An error is a straying from the truth, something believed wrongly; it is a mistake, a misplay, a deviation from a standard of expectation or judgment; it is the result of ignorance, inadvertence, or the inability to achieve what is right.

Individuals in organizations, and organizations in relation to their clients, the public, or their own staff, get involved in four major errors. These four broad categories are called *marginal, common, articulation,* and *control* errors. They are errors because they are unwanted events that can result in unpleasant, negative sanctions.

Marginal errors happen all the time. They are the "normal errors" of everyday life, the small mistakes in production we are accustomed to expect. It is the bad pea in the pea pod, the bit of shell in the oyster meat. *Common* errors also happen often. They are the consequences of actions on others who are not linked to or who do not participate in normal transactions. For example, the factory pollutes the river, killing the fish that the people who live downriver catch for food. *Articulation* errors arise from the complexity of the world economic system. They are the consequences of rapid changes in demand or supply. They are the unsold goods or the unemployed job seekers. *Control* errors are a different breed of organizational error. They are the consequence of organizational attempts to control their work environment. For example, you want to buy a small part that you need for your washing machine, but the manufacturer will not sell you that small part. They oblige you to pay ten times the cost of the part for an entire assembly that includes the part. If the organization controls enough clients, or if it controls the market, it does not need to adapt or innovate.

Marginal Errors

Mistakes are made at the margin of normal operations. Confusion at the hospital sometimes results in the patient being operated on for a different operation than the one required and ordered. It happens rarely, but it happens. In some cases, "marginal" errors may be quite important, but they are the result of human or equipment failure; they are the production imperfections that happen over and over again and are usually predictable. Some technologies require high quality standards, and so called error-free processes and safety procedures are introduced to guard those standards. For example, at the substation of the electric company, a spare transformer is kept on hand to rapidly replace any of those in operation that might fail. But as Perrow (1984) points out, high-risk technologies always carry an element of risk, notwithstanding all the layers of redundancy and protection that may be introduced. The spare transformer may have deteriorated and thus may also fail. Even if we use two or more spares, failure is still possible, sometimes even more probable. Moreover, redundancy introduces a new set of opportunities for failure. Spares or additional controls have to be checked and maintained, so that the more we add redundancy, the more we also add new opportunities for failure.

Marginal errors imply a tolerance level. In all organizational settings, there is an accepted tolerance for mistakes. Clients who seek quality, seek a low tolerance for mistakes: for example, how many times does the dental assistant cleaning your teeth have to cause you pain before you decide to try someone else? Clearly, there is a threshold zone, and the definition of acceptable risk is culturally bound (Douglas and Wildavsky, 1982). Attitudes change as errors are repeated, but perceptions of risk or tolerance for marginal errors are also related to our perceptions of our ability to control the situation (Heimer, 1985). In other words, we may be more willing to take risks when we know that we can control the situation than when we know we cannot. We are more willing to drive a car on a very long journey if we know that we can have it repaired on the way than if we know we cannot.

As technologies become more complex, control is not reduced, but it is displaced. The scribe could always sharpen the pen, but the typist with the faithful Royal had to call the local typewriter repair shop. At least the typist had a good idea what was wrong and could even perform some adjustments. With the computer, distancing is increased; as the technology becomes more complex, it also becomes more opaque to most of those who use it and therefore more difficult to control (Weick, 1990). This does not mean that more complex technologies increase the level of marginal error, but it means that as human error is replaced by equipment malfunction, centralized controls of operator behavior become less significant than reliance on external expert interventions.

Marginal errors per se do not concern management in organizations; what matters is avoiding a level of marginal error that goes beyond the accepted tolerance level. The dental assistant is not so much concerned with not causing you any pain at all as with not going beyond your tolerance to the point you may complain, seek help elsewhere, or even bring a legal suit for malpractice.

The Future of Marginal Errors

Marginal errors affect clients. They also affect operations within the organization. Let us examine how marginal errors affect clients and operations in the future:

- *The increased availability of more and better informa-*

tion tends to reduce tolerance levels. When we have readily available reliable information about the performance of different hospitals—for example, how rarely or frequently they perform the wrong operation—we expect better performance and seek access to the better hospitals. In other words, as our overall tolerance level drops, we begin to act politically, we complain, we vote, we demonstrate, or we simply seek other providers. At present, we may be quite resigned to high levels of marginal error in the post office. The wrong mail may be delivered at least once a week, mail may be delayed, and so on. But as we acquire more information about the performance of mail systems in other cities or countries, we begin to demand higher quality control standards.

Lower tolerance levels either result in greater political pressure to modify and improve service or in the search for alternatives. In the case of mail services, the rapid growth of alternative communication channels could result in the gradual displacement of conventional mail. In a new competitive communication market, increased information may well result in lower tolerance for and increased concern with levels of marginal error.

• *More opaque technologies increase distancing and apathy.* Concern with marginal error shifts when human error is displaced by equipment malfunction. As human operators become less able to control or even attend to the equipment, it becomes easier to place the blame for errors elsewhere. Attributable human errors tend to be easier to correct because those who make them know they make them and can attempt to improve or change their performance. The old-style tailor who cuts my pants too long can see and correct the mistake when I try them on. The operators of the Three

Mile Island nuclear reactor had no clear idea why they were unable to control the temperature of the reactor of Unit 3 on March 28, 1979. As technological complexity increases, there is more distancing: "It is not possible to process your claim today. The computers are down." Paradoxically, while there is more concern that unpredictable equipment malfunctions will cause widespread damage, the belief that these are apparently unavoidable leads to apathy: "Nothing we can do about it. The computers are down."

• *Decentralization lends new importance to delivery points.* As more complex products and services are introduced, clients have less information about what is or is not acceptable. As quality comes to matter more, clients become increasingly dependent on the services of workers at delivery points. These, in turn, are the organization's principal sources of information about clients' needs. Thus workers at delivery points accrue importance as communication links. In contrast, when the products and services of the organization are standardized, delivery points matter less. The first Ford automobiles were exactly alike. But standardization is no longer the way the game is played. The delivery of tailor-made products depends on a shift of importance from the center to delivery points.

The dental assistant notices (or should notice) that I am uncomfortable; the oyster worker knows about the shell fragments. Supervisory quality controls may also generate information, but improving quality, or reducing marginal errors, is a decentralization issue. When we discuss adaptable organizations being staffed by highly educated workers, who are given considerable autonomy and discretion, we imply that these workers have to be able to handle marginal errors. Given opaque technologies, frontline workers must be able to communicate directly and rapidly to obtain expert help when it is needed. As complexity increases (that is, as technologies become more opaque), pressure increases to decentralize operations. The oyster worker and her supervisor have to be able to act quickly and obtain the necessary help. In their case, the technology is terribly primitive. Another oyster factory uses automated processes, and the operators of its machines have direct responsibility to maintain quality. They have to be able to communicate directly with sources of expert help or become experts themselves, with enough discretion to act.

The question still remains: will the oyster worker tell her supervisor? Consider her situation: she might be blamed, judged incompetent, or deemed less competent than other oyster openers. What matter are her sense of professional pride, her trust in the organization, her sense of the firm's concern with maintaining product quality, and the ethos of her work group. As the technology becomes more complex, more opaque, and opportunities for marginal errors increase, workers' commitment becomes more important. In other words, a gradual shift takes place: output and procedural controls come to matter less; input controls—namely the training, the expectations associated with the role, the ethos and shared values of the workers and professionals—come to matter more. Outcome controls—namely reducing the number of people who spit shell fragments—matter much more. In the management of marginal errors, maintaining quality is increasingly a decentralized activity, and the rules that matter have more to do with internalized values and long-term outcomes than with routine procedural controls or narrow output measures. The organization depends much more on the loyalty of the staff.

Today, management is well aware that to maintain high levels of quality control requires highly decentralized error avoidance behavior on the shop floor. Moreover, the more complex the technology and decentralized the production process become, the more it becomes necessary for the shop floor worker to be involved in teamwork to maintain high levels of quality performance. The operator of the set of robots in the high-tech factory of the future is centrally concerned with avoiding malfunctions, or with correcting them as soon as they happen. The automated factory of the future working on real time will increasingly rely on the skills of work force teams (Drucker, 1988; Kraus, 1980; Shaiken, 1985). In these jobs, a more professionalized segment of the work force is necessary to maintain high levels of performance, particularly when much of the routinized work has been automated.

The team of workers in the imaginary magnetic vehicle assembly facility described in the previous chapter face many contingencies. They have to meet specifications set directly by their consumers, select appropriate designs for the assemblies, activate orders for components, schedule productions, guarantee tolerance levels, and during all that time, operate complex robots and watch for possible malfunctions and failures. The futuristic workers in our scenario are involved in complex tasks requiring problem-solving skills. They are given considerable discretion, but the importance of the task they perform makes error avoidance crucial to the success of the enterprise. Therefore, their motivation matters more than that of workers now. Also, they are more educated or at least more credentialed than today's workers, and have different aspirations. New controls are used: there is much more emphasis on the ethos of professions and on professional accomplishments.

Key Issue

The key issue is how to succeed in designing highly decentralized organizations where innovation takes place in response to client needs without going in all directions at once. In the discussion above, better educated or credentialed workers are not only given discretion to operate under general guidelines, they are also expected to innovate. They design or adapt designs to meet client specifications. If everyone can innovate, how does the organization maintain cohesion? How are individuals motivated to act? How is it done?

Obviously, we will return to these themes in the next chapters, but as the reader will quickly discover, this book places much emphasis on professional trust, ethos, and responsibility; on the inventive use of new reward concepts; and on monitoring to permit far more flexibility than is possible today.

Common Errors

Marginal errors take place in direct relationships: the dental assistant hurts me; I am the client and the dental assistant is the provider of a service that I want. In contrast, common errors involve parties that are not in a direct relationship. The children of my new neighbor, whose windows are only ten short feet from mine, love to play music. They have a taste in music that I do not share, and in addition, they seem to love very loud music. Even with their windows closed and mine also, I hear the deep thump thump of their large loud speakers. My entire wall facing their house seems to reverberate to the sound. At times, they leave, and peace returns for a while. I am waiting, but I know that at some point I will have to do something. For the moment it is still tolerable since it is winter and the windows are closed, but what about spring? Sooner or later I will have to seek a remedy—either directly, by appealing to the parents and to the children to spare us, or, if that fails, by appealing to my elected representative on the city council: there must be some applicable city ordinance against excessive noise.

Common errors often result from rational choices. My neighbors must be hard of hearing and their children will soon lose their own ability to hear sounds, but meanwhile, they do what they like best—play it loud, play it very loud. In some ways they are just like the polluter who sends chemical wastes downriver, knowing or caring little about the fish species that will be affected, the fishing industry that will go into a tailspin, and all other possible consequences.

Most common errors require external interventions. The basic problem is that the affected and affecting parties have no direct relationship. Therefore, common errors are connected through government intervention and regulation. Redress is sought through the political and legal process. The political process is particularly effective when those affected are informed, have time to act, are sufficiently numerous, and are organized and able to influence the regulatory process. But avoiding or correcting common errors is costly, and these costs are not necessarily shared evenly. Resistance to regulation and conflicts between regulators and regulatees generate new sources of uncertainty. The correcting of common errors is not as problematical as the uncertainties associated with the regulatory process. The problems are threefold:

First, regulatory interventions emanate from legislative actions or judicial decisions and therefore tend to be heavily oriented to procedural controls, namely controls that can be defended in a court of law. But procedural controls are by definition designed to reduce discretion, and discretion is important in any process of innovation. When a set of rules curtails discretion, workers may not be able to be creative and innovation will not take place.

Second, the uncertainty associated with regulatory interventions is tied to the conflictual nature of regulation. Regulations are usually designed carefully, with every effort being made to create fair, consistent, and reasonable standards. Even so, they are bound to appear to affect some people more than others, and conflicts are bound to take place, even if regulatees are in favor of the intent of the regulations. As a consequence, most regulations are challenged in court and elsewhere; most are modified, expanded, and continually altered, resulting in more uncertainty.

Third, the ability to change and innovate is not a preoccupation of regulators. Queuing time for ideas to become action is simply not taken into account. Moreover, conflicts and the intervention of the courts and legislatures in the codification of regulatory law result in a cumbersome, slow-moving apparatus. In other words, the regulatory process is part of the problem. External regulatory interventions are concerned with issues of fairness, consistency, and reasonableness. Therefore, issues are defined and shaped by concerns of the legal profession because the courts can or will intervene as soon as conflicts are brought before them for resolution. Their concerns are different: they want to know whether procedures have been followed correctly and legal enforcement obtained, whether compliance is taking place, whether the procedures that were followed can be enumerated, whether the necessary hearings were conducted, whether a complete environmental impact statement was prepared, whether it included the necessary cost-benefit analysis.

The Future of Common Errors

Common errors affect the regulatory process. Since the regulatory process is of concern, let us now examine how the organizations of the future handle these errors:

• *Common errors increase as technological innovations multiply.* New technologies result in new threats to the environment, to safety, and to third parties. As a consequence, the regulatory process intensifies. But a dilemma arises: the more we have regulations, the more we have delays and conflicts, and the more controls seem to focus on procedural practices. These controls are usually designed to limit discretion and consequently hamper innovation. The controls become very expensive. Therefore these questions emerge: Is the current regulatory model valid for the future? Does it increase queuing time excessively?

• *Time for external intervention is sharply reduced.* In the twenty-first century, the median lag time between innovation and impact on environment or safety is likely to be reduced. Many innovations have an immediate impact. For example, in genetic engineering, developments in the research laboratory have consequences in the test tube, or as soon as the idea is generated. When government does not

71

have the necessary lead time to intervene, regulation tends to become ineffectual because it is after the fact, and it tends to legitimize errors instead of preventing them.

• *The internationalization of the economy generates new pressures for the international harmonization of governmental regulatory policies.* At the same time, evasion of regulatory interventions is facilitated as plant siting and outsourcing take place on a world scale. As a consequence, uncertainties about the vagaries of regulatory interventions tend to increase; rules and regulations are constantly changed because many governments compete to attract investments and trade. Conflicts between organized pressure groups, regulatees, and regulators take place simultaneously in the legislatures and courts of many nation states, and the politics of regulation become international in scope.

• *Higher levels of education and training and the corresponding increase in the participation of the work force in management tend to reduce the ability of organizations to avoid whistle-blowing* (Bowman, 1983; Elliston and others, 1985). Moreover, much greater citizen involvement in political action, not only in the United States or Europe but in developing countries as well, tends to enhance and protect the role of whistle-blowers.

• *The mechanics of whistle-blowing change markedly.* New information technologies facilitate whistle-blowing by providing new means of interaction between would-be whistle-blowers and the public they seek to reach (Fulk and Steinfield, 1990; Rice and Shook, 1990). The growing importance of informal networks within organizations also provides greater opportunities to foster and defend would-be whistle-blowers.

• *Informal groups and networks within and without or-*

ganizations provide new structures to politicize organizational life. Informal networks increase the role of professional bodies whose allegiances are both internal and external to the organization. These informal yet useful structures provide both legitimacy and protection for increased levels of whistle-blowing, which alter managerial attitudes. At the same time, uncertainties increase as internal organizational decisions become subject to public scrutiny and are politicized. The costs of the regulatory model become excessive. It therefore becomes increasingly difficult to manage the protection of the environment or of the public interest *from outside the organization.*

The current regulatory model becomes dysfunctional: it cannot respond fast enough because it is far too time-consuming and conflict ridden, and it generates far too much uncertainty. Increasingly, regulatory interventions have to take place before the research is completed—that is, one has to question whether the research should be undertaken in the first place and whether the experiment should be completed. Early questioning has to take place *within the organization,* which means that the organization has to be able to address environmental or safety issues that go far beyond its own narrow purposes.

Key Lesson

The lesson here is that competition may be directly tied to the ability that some societies may acquire to internalize within each organization some regulatory missions that are now considered government's responsibility. This is a very important problem, but not a simple one. And obviously, this is a bold departure. I present it as a topic for discussion, although later in this book I will present a rough outline of a possible approach using professional bodies to make this adjustment. What the future really holds, I cannot guess or tell, but this book assumes that new professional institutions will be created. The professions will play a new and much broader role in the organization of the future: they counterbalance the narrower yet legitimate interests of management. To do this, the professions will require a new role in the governance structure of the organization and they will need to be linked directly to new external professional institutions that set the standards of "good and desirable practice." (See Chapter Five.)

Therefore, the new structures of governance in organizations will become partially participatory. This will have direct implications since it permits increased levels of decentralization. Small or middle-sized groups will run autonomous operations; they may link with others; they may be part of larger conglomerates, but control will be increasingly vested in decentralized units. In the future, the successful management of both marginal and common errors will result in greater levels of professional participation in management. This implies totally new governance structures, where new professional institutions might balance *within the organization* the more narrow interests of management and of owners.

Articulation Errors

Articulation errors are the partial or total lack of fit between what is wanted and what is available. They are the result of a lack of coordination between supply and demand. In contrast to common errors, articulation errors take place between parties who want to transact business together but are not able to reach a satisfactory agreement. You and I have been exchanging my widgets for your gadgets and now you no longer want widgets. In fact, you need fidgets and cannot find them anywhere. This is an articulation error, and obviously articulation errors are a very important dimension of organizational life.

Articulation errors contrast with marginal errors in their scope. Getting the wrong operation at the hospital is certainly a lack of fit between supply and demand. We labeled that possibility a marginal error because the patient goes to the hospital wanting an operation and the error was not expected to happen. A marginal error involves providing the wrong service or product in a *small* percentage of cases, as a result of uncontrollable events, within an "acceptable" tolerance for quality control. In contrast, an articulation error is providing the wrong service or product, or not providing a needed service or product, to a *large* number of potential or existing clients. To be sure, excessive marginal errors can also result in articulation errors. If the hospital acquires the reputation of performing too many wrong operations, the entire clientele may go elsewhere and we would then label this flight an articulation error: clients demand individualized health care, not randomized medical interventions.

Articulation errors can result from the division of labor: I produce widgets, you produce gadgets, and we exchange. The French sociologist Émile Durkheim (1933) emphasized that exchanges are the glue that binds the social system. Organic solidarity, as he called that form of integration, is based on differences, and the rules of exchange provide one of the mechanisms that make a mass of different individuals a unitary, coherent whole (pp. 397–398). When Durkheim wrote, just about one hundred years ago, the rate of change made it relatively easy to assume that articulation took place without difficulty. Durkheim described a hatter making hats in response to the demands of ladies who made requests for styles that pleased them. Whenever errors crept in, and the hats were unsuccessful and unsold, the hatter could always learn from his mistakes and even modify the unsold hats. Durkheim was not particularly concerned with articulation errors. He described these problems as "pathological"; they were irregularities in the overall integration and equilibrium of the social system (p. 271). Obviously Durkheim and his contemporaries had already witnessed many massive transformations of the economies of Europe, but his concept of an integrated social system could sustain "pathologies" that could have vast human repercussions without causing too much concern since these were, by and large, caused by the hidden hand of the market and were therefore somewhat beyond the control of institutions or individuals.

What has changed and continues to change is the time framework within which adjustments take place. Durkheim's hatter could learn from his mistakes because notwithstanding the fickleness of fashion, he always could sell some hats and dispose of or even readapt those he failed to sell. His ability to learn, adapt, and create provided him with new opportunities for good articulation and equilibrium. The new hat is that much more desirable since no one has ever seen anything quite like it.

Articulation errors are directly affected by organizational ability to foresee demand and adapt to it. Given sufficient information about the expected demand—or given sufficient imagination to surmise what will be in demand—and given the necessary time and resources, the organization learns, adapts, creates, and avoids articulation errors.

Failure of the Soviet Experiment

Accelerate the rate of change, eliminate the necessary lead time, or make resources for experimentation and innovation less readily available and you increase the probability of articulation errors. The largest experiment to reduce articulation errors took place in the Soviet Union. The Soviet experiment attempted to curtail articulation errors by controlling most of the economic system. A centralized, planned, and directed economy was supposed to be able to rationally allocate resources to meet wants. The problem was not so much the absence of lead time as it was the tremendous inertia of the decision process. Demands or needs were changing on too vast a scale to allow decision makers at the center to digest the information and act to meet needs on the periphery. Lack of incentives led Soviet bureaucrats to avoid taking risks. As a consequence, organizational learning and adaptability became totally insufficient. Inertia led to corruption. The only way to make the system work was to use the "back door" and arrange matters behind the scene. The collapse of the Soviet system may seem to some, after the fact, to have been unexpected, a major historical transformation no one would have predicted five years before it happened. Yet all students of the Soviet system were well aware of the problem. Granick's (1955) study of Soviet industrial firms described in great detail the complicated "behind the back door" arrangements plant managers were obliged to make to try to achieve the directives of the central planning body. Much of the literature of that period highlighted the Soviet difficulty in handling articulation errors (Azrael, 1966; Ryavec, 1975).

Few Mechanisms to Correct Articulation Errors

Large-scale articulation errors can result in the demise of organizations and of regimes. They are a central preoccupation, not only within organizations, but in the larger body politic. They are the principal source of uncertainty at the higher echelons of organizational life, not because these errors sometimes result in the demise of organizations or regimes—but, more importantly, because individuals and groups know that making too many wrong decisions can directly affect one's career and well-being.

Articulation errors differ in one important dimension from marginal and common errors. Many fewer formal organizational mechanisms exist to deal with them. Regulatory processes exist to remedy or reduce the occurrence of those marginal or common errors that can have strong repercussions on the public, consumers, or workers within the organization. Government intervenes to make certain that acceptable quality and safety standards are met by a wide range of organizations. Thus we have regulatory interventions in construction, food processing, and atomic energy, or we have the Clean Air Act, the Environmental Protection Agency, the Occupational Safety and Health Administration, and the Food and Drug Administration.

But the articulation error is another matter entirely, because market or political mechanisms cannot be tampered with without obvious costs. Unemployment insurance is a remedy for articulation errors; retraining programs and subsidies to large ailing corporate giants are indicators of the nature of the dilemma. Planning, of course, is one way society or organizations attempt to reduce articulation errors by deciding ahead of time how the pieces of the puzzle should fit together. Planning is still poorly understood in the United States. At the macro level, it requires close cooperation between government and the private sector. I have described the planning process at some length elsewhere (Benveniste, 1989), and I will not repeat all of that discussion here. Suffice it to stress again that planning is both a technical and political discourse about the future, where coalition formation and negotiation are central. Planning is necessarily sharply limited by our inability to foresee correctly and can only be fragmented, partial, and incomplete. The lessons of the Soviet Union do not eliminate the utility of planning, they simply highlight the excessive costs of errors engendered within the rigidities of a centralized and bureaucratic planning process. Planning can easily become bureaucratized and sterile. To avoid bureaucratization, planning needs to stay action oriented. Planners need to become managers of the change process, relying on informal networking to create coalitions of support. Given all these factors, planning cannot prevent all errors (pp. 263–286).

Articulation errors suggest insufficient organizational learning and adaptability. They indicate that the organization is simply not in sufficient touch with or able to respond to its environment. Thompson (1967, pp. 159–160) lists three uncertainties deriving from the possibility of articulation errors:

• *The absence of a workable theory to explain how things work and what will happen next.* We are simply unable to predict outcomes and have to make decisions "in the dark." For example, bureaucrats might implement a policy without knowing how the electorate might react because they have no previous experience, information, or valid opinion surveys that can be used as clues.

• *The myriad linkages between the organization and all the elements in the organizations' environment.* In a complex technological world economy we are increasingly linked to others through innumerable social and physical interconnections. It becomes increasingly difficult to keep up with all the relevant events taking place in Singapore or in Henley, Missouri, that might affect our life's chances, even if we understand how these events affect us.

• *The internal interdependence of the organization and its ability to respond to its environment.* Even if we understand our environment and manage to keep up with events that may affect us, there are still the uncertainties in our own responses: We may not be reading the data correctly. We may not be doing the right kind of research. We may not be investing enough in marketing. Marketing may not be doing its job properly. Production may not understand what marketing is doing.

The Future of Articulation Errors

Articulation errors are likely to increase in coming decades as the world economic system becomes more interconnected. Moreover, the magnitude of these errors will doubtless intensify. It is not only a matter of plant closures or offshore siting and sourcing. The economic flows alluded to in the preceding chapters carry the potential for major disarticulation and transformation of the economy over large regions. These will probably take place at frequent intervals as new technologies and patterns of production and consumption alter the relative advantage of competing economic systems. Watching and surviving at the macro level imply watching and surviving at the micro level. It is not only a matter of large-scale disarticulation but also of myriad small-scale consequences and myriad small-scale disarticulations taking place all the time. The stress of work life increases as the puzzle becomes more difficult to put together and careers and life chances are perceived to be endangered. The question becomes Can the system learn and adapt fast enough? And the answer in a world of economic competition is simple: organizations that reduce queuing time for ideas and translate ideas into action faster and more correctly will overtake those who do not or cannot. But once we have repeated this relatively self-evident truth, we are still faced with a dilemma: how does the organization of the future deal with a much increased potential for articulation errors? Two factors may affect the answer:

1. *As the danger of articulation errors increases, organizations may tend to avoid innovation and try to control their clients instead.* This is facilitated by the opaqueness of technologies. For example, an organization will sell us black boxes that cook, talk back, or move people around, but we will have to replace major components any time a small part fails. This kind of control will take many more dimensions than just obliging you or me to buy parts we do not need. We have to assume that organizations will constantly seek to manipulate their environment—*unless* we are able to invent ways of reducing the consequences of articulation errors. We will discuss this at greater length in the concluding part of this chapter, but for the moment suffice it to emphasize that it is not realistic to assume that organizations can greatly increase the rate of innovation unless soci-

ety can reduce some of the consequences of articulation errors.

2. *A more educated and active citizenship tolerates articulation errors less.* Our previous discussion about the role of an enlightened, educated work force, clientele, and citizenry in dealing with common errors applies directly to articulation errors. If we assume increased flows of capital, ideas, and other resources in a future world economic system, we also have to assume that workers, clients, and citizens will become far more concerned about the consequences of articulation errors. Already resistance to major plant closures is mounting. It is difficult to imagine that in the next century it will still be politically possible for firms or government to disregard the wider social and economic consequences of moving production, distribution, or R&D factors from one geographical location to another.

The ability to adapt is not only constrained by internal organizational defensive considerations. It is also constrained by external communities and the larger society. In the nineteenth and twentieth centuries, large-scale economic transformations have taken their toll, but the process of change has usually been slow enough not to necessitate intervention. Let me just give you one striking example: Prior to World War I, Chile was the world's largest exporter of natural nitrates, accounting for more than 60 percent of total world consumption. When nitrogen fixation from the air replaced natural nitrates, Chile's exports went down, but the process was still very gradual. Forty years later, at the end of the 1950s, Chile was still exporting about half the volume of nitrates it had exported before World War I, although its share of the world's market had dropped below 5 percent.

Current transformations tend to be far more radical and

rapid *because they are social and economic transformations tied to technological innovations.* In contrast to the forty-year Chilean example, in the ten short years between 1979 and 1989, the city of Pittsburgh, Pennsylvania, lost a hundred thousand jobs or so, mostly as a result of the displacement of American steel production by foreign competitors. This massive shift in the location of production was a direct consequence of the availability of new technologies and far lower costs of production in Korea and in other countries. Modern steel plants were built abroad, not in the United States, and American producers simply lost their competitive advantage, which resulted in plant closings.

We can assume that these trends will continue and accelerate in the future, even if government and others increasingly plan for "acceptable" levels of change as they protect or encourage selected economic sectors.

As the rate of articulation errors increases, defensive strategies also increase, and defensive strategies dampen innovation. Countries that become prey to larger levels of defensive strategies—for example, ones that refuse to change to protect the way they have been doing things because jobs, plants, or towns will suffer—will stagnate. Countries that stagnate will become increasingly dependent on the accomplishments of countries that do not. But countries that do not stagnate will be able to innovate because they are able to create new and necessary institutions whose task is to correct for the impact of articulation errors and thus reduce the natural propensity of individuals and organizations to pursue defensive strategies.

Key Lesson

Again, we are discussing a vast problem with many ramifications. The lesson that is emerging from this discussion is that the ability of organizations to change and adapt is directly linked to the wider society's ability to change and adapt. The design of new organizations suited to the competitive environment of the future is not only an organizational problem, it is also a much wider governmental, political, economic, and societal problem. This is one reason cooperation between private and public institutions becomes far more important in the next century.

One response that I propose is the formulation of new institutions to begin to address the problems raised here. Such institutions would provide limited but significant means to correct articulation errors *after they happen*. This does not mean that they would finance all the poor choices or bad mistakes investors may have made, but they would provide sufficient means of maintaining continuity to individuals, groups, or communities caught in difficult but short- or medium-term transformations, to reduce political and social opposition to change. Since this is a complex task, and one that government would not easily undertake, new professional bodies, neither private nor public, might undertake this work. Again, this is not a prediction. It is only a tentative image, but a plausible one, worth thinking about.

Control Errors: Uncertainty and Nonadaptive Strategies

Control errors are the successful attempts of organizations to impose goods or services that are not wanted. Most if not all organizations practice some form of control on their environment because the exchange relations between consumers and producers or between voters and elected politicians are necessarily imperfect. When the local drugstore

84

does not carry the less expensive toothpaste brand and you are obliged to purchase a more expensive brand, this is a control error, but it is not a very important control error. You may decide to spend more or drive ten blocks to find the brand you want. But important control errors take place in social life and they reflect the distribution of power in society. Those who have power can decide to use that power to impose on others goods and services they do not want or to deny goods and services they want. How and why are such decisions made, and what are the consequences?

Thompson (1967) conceives of complex organizations as *open systems.* He wants to understand how organizations fare in changing and uncertain environments. He points out that organizational learning does not take place automatically. When change is very rapid and the future uncertain, there may not be enough time to act, not enough information to know what to do, and considerable confusion as to how to proceed. Moreover, even if one is quite unsure how to proceed, one must still justify whatever action is taken, both to oneself and to others. That is, the more uncertain the future, the more one has to find legitimacy for one's actions. Thompson suggests that decision makers might decide that they have no rational way of making a choice, and that flipping a coin provides as good a way to choose as any. Or decision makers might find solace in an elaborate analysis of inconclusive data, or more simply, rely on past experience and continue what they have been doing all along. Thompson suggests that in such situations decision makers tend to want to avoid discretion (p. 119). The situation is uncomfortable because these decision makers know they have to act, and even if they do not act, their inaction will have consequences that will include potential unpleasantness, which they wish very much to avoid. They therefore need a justification—some attenuating explanation—should the course they pursue turn out to fail. They will often find such justification and protection in rules. Rules provide a defensive strategy: they become the justification for whatever actions are taken.

Since Thompson's pioneering work, much has been written about organizations and environmental uncertainty (Lawrence and Lorsch, 1967; Galbraith, 1977; Jauch and Kraft, 1986). This literature makes it clear that organizations handle uncertain environments in various complex ways. For our purpose it is useful to distinguish among the following patterns of response:

• *The desirable response:* The organization scans its environment, learns, invents, and adapts: it responds to external changes by changing or it initiates changes that the environment discovers desirable.

• *Control errors:* The organization attempts to control or structure the environment to fit its own needs. It does not respond to external changes and attempts instead to contain or channel changes in directions more suitable for the organization.

• *Hiding while failing:* The organization scans its environment but is unable to act upon the information it obtains. It can neither invent new solutions nor does it have sufficient power to control its clients or the public. It will instead attempt to deny it is making a mistake and attempt to lull its clients. It will attempt to convince them that it is doing what is right even if the clients suspect something is wrong. The organization will hide control errors, at least for a while. It may gradually lose its market or the support of its clients. But meanwhile, by hiding control errors it delays action.

Hiding control errors is particularly prevalent in public services such as education, social welfare, and public health, where it is difficult to define and measure what is accomplished. In such organizations, there is a tendency to use elaborate sets of rules and procedures to justify behavior, and considerable emphasis is given to evaluation and to proxy measures of accomplishment, such as test scores, that give the appearance but not the reality of what clients want.

• *Innovating and failing:* The organization scans its environment and decides to adapt. It innovates, but the innovation turns out to have serious deficiencies. For example, an organization develops a silicon breast implant that turns out to leak in some patients. These leaks cause these patients to have strong negative reactions, but the organization disregards the information. The organization perceives the problem as a minor marginal error: "Some women cannot handle implants." But as time passes, the problem receives more and more attention, and what was perceived as a minor marginal error is suddenly converted into a major control error that turns into an articulation error. Regulatory interventions take place; silicone breast implants are suspended until further evidence on their safety becomes available. The organization takes heavy losses and so do all the women who had breast implants. Even those who had successful implants are left to worry that they may face difficulties in the future. Was it a control error? Did the organization hide the facts about implants? In any case, many have been affected and the costs are high.

The Future of Control Errors

What happens to organizations if and when the rate of innovation accelerates? Will there be a greater tendency toward control errors? Specifically, will innovation be curtailed—or will organizations increasingly tend to adapt and innovate? Let us summarize the threads of the argument:

In a competitive international economy with higher levels of information and education, clients and the public become better organized, have access to new monitoring technologies, and consequently make it more difficult for organizations to maintain or hide control errors. There is more power balancing. If organizations control the necessary information and control access to goods and services, and if you and I have needs that cannot be met elsewhere, it will take considerable effort at client organizing before we can deal with control errors. Nevertheless, in general, with more education and far more resources to organize with, and with access to information, clients and the general public of the next century will have far more clout than they do at present.

The other side of the coin is that in a far more sophisticated technological environment two contrary forces come into play. First, the more complex the technologies, the more expertise is held by fewer individuals, making client or public access to and ability to interpret information that much more difficult. Second, as new technologies are invented to help access information, new technologies are also invented to protect information. In other words, power continues to matter, and power can be defined here as access to resources, technologies, experts, and information. Power will remain distributed, but I nevertheless believe we will see a downgrading of control errors. Let me explain why.

The greater importance of informal linkages in innovative organizations tends to place a premium on trust. But increased trust tends to go against secrecy. In other words, as informal groups and networks, particularly networks reaching outside the organization, are nurtured and managed, it becomes somewhat more difficult to maintain secrecy inside and outside the organization. Moreover, given that secrecy may have to be maintained to protect new ideas from competitors, secrecy itself becomes a scarce commodity: organizations attempt as much as possible to maintain trust, and to do this they keep as many lines of communication open as possible. It becomes counterproductive to engage in control errors and to try to hide them.

While new technologies to protect against information leaks are bound to be invented, the more organizations build technological fail-safe devices to maintain secrecy, the more these organizations will be at the mercy of technological failures. Given the higher cost of being exposed or caught, organizations will tend to reduce or avoid excessive reliance on technological means to protect secrecy except in areas where such practices are considered legitimate.

Centralization of international conglomerates discourages highly innovative and flexible practices. During the nineteen sixties, seventies, and eighties, we witnessed the beginnings of the internationalization of economic activity and the rise of multinational corporations. The characteristics of this phenomenon are already well documented in the early literature on multinational corporations (Barnet and Muller, 1974; Dunning, 1972; Eells, 1972; Rolfe and Damm, 1970; Vernon, 1972). Many factors were at work in that period of time: expansion and emergence of new foreign markets, taxes and other incentives offered by governments, access to new financial markets, availability of foreign labor, and so on. At the same time mergers and acquisitions at home and abroad provided many new opportunities to diversify and expand into new areas. But the basic phenomenon was organizational spread, namely the merging and linking together of many previously independent organizations into much larger conglomerates. These conglomerates have numerous defensive advantages: they provide access to resources and talent; they provide insurance in uncertain markets by greatly diversifying their own activities; they provide profits, and therefore capital resources; they provide vastly expanded career paths to a new breed of international managers; they provide an international arena in which to avoid the laws of specific countries; and finally, and most important to our discussion, they aggregate power to maintain control errors.

The management of increased levels of potential marginal and common errors requires greater levels of decentralization and of partial participation. Greater numbers of control errors imply centralization and corresponding increases in marginal and common errors. These in turn translate into increased numbers of articulation error. Therefore, the organization of the future will rely less on defensive postures and more on its ability to learn and adapt.

CHAPTER THREE

Rules, Structures, and Rules for Breaking Rules

This chapter explores the ways organizations adapt rules and structures to suit their needs for transformation. I briefly mentioned rules at the beginning of the last chapter. Now I will discuss at much greater length one of the most important elements of organizational change: the ability to break rules. I will approach this topic from an unconventional angle. Instead of discussing organizational rules, I will use rules of etiquette. Why? In rules of etiquette the quandary implicit in any rule breaking is sharply drawn: the existence of and need for meta rules. Rules of etiquette evolve in social milieus, and in contrast to organizational rules, there is no management in charge to change them. Therefore, the meta rules of etiquette are more visible and can be better understood than those of the business world.

The second major topic of this chapter is controls and the governance structures of adaptable organizations. Several governance models exist in which management enhances the participation of professional staffs as a prelude to giving these staffs new responsibilities. Some of the main lessons from the previous chapter carry over to this discussion: the need to decentralize and still maintain cohesion, the need to find ways to reduce the costs of external regulatory interventions by internalizing some of these, and the need to improve society's ability to adapt and change.

Rules and Meta Rules

Innovating often involves breaking rules. Rules are statements about the ways we expect ourselves and others to behave in given circumstances. For example, rules of etiquette tell us how we should address an elderly visitor, how seating may be arranged at the dinner table, or in what order we should enter the dining room once dinner is announced. Rules clearly reduce uncertainty since they guide our behavior by giving us shared expectations.

As dinner is announced, the young widowed lady of the house gives her arm to the man who is her guest of honor that evening and they lead the way into the dining room. All the guests know that this is expected. It is the rule. In that dining room, in that year, in that culture, this set of rules, or expectations, works. The other guests follow, find their places at the table, and enjoy a gracious dinner by candlelight, served by waiters wearing white gloves. Let us consider the various purposes that rules serve.

• *Rules reduce potential conflict.* Etiquette dictates who precedes whom, who accompanies, who opens the way, who helps with the seating, who sits at the right and who at the left of the young widowed hostess. Personal pretensions and potential affront are avoided because the rule is impersonal; it applies to everyone in the room.

• *Rules legitimize behavior.* We accept the seating arrangement because it is dictated by a set of accepted norms.

We know we are seated where we should sit, given our relationships and those of the other guests in the room. Should we complain, later on, that our partners at the table were terribly rude and dull, the hostess would answer with that charming smile of hers, "I know. I am so sorry. I wanted you close to me, but you know the rules."

• *Rules provide for discretion.* Rules can always be broken, and most rules include specifications of when they do not apply. The red traffic light at the intersection is a rule that says "stop your vehicle." The green light says "go ahead." The fire truck runs through the red light, sounding an alarm that tells us that the green light does not apply and that we should let the truck speed by. But discretion to break rules can also provide opportunities to exercise power and influence. The hostess breaks protocol and has a young man sit at her right instead of the guest of honor. Is she sending a message to other pretenders who have been courting her?

Breaking Rules

Although rules can be broken, they generally maintain the status quo since the behavior they regulate is predictable and accepted. As we enter the dining room, we know what will happen because the hostess is following the rules and she has done so for years. When she seats the young man at her right, we are taken aback and we are not sure what is happening. Is she sending a message? What is her relation with the young man? Is she attempting to embarrass or is she expressing strong displeasure with the guest of honor? But breaking the rule does not yet alter the status quo. The guest of honor is still the guest of honor. The young man is just a young man, and expectations are not yet changed.

But breaking the rule has opened the possibility for a change to occur. It has created the opportunity for a new interpretation of the situation.

How Rules Shape Change

To know how to behave in a changing environment still requires rules. The First World War is raging and our still-widowed hostess is actively helping the Red Cross cope with wounded officers billeted at her residence. New procedures are now in force at lunch and dinner. These procedures are brought about because our hostess is a problem solver. It is no longer possible to serve dinner in white gloves, and entrance and seating in the dining room have to take place on a first come, first served basis. The new rules are instituted to meet the new circumstances. Only our hostess's seat is still reserved. Her suitors are now away at the front. This may seem self-evident behavior to you and me, looking in from outside after the fact. Yet not everyone in the social circles of our hostess adapted the way she did. Other families continued with their lives, "suffering the inconveniences of war," keeping their older male servants (the younger males were in the army). In those families, the old rules were kept and service in white gloves continued throughout the war. Our hostess, in contrast, adapted manners and etiquette she was already familiar with. The simplified procedures she instituted were roughly those used during the hunt when hunters were served some brief collation in the field.

When the hostess seats the young man where her guest of honor should sit or when she adopts new seating rules, she is changing rules in order to be creative.

When she seats the young man next to her, she provides new opportunities for her two suitors, who are threatened, to attempt to communicate with her. The guest of honor, faced with an unexplained slight, is obliged to play his role differently. He publicly interprets what is happening, acting as if he had asked for the young man to take his place. The dinner becomes theater where the actors have to improvise a new play. The two suitors downplay the guest of honor and the young man is very confused. The hostess is charming as she assesses who plays well and who does not.

When she adopts the rules of the hunt collation in her dining room, she changes rules to solve a problem, but in both cases what mattered was her ability to change rules without destroying rules. Her dinner with the young man was a success because she shifted the rule without abolishing it. She increased uncertainty to a tolerable level within an accepted overall normative order. When she adopts the rules of the hunt, she does what others in her circles do not do. She uses new rules to solve problems.

Meta Rules

To shift rules requires meta rules. Why is our hostess able to adapt to wartime circumstances? Because she is willing and able to alter the existing rules. She is able to alter rules because she shares with her guests an accepted internalized normative order. They appreciate and understand what she is doing. Within this normative order, she is able to step back, observe the situation, and conclude that circumstances call for a different way of handling the way one proceeds to the dining table. It is her ability to step back, observe, and describe a new way of behaving that makes her different from other patrician families in her neighborhood. She invents a myth of the future. She says, "In war as at the hunt." This is a new language, a new image of the future.

Why was she able to judge her suitors' talents? Because she obliged them to play out a role they had to invent at the moment. Again, she was able to step back, change the scene, observe the action, and reach her conclusions.

To step back requires meta rules. What are meta rules? A set of understandings, a culture, beliefs, expectations, ideologies, and myths that allow one to change rules. Our hostess acted purposely. She knew she was breaking the rules. It did not happen by accident; it was not an unconscious act. But she maintained her identity, her status, while she innovated. She had the ability to step back, observe, and in the context of her culture, decide differently.

From this example, we see clearly how the organization of the twenty-first century may also be able to step back and observe itself, and how it can use shared understandings, including ideologies and myths, to decide to act differently. These shared understandings are the meta rules of the organization.

What does it mean "to step back"? It means that the organization is able to interrupt existing rules so that new rules can be considered. It means meta rules can be invoked. What differentiates meta rules from rules? Meta rules precede rules. Our hostess is able to announce that the small ceremony preceding dinner will be completely altered because the meta rules we all share permit her to make such a decision. She creates a new understanding, or new myth of the future, which we come to adopt. The meta rules formulated around her social lineage, the death of her husband, and her role as young widow and hostess provide her with the legitimacy and ability to change the rules of the household, and she does it.

In the organization of today, meta rules are handled by management. Management has both the authority and ability to change the rules. It acts as our hostess did, although she pioneered and had much less authority to do what she did. What is interesting is that in the organization of the future, the ability to change rules will be decentralized. There will be, therefore, much less authority to change rules. The ability to change has to come from meta rules, namely shared understandings within the work force. This is why the professionalization of the work force is so important.

How Organizations Use Rules

Let me expand further on this line of thought. Organizations have a distinct advantage over our hostess. She follows, interprets, and even innovates with the rules of etiquette of her social milieu, but her ability to invent new rules is constrained by social practices, traditions, and the roles of elites that set the tone of accepted practice. In contrast, organizations specify the expected behaviors of their members. Management can change these specifications whenever a need arises. Organizations are able to change rules readily, but the process is complicated because rules serve not only to reduce uncertainty or provide legitimacy but also to control behavior.

Rules ensure that individuals will be guided as to what is expected of them. To the extent that they are enforced through rewards and punishments and are complied with, rules also become powerful instruments of organizational control. They permit the coordination of work and, more importantly still, establish standards of expected performance—and therefore deter much corruption. Rules limit arbitrary behavior. For example, rules about sexual harassment specify undesirable behaviors and procedures for redress. Rules limit discretion, and this is both a very important contribution of rules and their major drawback. Rules are routinized orders, and the very reason they may be so effective—namely, that they permit the coordination of work and establish the standards of performance—also explains why they can be totally dysfunctional: rules limit discretion.

As we well know, rules are effective when the future is relatively predictable, so that it is possible ahead of time to make rules that will work, and sufficient discretion is left within the rules to allow problem solvers to address significant new, unique, or rare events. But in a rapidly changing environment, when even the exact definition of the work to be performed may be in doubt, and when organizations have to adapt, learn how, and invent, it is discretion that matters. Discretion is needed within rules, but more importantly, discretion to step back and change rules when these are no longer appropriate is essential.

Discretion within rules implies a problem-solving capability, namely a skilled or a professional attitude toward work. The more work is routinized, the more it is repetitive, the more it requires limited skills. The more discretion within rules is enlarged, the more diverse skills are needed. Discretion to step back and change rules requires meta rules, namely a professional attitude toward work that provides new overall visions of the purposes pursued combined with the authority to participate in the invention of shared beliefs, ideologies, and myths that reorient behavior.

In the organization of the future, rules per se will be less important because they can be changed readily. The shared beliefs, ideologies, or myths about the future from which goals are derived are a more important source of behavior control. But if the organization relies less on rules and more on shared beliefs, this means a higher level of participation of important segments of the work force in governance. They and management will create the beliefs, ideologies, myths, and meta rules needed to innovate. In the future, flexibility is achieved because trust in common purposes guides action.

Let me illustrate what I mean. Today, management may delegate authority, give decision-making capability to others, but as we all know too well, problems often arise that have not been delegated. People dealing with clients suddenly encounter a problem they are not allowed to solve. They have to seek authorization from their superiors. That is what I am discussing here. In the organization of the future, some or many delivery point workers may act independently. But the only reason these workers can act without clearance from above is that they share management's overall vision of the organization's purposes, and they can independently reach the same decisions management would have made if management had been as fully informed as they are.

How Organizations Control

Organizations control by regulating inputs, process, outputs, and outcomes. If we consider a worker in a factory, we may say that this worker receives incentives such as salaries, training, materials, and equipment to work with. These are inputs. Then we say this worker is expected to perform a number of operations, and we describe these operations.

This is the process. Then we say that this worker produces sixty widgets per hour. This is an output. Finally, we might go further and speak of outcomes. We would say, for example, that as a result of this output, sales increased 10 percent, the sale of widgets increased well-being in the community, or this increase is related to the overall growth of the economy.

Organizations control inputs, process, and outputs. Today, outcomes are more rarely used, although in the future they may become a far more important control instrument. In the classical control situation of the beginning of this century, the worker was paid a salary that was related to his or her attributable output. In addition, many rules of procedure were instituted. This worker was tightly controlled and given very little discretion. The work was highly routinized. That salary was tied to production should have ensured motivation to perform the routinized task expeditiously. Many procedural controls monitored by supervisors protected workers and equipment, and helped reduce marginal errors.

This form of overall control is still widely used in most twentieth-century organizations. It is used in factories, commercial establishments, and government agencies. To be sure, input controls cannot always be tied directly to specific outputs, and performance is often assessed by supervisors who control both process and outputs. Thus in some schools, principals evaluate teachers by assessing their adherence to and compliance with expectations of how they should teach. The principals visit the teachers in their classes and score them on a set of indicators: Do they have a lesson plan? Do they follow it? Do they engage students in interactions? Do they maintain discipline? And so on. These are process rule evaluations and controls. Later the students' performance scores on national, state, or school tests can also be used to evaluate the effectiveness of the teacher. These are output measures. Both the class visits and the tests become controls when they are perceived to affect valued incentives (pay increases, assignment to better classroom, small grants for materials, or whatever the school can use to motivate teachers).

Process and Output Controls

The problems with process or output controls are many: we may not know what process results in what outputs, we may not measure or evaluate significant outputs, or if we measure outputs correctly they may be much less important than other outcomes. More importantly, once rewards and punishments are tied to specific process rules or output measures, innovation is hampered. If the principal is perceived to like a certain way of doing things, teachers who experiment and do things differently may fear they will be evaluated negatively. Process or output controls deter innovation anytime rewards and punishments are tied to or are perceived to be tied to status quo processes or outputs.

If the organization is involved in rapid change, and organizational learning is a central preoccupation, reliance on process or output controls is dysfunctional. Or, to put it more exactly, the inability to change process or output controls hampers innovation. The control system of the organization is an important factor in facilitating or deterring innovation. The more the organization relies on controlling process or outputs, the more innovations dealing with process or outputs may be hampered.

The collapse of the Soviet system had much to do with the imposition of strict output controls. The plan specified desired production targets and tied rewards to them. When output had to be changed, the production units did not have sufficient discretion to respond to changes in the environment. Similarly, process controls that dictate the "best" way or the "right" way to perform a task hamper innovation when the controls are no longer working.

Who changes process or output controls? Top management does, but top management will not be able to attend to the great diversity of changes that will have to take place in the future at delivery points. The adaptable, innovative organization will be so because it allows change to take place where it matters: at the delivery points where the organization affects its clients and the public. Therefore, the success of organizations in the future will depend on a radical shift away from process and output controls toward greater use of input and outcome controls.

In other words, the organization of the future will need to depend much more on the attitudes and internalized norms of its workers. These workers, as I suggested in the discussion of coming trends in Chapter One, tend, in the aggregate, to be better educated than workers of today, although, inevitably, there will be considerable variation. This strongly suggests that participation in the governance of the organization will tend to be selective. But there will be new structures of governance, which, in some respects, may be much more democratic than the ones we have now.

Commitment to the organization will matter much more in the future. This means that some workers, or many workers, will tend to identify closely with the organization. As I suggested in Chapter One, one of the consequences of the

102

feminization of the organization will be the gradual blurring of what is organization and what is family. I cannot expand too much here on this topic, but I would suggest that contrary to current practice, where long-term commitment seems to be decreasing, we have to expect that in the future the reverse will tend to take place, although, as we shall see in the next chapter, commitment may shift from the organization per se to what I will describe as the creative milieu, namely the ever-changing set of organizations where individuals work and pursue careers. Put differently, high levels of commitment will be maintained even as organizations change, evolve, and are transformed. But for this to succeed, new institutions providing continuity may be needed.

Outcome Controls

At the beginning of the twentieth century, bureaucracy became the tool of reform. Process controls and sharp limits on discretionary behavior were intended to reduce corruption and plunder (Osborne and Gaebler, 1992). Careful monitoring of behavior was designed to ensure that people in organizations did what they were supposed to do and did not use the organization to advance personal or family objectives or to enrich their own pockets.

During the twentieth century, as the costs of bureaucratization became excessive, reliance on process and output controls decreased. Nevertheless, these controls remain important for the simple reason that outcomes are often difficult to measure. How does the barber measure outcomes? By the number of haircuts? Or by the looks of customers? This problem has received much attention in many sectors including health care since controlling outcomes can have much to do with effectiveness (Heithoff and Lohr, 1990).

Output controls are useful when the measures do not distort what the organization is supposed to accomplish and when the measures are valid and reliable. Yet, as we shall see in the following pages, outcome measures are increasingly becoming more relevant simply because outcomes are usually far more significant than more narrowly defined outputs. Increasingly, outcome measures are used to assess how well the organization is performing, particularly where market mechanisms do not operate.

As mentioned previously, as the organization grants greater discretion at all levels of the hierarchy, more individuals are empowered to change rules. But the organization remains integrated through new forms of selective participatory management and the invention of a shared vision of common purposes. Outcome measures and outcome controls become more important because they more closely reflect a shared vision of the future. The organization is saying to its workers: "Here are the resources, here are desirable images of what we want to accomplish; we have trained you, go to it, and it is overall results that matter."

Outcomes Versus Outputs

Outcomes are broad collective results. They are the results that matter most to clients and citizens. Firms or governments produce outputs. What happens when outputs are used as outcomes? They involve a subjective element of evaluation because they involve human preferences; they reflect what pleases and does not please those who buy products or use government services (Levy, Meltsner, and Wildavsky, 1974).

Outcomes differ from outputs. They are the consequences of outputs. I study engineering and graduate. My
engineering school's output might be considered the rate
of graduation. I obtain employment and contribute to the
community where I live; now we are in the realm of outcomes.

Outcomes are affected by external factors that may be
beyond the control or responsibility of the organization that
generates outputs. The concept of outcomes carries both a
longer time dimension—namely, they often happen long
after outputs take place—and a broader connection to factors the organization does not influence directly: the fact a
well-paying job is available might not be directly attributable
to my engineering school. As a consequence, outcomes are
necessarily much more collective; that is, they are influenced
by the work and actions of many. For example, say that the
engineering school receives large financial incentives for
the contributions of its graduates to a general measure of
collective well-being, say the annual rate of economic
growth in the region where most of its graduates find employment. This would be an outcome reward. Presumably,
the graduates of the engineering school contribute to the
development of the region and the state government has
decided to link this development with the dollars the engineering school obtains or the bonuses it pays.

Many other factors impinge on the economic growth of
the region, factors that have nothing to do with our engineering school—for example, consumer confidence, rates of saving and investment links to other economic regions, competition from abroad, weather patterns, the price of energy,
and so on. Therefore, it is both difficult to attribute the contribution of our engineering school to whatever growth is

105

achieved and, at the same time, it is difficult to know exactly how the engineering school can or should contribute to the region's economic growth. Nevertheless, if controls are so designed, an outcome measure, such as the annual rate of economic growth, can play a significant role—not necessarily dominant, but significant—in fund allocations. It follows that to the extent that staff and management of the engineering school perceive ways to contribute to economic growth, they will do so. What matters is the creation of controls, including rewards, that are sufficient to create the necessary cooperation and articulation that permit members of a complex system to pursue common objectives.

How Outcomes Are Selected

Organizations select outcomes that are important to their success, to the perceptions of owners, clients, and the general public regarding their contributions to the general well-being. Various outcomes may be used. For example, the manufacturers of our magnetic vehicles might have instituted outcome bonus plans based on (1) measured satisfaction of clients, (2) annual cost reductions, and (3) productivity gains and profit margins. In addition, they might have additional bonus plans designed to increase cooperative work with other organizations. In contrast, government agencies might tend to have bonus plans linked to very general measures of collective well-being, such as economic growth, crime reduction, maintenance of economic infrastructure, and so on.

As mentioned previously, the reason outcome measures will have to be used more widely in the future is closely related to the problem of cohesion maintenance. When innovation is decentralized, discretion is provided so that everyone can invent, experiment, go in all directions at once. Therefore, strong motivators are needed to maintain cohesion. Outcome measures usually translate into collective rewards. In our earlier example, the entire engineering school was rewarded when economic growth took place in the region. But this still leaves the problem of free riders: what about members of the staff of the engineering school who let others do the work since they will be rewarded in any case? To work, collective rewards that reflect individual contributions are needed to avoid free riders. Therefore, when exact contribution cannot be determined, collective rewards that approximate contributions have to be invented. For example, if annual bonuses are based on the overall rate of economic growth of the region, government workers who affect or contribute in some way or other to economic growth will still seek to make contributions as long as they feel that their counterparts are contributing and as long as they know that those who do not contribute will not be rewarded for the collective endeavor. If free riders are allowed, contributions are lessened since it is clear that it is not worth making special efforts to work collectively. Therefore, free riders cannot be permitted. Reward systems based on outcomes have to use performance evaluations to trigger outcome rewards. In other words, individuals need to be evaluated according to norms of performance that are negotiated—and their evaluations, positive or negative, trigger or do not trigger rewards based on outcomes.

Bureaucratic Versus Professional Structures

Today, many organizations or portions of organizations already have a professional structure. For example, most research and development (R&D) departments tend to be organized in an unbureaucratic way, giving a more important voice to professional workers. The same is true of hospitals, think tanks, research universities, law firms, theater groups, and even unconventional innovative organizations (Miller, 1986; Harris, 1985; Benveniste, 1987). In these new structures, rules and regulations are less dominant than professional judgment. Control is exercised but there is more reliance on trust, therefore more reliance on input and outcome than in process or output controls.

In the bureaucratic model of organization we have the usual pyramid of supervision and control. Management is sharply distinguished from workers. In many organizations, workers are organized into unions to defend their interests in negotiations with management. The structure of the organization is highly centralized, and responsibilities for goal formation, coordination, and monitoring of performance rest very much at the top of the pyramid.

Today, workers do not share many of these important responsibilities with management. For example, when General Motors announced in February 1992 that it was planning to close several of its more important plants, including the Flint plant and one at Willow Run in the state of Michigan, the workers at the Willow Run plant near Ypsilanti township, who had heard rumors that their plant would not be closed and that a sister plant in Arlington, Texas, would be closed, were taken by surprise when the opposite decision was announced. My point in mentioning this is to stress our current very sharp distinction between the responsibilities of management and those of the work force.

Professional Models

Professional models are structures wherein professional workers (as contrasted with ordinary workers) share many responsibilities with management or even manage by themselves. The three most common professional models of governance are the partnership, the senior staff model, and the dual governance model. I have described these at length elsewhere (Benveniste, 1987).

The Partnership. The partnership model gives senior partners—who are professional workers—all the responsibilities of management. The partners may select a chairperson, or some partners may be more influential than others, but by and large, they are collectively responsible for running their organization. To be sure, not all workers share these responsibilities equally, and many professionals—for example, in law, investment firms, and medical practices—start at the bottom, doing what they are told for many years before they climb the professional career ladder, become recognized, and are invited to become full or senior partners. Others' specialties or interests are such that they will continue to work for the senior partners throughout their careers. But, in contrast to the bureaucratic organization, the partnership gives senior professionals, who still carry their original professional tasks (that is, work as lawyers or medical doctors, as contrasted to working as managers), the entire responsibility for managing the organization. The partnership has many advantages and disadvantages. It works when the partners' work can be easily coordinated and when consensus is maintained. Nevertheless, as Auletta (1986) has shown us in his account of the fall of the house of Lehman on Wall Street, conflicts between partners can easily become highly dysfunctional.

Senior Staff. In the senior staff model, a group of professionals run the organization, but this group is headed by a manager who shares all or most managerial responsibilities with the senior staff. This is the way think tanks, research units, and other R&D operations tend to be organized. The senior staff model has the same advantages as the partnership, in the sense that individually or collectively the senior staff will be involved in goal setting, in strategic planning, in task assignments and coordination, and in all other relevant managerial responsibilities. But this model offers the benefits of centralized decision making; conflicts, for example, can be adjudicated by the manager because he or she has the necessary decision-making authority. This model is particularly useful in organizations that require considerable internal coordination (in contrast to the partnership, which is not particularly suited to intensive internal coordination) but that require the decision-making capabilities of professionals—namely, their ability to act on the basis of internalized professional norms that are far less restrictive than conventional process rules or output measures of performance.

Dual Governance. The dual governance model involves two hierarchies, one professional and the other managerial, that share distinct managerial responsibilities. This is the model used in some hospitals, where separate professional committees typically run certain hospital activities (such as allocating resources or purchasing new equipment), and in research universities, where faculty members have distinct responsibilities for developing curricula, approving courses of instruction, granting promotions, determining retention and hiring of faculty, and so on, while the administration maintains independent control of budgets, space, student records, and so on.

This model is not particularly well suited to organizations facing rapid change because the governance structure tends to be diffused; power is shared by many. Moreover, the ability of the professional staff and the administration to cooperate depends on the level of consensus that can be achieved among the groups involved. Elaborate procedures of participation makes it difficult for the organization to respond quickly, but it benefits from the wider, more democratic participation of the entire professional staff (in contrast to the partnership and the senior staff models, which limit participation to a professional elite).

Given the difficulties professionals may have in resolving their own conflicts, the dual governance model is sometimes referred to as a political model of governance because the endless conflicts these professionals nurture (for example, the conflicts within the faculties of departments in universities) is reminiscent of the political arena (Baldridge, Curtis, Ecker, and Riley, 1978).

The model most relevant for the twenty-first century organization is the senior staff model, or appropriate modifications of it. The reason is not that greater levels of participation will be possible and desirable, or that organizations will tend to become completely democratic. The ability to scan the environment, to move rapidly, to coordinate disparate elements, to mass resources, to organize and assign tasks will always require a high level of centralization to be successful. But at the same time, the ability to invent—to change rules, to invoke meta rules, to create myths and ideologies that orient collective behavior, so that one can take risks and carry ideas into action—requires a far greater degree of freedom than is possible in conventional hierarchical organizations where most workers are precisely controlled and accountable.

The organization of the future will likely differ from today's organization in this important dimension: it will place far more discretion at much lower levels of the hierarchical pyramid than is the practice today. Yet, overall control will be maintained, but in a much more fluid and informal manner than at present. Most of the critical tasks and activities will be handled by professional teams, who will be responsible for carrying out the purpose of the organization or even the purposes of many organizations. These teams will be headed by professional senior staff members who have a direct link to the higher decision centers.

Participation will have to increase, but very selectively, allowing hierarchies within the senior staff to modulate, articulate, and represent the increased voice of professionals within the decision centers. As we shall see more clearly in the next chapter, the granting of discretion—the decentralization of power to create new rules of the game tied to multiorganization involvement—will result in large-scale networking and lead to new startups and spinoffs.

Envelope Supervision

In the last chapter we imagined a team of future workers at a plant producing high-speed magnetic vehicles (vehicles that levitate in magnetic tunnels and can be programmed to form trains so as to achieve the advantages of both private and mass transportation). These workers formed task teams endowed with far greater autonomy and discretion than are practiced today. For example, the production teams were able to have direct linkages with their consumers and were therefore able to tailor vehicle designs to meet consumer specifications. Operating on the senior staff model, they could network with suppliers and use scarce internal resources competitively through pricing mechanisms. Their work and performance are monitored, but they have much larger degrees of freedom as they link interorganizationally.

The concept of envelope supervision is useful to understanding how monitoring is achieved in a participatory decentralized production process. Envelope supervision involves mutually agreed upon definitions of (1) the scope of discretion and (2) performance expectations based on outcomes. The professional task team staff, working within the governance structure—for example, an executive committee representing the entire professional staff—would establish with their colleagues a broad agreement on those areas where they are given complete discretion, the information tools they will use in making choices, and the precise expectations that will be used by the same executive committee to monitor performance. Error avoidance is achieved by monitoring. Given advances in technology, in most task situations more information is collected than can be used to monitor and evaluate, but the point of envelope supervision is to create and enlarge the autonomy of task teams to allow for experimentation and innovation.

Some tasks are well understood and can therefore be routinized. But the organization of the twenty-first century will need to allow for adaptive, nonroutinized behavior much more often than is practiced now. Why? First, because change and adaptation have new importance in a competitive environment; second, because an increasingly educated labor force is not motivated to perform unless it is able to exercise some discretion and adopt work practices of professional workers; third, because the professional work force assumes far greater responsibility for reducing marginal common and articulation errors; and fourth, because new information technologies permit independent decision makers to make choices that take into account overall needs and purposes.

The importance of envelope supervision lies in the mutual agreements that establish the parameters of discretion and performance expectations. These mutual agreements are the rules of the game while they are in force, but they can be reexamined and changed by the parties. The agreements provide the necessary structure for the maintenance of organizational integrity. For example, while the workers in our magnetic vehicle plant are given broad discretion in design choice, they are still expected to use available design components.

These workers are evaluated and rewarded in light of significant outcomes, such as the known satisfaction of purchasers. But while they have considerable discretion, they are still expected to perform within a well-defined set of expectations. More importantly, if they find that these expectations no longer make sense in their environment, they are *expected* to suggest changes. In other words, when agreed-to expectations no longer fit reality—say that available components are no longer wanted by clients and our workers find they should play a role in designing new ones—the terms of envelope supervision are altered. A new understanding is reached, new rules of the game are agreed to, and our workers submit new component specifications and designs. They change the rules.

Senior Staff and Other Professional Workers

In the senior staff professional model, the old distinction between management versus workers is sharply altered. We now have two hierarchies of workers. First, we have senior professional workers, who have considerable discretion, change rules, operate teams, network, and share many managerial responsibilities with management. Second, we have large numbers of other professional workers, who operate in fairly controlled situations, although many exercise considerable discretion. Discretion is not granted hierarchically. One finds professional workers with high levels of discretion operating at all levels of the organization. It is the characteristics of the work to be performed that determine workers' discretion. Symbolic analysts, technology operators, and even in-person service workers need to have discretionary capability.

Professional workers are managed through input and outcome controls. Today routinized workers are controlled through process and output controls. In the future, "professional" work will not be limited to the narrow definition of professions such as engineering, medicine, law, and so on. Instead, professional workers will be defined as those given considerable discretion. Workers are given considerable discretion when the task requires it, and are given training to enable them to assume their new responsibilities. Professional workers share responsibilities with management, and as we shall discuss at greater length in the next chapter, participate in networks that remove them from direct supervision. Long-term outcome controls orient collective behavior.

Another consequence will be that the union-versus-management dichotomy will have less utility in this new context. Unions will still exist, but will deal with marginalized workers. It is likely that some unions will have been largely transformed into completely new professional organizations that play completely new roles both within and outside the organization. These new professional organizations will share management's concerns and will be seen by management as the cooperating representation of all the involved professions, each of which takes responsibilities for defining what is acceptable practice, attending to the ethical dimensions of the work to be performed, and carrying considerable responsibility for the avoidance of marginal, common, and articulation errors.

The scenarios in Part Two incorporate this assumption; my hope is that the reader will shift into the science fiction mode of this book with me, to play out this and other assumptions. For example, these new professional institutions would not resemble our current professional societies and associations. They would have a much broader mission and would be funded to carry it out. The new institutions would therefore be central to the restructuring of the organization of the future. They would ensure the entrepreneurial role of the professions in the adaptive and learning organization. In Chapter Five I will describe such a set of institutions. Obviously, this description is pure fantasy, but my purpose is to suggest that if organizations of the future are going to be much more adaptive than present ones, some new societal arrangements will have to be invented.

CHAPTER FOUR

Networks, Risks, and Conflict Resolution

The organization of the future innovates; therefore it takes risks. It is a learning organization (Senge, 1990). It delegates power, empowers its entrepreneurial members, links with other organizations, and avoids errors. In the first part of this chapter I focus on selected characteristics of decentralized, innovative organizations, particularly on the notion of the porous organization. A complementary concern is the importance of stability and continuity. In this chapter I explain how an innovative milieu of professional group networks and interrelated organizations might function as the perceived basis for stability in the midst of change.

In the second part of the chapter, I discuss the characteristics of groups and networks and show how they differ from our current concept of the formal organization. I focus on the role of women in networks and on how women will play more important organizational roles in the twenty-first century. Networks are likely to be extremely important when decentralized organizations attempt to innovate. Consequently, when groups and networks are in a formative stage, they will need access to resources. In looking at ways

117

this access might be ensured, I also consider rhetoric and the ethics of communication. For example, does more openness imply full participation?

This chapter concludes the analytical portion of this book, which provides the theoretical bases for Part Two, where I use fictional narrative to describe some of the new institutions that might be invented and the way "typical" future organizations might operate.

Facilitating Risk and Innovation

Organizations of the future will not be able to afford to merely pay lip service to a rhetoric of change. They will recognize the hard fact that change depends on beliefs and on persuasion (Majone, 1989; Weiss and Bucavalas, 1980). Since beliefs tend to be based on experience, if management says that change is desirable but rejects any new ideas that individuals come up with, workers rapidly stop innovating. More importantly, if workers who innovate and fail are severely punished, they will think twice about innovating again.

The organization of the future will have to manage risks and errors, in sharp contrast to much of current practice. Today, typical government agencies and the many private firms that are not particularly innovative pay lip service to the rhetoric of change. They exclaim about the importance of meeting new needs by developing new services and products, but they have not thought through policies regarding risks and possible failures. They want change at very little cost and risk, and too often they immediately punish innovators who do not succeed on the first try. There is much bemoaning of the lack of creativity in many public and private sector organizations (Altshuler and Zegans, 1990), but creativity and innovation do not just happen by chance. Like rare flowers, these processes require a supportive environment; they require conditions that facilitate their development.

Direct Links with the Exterior

Art in the form of small, intimate, and delightful paintings flourished in seventeenth-century Holland because of the bourgeoisie's newly acquired taste for such pictures, which decorated the homes of the more affluent merchants, traders, and other well-to-do urban dwellers. In contrast, in seventeenth-century France, paintings were used mostly to decorate churches, public buildings, and the stately homes of the nobility. Thus the market for painting in Holland resulted in an abundance of paintings depicting the warm interiors and genre scenes of the bourgeoisie for whom they were intended. In France, seventeenth-century painting depicted religious motifs (for the churches), heroic battle scenes, hunts, and classical allegorical scenes (for public buildings), and all of the above plus portraiture (for the homes of the nobility, such as Versailles and Vaux-le-Viconte). Given that in the seventeenth century there was much exchange of information about painting, these differences are striking because they show the extent to which market demand drives artistic creativity.

As we saw earlier, the adaptive, change-oriented organization is closely linked with its clients and environment. Links with the market have to be numerous to permit close cooperation in the creative activities that lead to adaptation and change. They have to be decentralized to increase the flow of information from users to producers. This is particularly relevant in the public governmental sector, where innovation is as important as in the private sector. As was discussed in previous chapters, the development or adaptation of new products and services needs to become the responsibility of most or all the workers, including those who deal directly with clients, and the reader will have no problem recalling the teams of workers in our magnetic vehicle factory who have direct contact with customers.

Innovation is a social process; the individual invents, but invention is nurtured by demand. Without demand, invention may persist but not flourish. Demand has to be felt and understood. The designer needs constant feedback, not only to reorient designs to client needs but, more importantly, to legitimize the inherent risk of invention. I would assume that the organization of the future will depend heavily on client participation in design. This may become even more important in the public sector. But links with clients, while well understood today (Drucker, 1992; Peters, 1992), do not capture the complexity of the decentralized organization of the future. Basically decentralization—the breaking up of vertically integrated large systems into smaller, more flexible units—implies constant linking, not only with customers or clients but also with all those who are relevant in creating or using products and services. This means links with producers of components, links with organizations providing complementary services, and links that reflect the more complex realities of the modern world (Kilmann, Kilmann, and Associates, 1990).

For example, we have already seen the automotive industry move into the finance industry to provide more attractive services to its consumers. I have to assume that competition for quality will inevitably translate into much more complex combinations of purveyors of services to provide more attractive packages. Maybe the automotive industry of the future will not only be in the car production and financing businesses but also in automotive rental and repair, in transportation design, in transportation education, even in overall transportation management. Links between private and public agencies will increase markedly as their functions become more clearly complementary. These transformations will certainly affect the public sector far more than the private sector, first, because public organizations deal with many problems where coordination is crucial—say delinquency, criminal behavior, welfare, or other urban problems—and second, because cooperation and coordination with the private sector in education, research, and in readying the environment for risk taking will become far more important in the future.

The Porous Organization

Innovation requires the rearrangement of resources to achieve new ends. The existing organizational structure was, at best, invented to fit the needs of the present. More often, it still reflects the needs of the past. Frequently, a plan for the division of labor dictates how the organization is broken up into distinct areas, or compartments. For example, within the Department of State in Washington, D.C., the principal compartments are determined by geographical considerations (for example, the country desks) or by functional considerations (for example, crisis management, economic affairs, consular services, and so on). Individuals in organizations tend to identify with the compartments in which they serve. For example, when I served with Cultural Affairs at the Department of State, we had a very prejudiced view of Economic Affairs. We did not think people in that part of the department wanted or were able to understand what we were attempting to do. The department has undergone many reorganizations, but each unit in it still has a separate culture, often a dominant ideology, its own stakeholders and clientele, its own access to congressional staff and committees, and a strong commitment to protect its own bureaucratic turf.

The leadership of the department constantly espouses the values of cooperation and collaboration across internal units and across external agencies. But within units, there prevails a culture of cautious protective behavior. Anyone who chairs one of the innumerable coordinating committees that dot the Washington landscape quickly discovers that unit or agency representatives are often not there to solve problems or even to coordinate their efforts. They are there to protect the home turf. Their main concern is that others not put claims on the resources they use or reduce the legitimacy of their claims. Once turf is clearly protected, it is possible to discuss mutually advantageous undertakings.

There are many reasons for this state of affairs, but one of the important ones has to do with perceptions of the reward system. People perceive that they will be rewarded in terms of their contributions and those of the immediate groups to which they belong. Compartments—meaning sections or units—are created to facilitate the division of labor, but perceptions of the ways rewards are allocated tends to constrain what division of labor requires: lateral coordination across compartments. Moreover, compartments may be highly dysfunctional to innovation when the labels on the compartments have to change. Resistance to change is often anchored in people's commitment to existing structures and in the strategies they pursue to defend those structures.

There will need to be a porous quality to the organization of the future. Compartmentalization or segmentation, as Rosabeth Moss Kanter calls the phenomenon (1983, pp. 28–35), will have to be reduced. The main reason this will be possible is that perceptions of the reward system will have been altered. Innovators at the bottom who decide to link with others and act as bottom-up entrepreneurs will know that they will probably be rewarded or at least protected if they make errors.

There needs to be an internal social context for innovation that will allow many participants to come together informally. For this to happen, management cannot be threatened by grass roots activity. Management in the next century will probably resemble English elites of the eighteenth or early nineteenth century. As Wallace (1982) has shown, English elites at the beginning of the Industrial Revolution were able to work directly with a wide variety of people coming from many layers of the social milieu of the time. Inventive artisans, small bourgeois entrepreneurs, merchants, recent immigrants, and all sorts of religious nonconformists were able to link up with elites to carry forward the transformation of the English economy. One reason elites did not fear the artisans, the recent immigrants, or the others with whom they worked was their perception of the continuity of the English class structure.

This does not mean that the organization of the future will have to protect the top or perpetuate elitist hierarchical structures. On the contrary, it means that individuals will not be living under the old Spanish saying: *Quita-te tu para poner-me yo* (Remove yourself so I can take your place). In the transformed organization sketched here, management will share responsibility with professional staffs. The organization will be both entrepreneurial and intelligent. The information revolution will have altered decision making and it will be possible to study the parameters of the new environment and make better choices. Therefore, professionals will have risen in importance because of their ability to access and analyze information and share with management the task of improving decisions. The culture of the organization will have shifted because what will matter in the next century will be the ability to innovate. *Quita-te tu para poner-me yo* makes little sense when it is the function of management to empower the bottom to change. Success at the bottom does not translate into the bottom taking over. It translates into an adaptive, creative organization, which is what management will perceive as its goal.

But as mentioned in the previous chapter, management will support bottom-up innovation and segmentalism will be reduced only if new reward structures are devised. Whether new reward structures based on outcome measures can be invented and made operational is beyond our scope here. But I am assuming that somehow, with new technologies, it will become possible to tie rewards to larger and more complex consequences of the activities of organizations. This means that everyone's contribution will matter if success is to be achieved. In other words, the new reward structures have to deter the kind of narrow bureaucratic turf protection that is so pernicious and costly today. Furthermore, such decentralization will give management a more important function. It will become responsible for the levels to which it allocates discretion. It will allow workers to change rules, but it will also become far more responsible for inventing the shared meanings, ideologies, myths, and rewards that orient collective behavior and maintain continuity of purpose.

Stability and Continuity

A major reason individuals in organizations resist change is their need for stability and continuity. Gather a group of teachers in an experimental school and tell them that they are free to innovate. Ask them to come up with big ideas and to suggest those major changes in education they think best for their pupils. The teachers will get together, talk for a long while, and finally cautiously suggest they would like to slightly alter the procedures for ordering textbooks. The bottom does not innovate automatically.

Innovations take place in creative milieus (Andersson, 1985; Aydalot and Keeble, 1988; Hall, 1990). The pressure to innovate comes from a demand, a market, a stimulus that causes instability: rules need to be broken or changed. But to break or change its rules, the organization needs continuity and stability. As pointed out previously, it needs meta rules. In the organization of the future, stability and continuity will no longer be provided by the organization itself. The environment or the milieu will also provide stability and continuity, in addition to the individual firm or government bureau. This assumption is very important to my argument: the organization will have to become somewhat less important than the milieu where individuals work and pursue careers.

What is the milieu? It is the set of individuals and organizations involved in the change process. Creative milieus emerge from firms, units, bureaus, and other organizational compartments. Networks form, grow, become spin-offs, grow more, become larger organizations, and ultimately wither and disappear. But for this to be possible, individuals have to identify with something other than their unit or bureau. Stability, careers, and rewards cannot come from only one source.

The nineteenth-century organization provided a unitary source not only of stability but also of continuity, careers, and rewards. The goals of the organization were what mattered. Rewards were, and still are, linked to the achievement of the organization's goals. To be sure, in the twentieth century, individuals have increasingly pursued careers across units, departments, firms, or government services. The concept of a career liberates the more successful from the domination of single organizations (Glazer, 1968). But perceptions of the reward system incite a vast majority to resort to caution and protective strategies. The teachers in the experimental school are extremely cautious because they fear getting into difficulty. They do not want parents screaming at them or principals, administrators, and school board members accusing them of not meeting the needs of the school district. They fear change, and as soon as they find a program that seems to work, they lose all interest in experimenting with new and different approaches.

The organization of the twenty-first century will no longer place stability, continuity, and all rewards in a single organization. The goals of the organization will have to matter less than the collective ideologies, myths, and goals of larger environments. But for this to be possible, it is necessary to think about new societal institutions that can somehow protect individuals and groups as they adapt. As the reader already knows, I am proposing some totally new professional organizations. These professional bodies would provide continuity. They would provide individual and collective career support and would facilitate skill reacquisition and employment transfer. I will describe such a set of institutions in the next chapter, and I will leave it to the reader to judge whether such a vision makes any sense.

In such a novel setup, the bureau, unit, or compartment is no longer perceived to have value beyond accomplishing the work it performs. As long as the structure is useful, it is kept. When no longer useful, it is discarded by those who used it because there is no inherent reason to protect it. The milieu has replaced the organization as the source of stability and continuity. The firm innovates, succeeds, and grows. New products are invented. The firm becomes obsolescent. It is dissolved. A new firm or several new firms are created. Old government bureaus are also closed and new ones created. Career continuity is provided by the new professional institutions. Schumpeterian innovators emerge, access resources, create new start-ups and spin-offs. The organization changes.

Groups, Teams, and Networks

Groups are informal sets of individuals within given units, departments, or even sectors of the organization. Groups are brought together by a shared collective interest in specific accomplishments, improvements, or innovations. In the organization of the future, informal arrangements will be more important than they are now, and as we shall see, informal action will be encouraged, even fostered. But allow me to make a few definitions so that I can be more explicit.

127

Teams are formalized groups. Once informal and incipient groups have demonstrated their ability to carry forward a new project and once they reach a given resource threshold, they obtain the approval of their supervisors. Assignments to teams cut across departments and can be temporary, long term, part time, or permanent. Interorganizational teams cut across organizations and can receive funding and support from various involved organizations. Interorganizational teams will probably be much more prevalent in the future since collective undertakings involving many organizations will become the dominant pattern of production and of service delivery (Kilmann, Kilmann, and Associates, 1990; Perrucci and Potter, 1989; Nohria and Eccle, 1992).

Networks, as I define the term here, are made up of members of affinity groups, that is, people who happen to have common interests, common purposes, shared ideals—something that brings them together. Networks are therefore informal but cut across units, departments, and organizations. Networks form when people perceive problems and opportunities. Networks (informal) are the basic initial formative stage of interorganizational teams (formal, established networks). Groups and networks have the following characteristics:

• *Groups and networks are invitational.* Groups and networks are self-selected. Because they are informal and task oriented, they tend to attract their membership. One can be a member of one or of many such affinity arrangements. Since they are informal, they usually have a minimal structure of their own, although there might be a founder or founders, a skeletal managerial function, or possibly a secretariat. But since they are invitational, they tend to form around problems or issues and are greatly facilitated by instantaneous communications. Networks cut across existing organizational boundaries and often lead to the emergence of formalized arrangements.

• *Groups and networks have access to resources.* In the organization of the future, groups and networks will have more ready access to minimal resources than is the case at present. Given discretionary resources at all levels of the organization, the members of groups bring with them the ability to act, and therefore the ability to create networks across organizations. As a consequence, one's commitment to and participation in a group or network includes early contributions that facilitate initiation, maintenance, and persistence of new groups and networks. These in turn become much more prevalent and important than at present.

It is plausible to assume that in the organization of the future, members of a group that meets from time to time, who have an idea and decide to carry that idea forward, could acquire automatic recognition and, as such, would be able to make modest claims on budgetary and other resources, or reorganize, or rearrange prototype production processes—without receiving formal approval or supervision.

Groups can work across organizations, create networks, pool resources, and move ideas. Sooner or later, of course, they need access to larger claims on budgetary resources, which may require authorization. But meanwhile, action is initiated. Such practices are already common in innovative organizations; they will become the norm in the future (Kanter, 1983).

• *Groups and networks accrue power.* Since they are problem solvers, groups and networks acquire power outside the formalized organizational structure. In 2050 when you join an organization, you will join an established, visible undertaking, but the groups and networks you participate in will acquire a reality of their own because they will acquire reputations. They will acquire reputations from their problem solving ability. In the next century, problem solving will be a more important source of authority than formal hierarchies. Groups and networks will remain informal, but informal links will often matter more than the formal established rules and procedures. Power will need to be redistributed in the organization, and a large proportion of power will be informal, in the sense that influence will be exercised outside formal channels of command. Groups and networks are not yet recognized—that is, they are not yet teams—but since they can act and solve problems, they matter. Moreover, given the importance of innovation in the organization, teams, once they are recognized as such—once they have access to budgets, once individuals are reassigned, or have reassigned themselves—will function on their own. Nevertheless, these teams will continually reconstitute to address new activities, and they will generate new groups and networks. To be sure, the power that groups and networks accrue at first will be limited. But the important difference between practice in the future and that of today will be the recognition that the bottom has a voice. Management will have let go far more than is conceivable today. There will be far more fluidity and a recognized accepted level of bottom-up innovation that will take place quite outside the purview of management and across organizations. Obviously, there will have to be a limit to the randomness; conflicts will have to be resolved; but the organization of 2050 will recognize that some randomness, disorder, overlapping, or deliberate lack of coordination is desirable, at least for a while (Peters, 1992).

• *Groups and networks are long lasting.* One might think that the organization of the future will keep generating new groups and networks as new ideas and approaches are pursued and consequently that it will keep shedding those that have completed their work. But groups and networks are affinity groupings. The reason they are able to organize themselves, appropriate resources, and achieve results without any formal structure is that high levels of trust exist among members. Members of groups and networks tend to work together, in similar circumstances, many times. They have common professional and ideological commitments. New members affiliate and old ones leave; a group or network may splinter, break up for a while, and reform later on. But by and large, the personal contacts remain intact and allow the group to continue to function over long periods of time.

In fact, it is not so much that the organization creates groups and networks. On the contrary, groups and networks emerge, begin to act, and, when they succeed, generate teams. In due time, these teams may spin off and become new organizations. Therefore, groups and networks should no longer be looked upon as "imperfections" of formal organizations. They need to be understood as indications of the underlying innovative strength of the organization. They evolve over time, their membership changes, the topics they address vary, but they are long lasting. This is the concept of the innovative milieu discussed previously.

In contrast, the innovative organization of the future will have temporal qualities. It will serve as an incubator for ideas, allow spontaneous relationships to form, help initiate and legitimize new ideas, and sponsor start-ups and spin-offs (Miller, 1986; Miller and Côté, 1985). It will have an inner resiliency (Lundstedt and Moss, 1989). It will be able to respond and to transform itself. But to do so, the power to effect change cannot be located only at the top. As one student of organizational change, concerned with the ethics of innovation, points out, there is a political aspect to innovation. When all power is at the top, all power is in the hands of a small elite group. This group is probably literate, educated, well informed, well heeled, and secure. Thus it is a group that can easily resist change (Mueller, 1971). The organization of the future will have to depend on different organizational structures, some of which I discussed in the previous chapter. But the principal new characteristic will be decentralized power, shared by several parties—management, the professional staff, some technical workers, and in-person service staff.

• *Groups and networks link with professions.* In the future organizational world posited here, the professions will play a much larger and more powerful role than they do now. The scope of their responsibilities will be vastly expanded. (I discuss plausible new institutions to accomplish this in the next chapter.) Groups and networks will receive direct guidance from the members of the professions that join them. In other words, the discussion of the desirability of actions will take place in a different context than at present. Organizational imperatives will remain dominant—but less dominant than they are at present since far more discretion will be granted at much lower levels of the hierarchy and resources will be available for action at the periphery of the organization or for involvement with members of other organizations. At the same time, the professions will have developed complex structures involving new professional agencies that will have totally new responsibilities. They will be asked to define what is good and desirable practice. These new structures will provide a mechanism to ensure the protection of clients and the public from the narrower interests of organizations.

• *Groups and networks require nurturing management.* Informal structures are in many ways far more fragile than formal, well-routinized arrangements. The managerial skill required to keep them going involves careful attention to detail since there are few rules to go by, attention to individual idiosyncratic styles, attention to the concerns and fears of others—in short, far more consideration of individuals' roles within the group. As mentioned previously, these management skills tend to be associated with women's leadership styles, which incorporate nurturance and emotional perceptiveness. The organization of the future is likely to be more fluid, less well defined, less precise than organizations are now, and the current research seems to suggest that women's leadership traits are well suited to such circumstances (Eagly, Makhijani, and Klonsky, 1992; Jurma and Wright, 1990; Fleishman and Hunt, 1973).

Thus, the trends described in Chapter One come to reinforce each other. Not only will there be more educated workers and more females in the work force, but the decentralized and porous organization of the future will be far more dependent on the traits such workers bring to it. Indeed, we can assume that in the next century gender differences in leadership styles will tend to disappear as men become more socialized to adopt what are now regarded as feminine styles. Correspondingly, we have to assume that

133

women will equal men in pay, status, and perceived worth to the organization simply because they are important problem solvers whose talents will be increasingly in demand.

The Role of Technical Assistance

I have described entrepreneurial innovators who come together, have ideas, translate these ideas into action, and presumably succeed. I have alluded to the need for support for those who fail and suggested that new institutional mechanisms might take care of this very real problem. Meanwhile, I have said nothing about massing resources and I have said little about who decides when ideas make sense and when they do not. I did suggest that the organization of the future would probably adopt somewhat more participatory forms of governance, and I suggested in the last chapter that the senior staff model might prove useful in the future.

In what is increasingly emerging as a professionalized organization, patterned somewhat after current R&D departments (Miller, 1986), technical assistance is playing an important role and should, therefore, receive separate treatment here (Huberman and Miles, 1984).

Berman (1986) differentiates between willingness to comply with proposed changes and mere ability to comply. One may want to innovate and still not know how. The teachers who were asked to think freely about priorities to improve education were cautious because they did not want trouble. But that is only one of many factors affecting their performance. It is also highly probable that they had never attempted to organize to improve the learning process in their school. It was not a task they were prepared to undertake. They did not have access to the necessary information and did not know how to ask the right questions. Had they decided to go ahead, they would have solved some evident problems, but they probably would have been much more effective with some outside help. For example, a repertoire of experiences and models exists, which they could obtain with minimal help. That is one obvious use of technical assistance.

There is another issue that needs to be addressed. Once innovation is decentralized and encouraged, once resources can be accessed to initiate change, and once rewards are perceived to be tied to innovative activities, it is still necessary to maintain or increase the sophistication of research efforts and to select the more promising innovations.

Moreover, once innovation and experimentation are perceived or known to be desirable, much pseudo innovation is also generated. This problem is very real as soon as innovative behavior is perceived to be rewarded. Facilitating innovation facilitates pseudo innovation, or innovation for its own sake.

But meanwhile, top-down control has been reduced. Bottom-up innovation has been facilitated by reducing hierarchical control, granting ready access to resources, and allowing networking outside existing hierarchical structures; thus nonconforming ideas are permitted to flower. In this perspective, technical assistance serves (1) to eliminate pseudo innovation and (2) to select more promising approaches. Technical assistance can help professionals within and across organizations to learn, and it ensures the sophistication of the exercise. More importantly, it becomes the participatory mechanism that allows a professional structure outside the existing hierarchical structure to reduce potential conflict, reach agreements, make decisions about massing resources, and maintain the cohesion of the enterprise.

The Synergy Factor

When Stanford Research Institute began in the late 1950s to develop programs for small industries in Third World countries (Staley, 1958; Stepaneck, 1960), it quickly became clear that change depended on the interaction of many factors. One did not develop small industries by simply giving advice without providing capital, assisting merchants to become entrepreneurs, providing the necessary infrastructure in industrial parks, or designing marketing cooperatives. It took the simultaneous interplay of multiple interventions to create both the demand and the capability for action. Moreover, in those early days, the ideas of François Perroux dominated the thinking of those who wanted to accelerate economic development in the Third World. Growth poles, he wrote, begin in selected locations when conditions are ripe, and entrepreneurs emerge. Initially, change takes place in specific localities and ultimately begins to spread (Perroux, 1961). Creative milieus depend on the energy generated by multiphased, diverse, complementary actions that sparks both the imbalance that generates new demands and the basic competence to solve and invent (Andersson, 1985; Aydalot, 1986; Aydalot and Keeble, 1988).

The organization of the future will have an overarching synergetic attitude and policy toward innovation. Beyond access to resources, incentives, and the facilitation of communication across hierarchical barriers and organizational compartmentalization, the organization will use technical assistance to facilitate the synergy factor. As Hagebak (1982) points out, it is easier to innovate, make errors, and seek forgiveness than to ask for permission ahead of time. The organization we know today is rarely able to activate the synergy factor because innovation requires spontaneous action on the part of many players. Asking for permission means delays or denials; it makes it difficult to bring together all the elements needed to try new approaches. Forgiveness is possible when a policy exists to grant it, when it is understood that some mistakes will be made, when making no mistake may appear to be suspicious. Those who do not make mistakes do not take risks and probably never innovate.

As mentioned previously, the reward system of the organization of the future will be designed to encourage those who make mistakes—perhaps not all the time, but possibly a good number of times. This is in contrast to normal practice today. As one disgruntled innovator put it to me recently: "Sure, the board and top management talk about innovation, but they mean they want innovations that succeed—and succeed in the near future. There is no place in their thinking for doing an experiment that fails. They want immediate successes so they can show results at the end of the year. All our managers are aware of this. They know they cannot make big mistakes. They will be reviewed; therefore, they have to be cautious. They too often go for the sure thing, which means they miss lots of potential big ones."

Accommodating Errors

Today in most organizations the bottom line is output measures that translate into annual appropriations (in the case

137

of government agencies) or sufficient profits (in the case of private firms). The bottom line is not the long-term innovative and adaptive strategy of the organization. Errors have to be avoided because they incur heavy short-term costs. As a consequence, there is an insufficient societal and organizational adaptive capability. In contrast, the organization of the future will have to be designed to sustain some mistakes. In some cases, synergy will be programmed in; groups will be brought together to address new problems. In many others, it will be fortuitous. Organizational design will encourage encounters and facilitate informal group formation. But in any case, the organization will be able to sustain mistakes, either through new institutional mechanisms, such as those described in the next chapter, or because networks provide career protection to their members, or because the organizations will have developed conscious policies to reward, support, and encourage innovators, even when they make some mistakes.

To be sure, even with synergy, the problem of balance remains. The more innovative organization can make some mistakes, but it cannot make too many mistakes. No society and no organization can sustain constant, repeated failures, however innovative these might be. So the question breaks into three components: How much error is desirable? How are the costs of errors apportioned? (In other words, who sustains the pain?) And, who is allowed to make errors? (To what extent is innovation decentralized?) Those are questions that management and the senior staff have to answer, and this is where technical assistance provides a mechanism within or across organizations to resolve such problems.

Channeling Group Cohesion and Conflict Resolution

The innovative organization must decide when and how to mass resources. Any change implies difficulties for some and pleasure for others, therefore change implies conflict. More importantly, we have to know how the agenda is to be set. How are shared meaning and purpose to be arrived at? How are goals and priorities to be set?

Let me backtrack a bit. Let us revisit the teachers who "innovate" by changing the book ordering procedure. If you interview them, sooner or later they will tell you why they thought book ordering was a good issue to focus on: "because changing how one orders textbooks hurts no one." You will also find out that teachers are always very concerned about not doing anything to generate conflict. "Teachers have to stick together to survive," they will tell you. It might be that teaching attracts individuals who fly from conflict, but anyone with experience in the schools will tell you that is not a good explanation. More likely, the teachers perceive themselves to be in a weak position and to the extent possible they stick together so that the group can defend itself against the pressures created by students, parents, administrators, school board members, and the larger community (Becker, 1953). When innovations are talked about, there is always concern for how they might affect oneself and close affinity group members.

But teachers are not unique, although the characteristics of teaching accentuate the phenomenon. Teachers practice a task everyone has an opinion about, and they practice this task on children who spend many hours with them, and these children are, in turn, in most cases, of great interest and concern to their parents. Therefore, external and resulting internal pressures on teachers are high, and group cohesion important.

In any work situation, one will find similar affinity groups, even when external or internal pressures differ. Let me give you an example from a small voluntary group because it illustrates the problems of participatory management. When I began studying an important citywide program for battered women in the late 1970s (Benveniste, 1987), I found patterns similar to those teachers evince. In an organization where innovation was very important, no one really knew how to run an effective battered women's program.

The goals of the program were vague. What should be done was not clear. Should Florence's Refuge—as I had called the organization—focus on raising the general levels of consciousness about battered women? Or should it spend more time getting other agencies to respond to the problem of battered women, and more specifically, of battered wives? The staff at the refuge had rapidly found out that many agencies—social work, church groups, and, more importantly, the courts and the police—were reluctant to step into what was generally labeled as a family dispute. The refuge could espouse counseling and therapy, along the lines of the healing professions, or pursue a more political agenda, as espoused by the strong feminist contingent on the staff. The refuge might only be interested in women or in men and women.

The organization was involved in constant experimentation, with two main strong and committed affinity groups, each with an ideology and a symbolic language. One wanted the refuge to serve as a symbol of women's oppression in a male-dominated world. The other wanted the refuge to serve as a symbol of the need for healing and understanding. The two groups vied to direct the collective effort into new but somewhat contradictory directions.

Florence, the founder and director, had trouble with her staff, and trust eroded: "Florence was taken aback by the behavior of many members of the staff. She expected them, somehow, to spontaneously gather around her and assist her. Since they did not seem to do what she thought they should do, she had trouble predicting what they were doing and they did not perform as she expected. Similar problems arose within the staff and trust was eroded further" (Benveniste, 1987, p. 110).

Florence was faced with conflicting views, but she did not know how to deal with the affinity groups: "She realized that, left on its own, the staff might go in many directions at once. She was, in all probability, tempted to assert her vision to maintain the Refuge on a reasonable compromise between the many factions at work.... The staff was small enough to be able to discuss the definition of what the organization was about. Florence apparently never really discussed the topic officially, although in daily contacts, she must have stated beliefs and discussed them. There were ideological cleavages among staffers and arguments about what the Refuge was or was not. Florence probably saved time by avoiding formal participatory discussions. She may have fomented internal conflicts in so doing" (p. 112).

Florence left matters to brew and follow their own course. She avoided conflict, but in avoiding conflict, she failed to channel group cohesion. By and large, events dominated the organization. Reality imposed itself, and the organization learned from daily practice: "In the midst of these discussions, learning took place. In most instances, the staff learned from direct experience. They learned from the battered women who came to them with real problems and had no desire to wait for the enunciation of more perfect symbols and better ideological definitions. Reality asserted itself. Cases had to be handled and cases determined practice. Here Florence lost out because she never involved the professional staff as much as she might have in experimenting with new approaches, creating different work teams, or exploring different alternatives to generate external support" (pp. 113–114).

Managing Group Efforts

Successful innovation requires affinity group involvement and the maintenance of trust across groups. More importantly, members of the organization need to agree about what it is doing. The organization needs to provide shared meanings and shared visions about the future from which members can derive goals and priorities. This requires participation and a much more transparent participatory process, where conflict is taken as normal. This is where some novel forms of nonbureaucratic planning can play a new role in resolving conflict (Benveniste, 1989). Coalition formation and networking become accepted forms of professional behavior as ideologies and goals are translated into action programs; when this happens, conflict resolution can be encouraged. Affinity groups exist in an organization because their members share an ideological stance regarding what is important, what has to be done. At first, many of these semi-independent groups may innovate in many different and contradictory directions. These early differing points of view have to be protected because innovations come out of such conflicts, but only if, sooner or later, the conflict is resolved. Decisions have to be made; the effort has to have purpose and direction.

The teachers who suggest modifying book ordering procedures have seen many "innovative" fads come and go. They have their own convictions about teaching practices and prefer to be left alone in the privacy of their own classrooms. They are suspicious of new calls for innovation and will not readily accept the idea of change unless they sense that what they have to say matters and that they can play a role in the change process. Florence's staff had good ideas, but they avoided the first task of any change process: they did not even agree about the goals of the organization, much less how to allocate resources and set priorities.

In the organization of the future, the processes of formulating change will need to take place at many levels and will require new forms of participation to accomplish partial planning, conflict resolution, trust maintenance, and rectification of any negative consequences of changes. These participative efforts can help the group to respond to real, task-centered need for change and to cohere during the change process. The principal reason these processes will probably work in fifty years, whereas they do not seem to take place readily today, has to do with the future importance of innovative milieus. In this scenario, individuals, as contrasted to organizations, are aware that whatever happens, they will be assisted so that they can adapt and perform in the change situation. Clearly, this is one of the more fundamental differences between tomorrow's and today's organization.

Managing Communications

In a bureaucratic, which is to say routinized, task environment, there is little need to discuss what is desirable and what is not because the routines seem to work. As long as routines seem to work, there are few questions to ask. Bureaucracies often have well-established ideological statements of what they are about: "We provide quality health care," or "We build to last." Bureaucracies use these ideological statements to represent themselves to clients, the public, and their own staffs. Divergences between the ideological statements and the realities of task performance may abound, but the momentum of routine allows the organization to disregard them. Clients, the public, and members of the organization know about these divergences. They understand that rhetoric and performance are not necessarily the same thing, and they base their expectations on their past experiences, not on the rhetoric.

In the routinized, therefore predictable organization, ideological rhetoric represents an ideal, not what is going to happen. The rhetoric does not eliminate uncertainty or tell us what will happen next, but rather, it suggests what *should* happen. Meanwhile, we may accommodate ourselves to lower quality service and goods. We know that the rhetoric is only rhetoric, while our experience tells us what to expect in the future.

In contrast, in a rapidly changing environment, the practice of the past does not help us to understand what will happen next because we are inventing, creating new programs, services, or products. Therefore, ideological statements of what should happen have to closely approximate actual performance, at least for those who are actively in-

144

volved in the performance. For example, when I visit the laboratory of Professor Frank X, a reputed biologist at a western university (Benveniste, 1987), I notice that the veracity of his discourse varies, depending on the topic. When Professor X discusses an ongoing experiment with Jerome, the laboratory assistant, his discourse is precise and matter of fact. He does not include any embellishments or rhetoric. He details precisely what has to be done and how it is to be done. In contrast, when the professor discusses the everyday routine of watering the laboratory plants (a task Jerome resents doing because he believes it to be unprofessional), the professor embellishes his discourse with rhetoric (p. 27).

Communications in the organization of the future will have to be differentiated. At one level, a new ethic of communication will seek to demystify the social context in which decisions and actions take place. At another level, the organization of the future will tend to provide opportunities wherein individuals have the same chances to speak; the same chances to express attitudes, feelings, and intentions; and the same chances to agree to or oppose arguments and to provide interpretations. Planning and change require greater transparency to coordinate task performance and behavior in a more uncertain and unpredictable environment (Kemp, 1985; Hart, 1986).

At another level, communications in change situations necessarily serve other functions, primarily the legitimization of new actions and, more importantly, the creation of advocacy groups and coalitions of support (Benveniste, 1989; Sabatier, 1987). These communications are not characterized by the openness needed during ongoing novel explorations because, as I have shown in *Mastering the Politics of Planning* (1989), the process of coalition formation in a change situation requires both credibility and some initial level of secrecy. Secrecy is needed to allow the coalition to take stock of its strength. Credibility is needed to ensure the group's conviction in the desirability of moving ahead. Therefore, while more democratic, porous, and transparent than today, the organization of the future will not always rely on increased levels of formalized participation: "Some authors argue that participation is always an important component of the planning process (Burke, 1968, 1979; Barber, 1984; Susskind and Elliott, 1983). But it is not participation per se that matters. What matters is maintaining open communication and trust, being able to identify ideas and to learn, and ultimately reaching agreements that hold. Formal participatory arrangements entail issues of legitimacy and create a structure with rights and privileges that focus attention on procedural issues. When these procedural issues cannot be easily resolved to everyone's satisfaction, distrust increases, conflict erupts, and the coalition finds itself in trouble" (p. 183).

I go on to argue that organizations change successfully by relying on informal groups or networks to fulfill many of the functions of formal participation without incurring the costs associated with formalized participation, particularly in terms of resisting change and providing entrenched parties with a pulpit to deter action. In other words, it is much easier to create coalitions, obtain a consensus, and even sign a peace agreement in the Middle East if negotiations take place in partial secrecy and if the participatory process is highly informal. But as we just pointed out earlier, informal groups, networks, or "skunk works," as some authors call them (Vaill, 1989), have an internal communication ethic.

Communications have to be open, transparent, precise, and sincere among group or network members because these individuals are problem solvers. The task requires the purity of language exemplified by the terse exchanges between mission control in Houston and the astronauts on a space walk. But in their relations with the external world, groups and networks need to use a more politicized language suited to the vagaries of the politics of change.

The organization of the future will need to use a politicized language to bring about group cohesion. It will need to invent myths and desirable futures, describe ideologies that motivate participation, and set broad goals and "incomplete plans" to orient action. Openness facilitates work at the bottom. But as we move upward, ambiguity still prevails to facilitate coalition formation and consensus building. It may seem contradictory, but to debureaucratize planning, it is still necessary to maintain some opaqueness.

PART TWO

Imagining the Organization of the Future

Much of this portion of the book is in the form of fictional narrative. My purpose in fictionalizing is to explore problems, to provide descriptions, and to ask: do we like these images of the future?

Some readers will not think the scenarios drawn here possible or desirable. There is little doubt that those who live in 2050 will have seen and experienced changes beyond what we can imagine, and will have invented many different approaches and solutions to situations they face.

Nonetheless, the fictional narratives here deal with three fundamental problems, which I raised in the preface: how higher levels of decentralization, discretion, and change can be achieved while maintaining integration and continuity, how some external governmental controls can be undertaken within the organization, and what it would take to actually correct some of the pain resulting from major economic dislocations.

Both Chapter Five, "New Social Institutions," and Chapter Six, "Inside the Future Organization," are presented in a schematic, artificial manner. They are, so to speak, moral fables, wherein good people seem to act correctly and big problems are eliminated. Yet these scenarios provide a way to describe and comprehend the magnitude of the institutional problems we may face in the future. I have, to the best of my abilities, attempted to show that all would not be well, even in the ideal world I present. Maybe perfection always escapes us. In this analysis happiness is elusive. But I will accomplish my aim if the reader is encouraged to think about alternatives. What is your vision of the future?

CHAPTER FIVE

New Social
Institutions

In this chapter, I attempt to present a plausible scenario: a "New System" that helps individuals, organizations, and communities adjust to rapid social, economic, and technological changes, and correct errors after they happen. In addition, I posit new institutions, within and without organizations, that provide incentives to individuals to pursue both collective and organizational goals and that define what are desirable practices and products. These new institutions permit organizations to internalize selected regulatory practices that greatly increase the costs of innovation. Moreover, these new bodies increase coordination and protect clients and public. I describe them as professional institutions with a much more important mission than that played by current professional associations and with new sources of funding that allow them to intervene to meet challenges.

This chapter is both utopian and fictional. It is not a prediction. Moreover, this scenario is not "mere" science fiction. It has heuristic value in that it obliges us to think about the possibility, practical implications, and desirability of rapid change. This is a scenario of a plausible future. We may not like it, in which case we should think how it might be changed.

The fictional narrative expands considerably on Part One, which only touches lightly on the idea that new professional institutions might emerge and undertake all the tasks described in the following pages. This role for the professions is based on the assumption that the organization of the future faces three important problems: that of maintaining continuity and purpose in highly decentralized arrangements where groups, networks, and even organizations come and go; that of reducing or at least delaying the very high costs of external regulatory practices; and that of addressing the apparent need for a more systematic approach to the problems faced by individuals, groups, organizations, and communities when rapid changes completely alter existing employment patterns. The discussion of the six trends in Chapter One also provided other insights about problems that would transform the workplace landscape, such as the emergence of a more educated or more credentialed work force that would aspire to professional roles, the importance of feminine leadership styles in organization, and concomitant implications for the blurring of family and organizational boundaries.

The emergence of new professional institutions follows somewhat from these trends, but I go further, suggesting that as unions lose some importance, professional associations will begin to address the issues discussed above. The reason I focus on professional associations is that they blur the sharp distinction between government and private sector. The reader may want to think of them as a new third force bridging the gap between public and private polarities.

How these new institutions actually come about is not

covered here, as there is not much point in my describing their fictional birth. Presumably they would require legislative and executive sanction, which would give them their mandate. Presumably they would begin as very small experiments and ultimately grow into full-fledged institutions. Presumably they would not resemble current professional organizations because their mandates would be very different. Instead of protecting professions and their clients, they would be charged with making organizations and the society that depends on organizations more competitive.

Whether these new institutions would function as described here is highly debatable. I only present them as one possible development for discussion purposes. At the end of the chapter I include several criticisms and attempt to answer some of these criticisms. But as the reader will see, the chapter does not answer every question. On the contrary, it raises new questions about the future. This is as it should be. My purpose is not to predict, but to invoke serious consideration of the plausible long-term future.

Elements of the New System

The new institutions are professional bodies. My scheme for them assumes that all work and living activities have been professionalized in the sense that every living individual is a member of at least one profession. Even infants have professional memberships, although theirs are held by sponsors who act on their behalf. But starting at six years of age, children begin to participate in and run professional bodies that handle their interests in a wide variety of matters. Sometimes adults still help them, but in the New System every individual is a member of at least one professional body representing his or her major occupation.

Thus many professional bodies exist for engineers, many for cooks, drivers, high school students, managers, housekeepers, artists, lawyers, doctors, landscape designers, and so on. (Both men and women work in about equal numbers at all types of jobs.) These professional bodies accomplish diversified tasks.

The scheme relies on four distinct professional institutions. First, as mentioned above, we have *Professional Governors,* who work at the micro level directly with individual members, helping them in their careers. Then, in addition, there are *Professional Councils, Professional Courts,* and *Professional Boards.* The Professional Councils play a macro role, dealing with sectors of the economy, preparing overall plans and policies, and defining what is "good practice" within their areas of responsibility. The Professional Courts handle conflicts and disputes. They are specialized and rely more on scientific language and evidence than courts do at present. The Professional Boards are elected bodies that appoint the members of the Councils and Courts and help elaborate the financing schemes that are necessary to maintain all of these new institutions. To explain them in greater detail, I will use fictitious interviews with experienced experts from the future, along with descriptive background information.

Professional Governors

The Professional Governors (PGs) help individuals with retraining, changing careers, or moving or waiting it out when major labor market disarticulations take place. They are relatively well funded by a special levy on private and government payrolls; therefore they serve as an insurance system.

The staffs have access to information about individuals' work histories, they provide career counseling and employment services, they provide reeducation and retraining grants tailored to individual needs, and they can access a wide variety of services. They are highly decentralized and the staffs of the various PGs are rewarded in terms of their ability to effectively help individuals find significant work. There is a minimum of paperwork because within each PG case workers decide with the applicants how to allocate resources earmarked for each case.

They are effective because the corps staff of the PGs are linked together through a multitude of networks, including planning networks. Counselors—say of thinking machine workers—have direct access to counselors in other fields. They also have access to tremendous amounts of information about activities and plans, which they use when providing advice. Small ad hoc advisory teams are easily created, further education and training are readily made available, and help in moving to different geographical locations is also provided. To give you an example, in some instances they provide help in finding new schools for children; employment for a significant other; help in selling, financing, and locating housing; help in moving; and most importantly, help in retraining and finding new employment.

Joseph Nielsen, 42, used to manage an electronic assembly plant in what used to be the Silicon Valley in California. His wife, Catherine, was a top professional. When they both found themselves out of their jobs, they went to see their PG. They were tested to assess proficiencies and preferences, given access to economic sector estimates, and assisted to consider moving into high-speed vehicle assembly, a growth industry at the time. The PG funded a six-month education program for both; helped both find high-level jobs; moved Joseph, his wife, Catherine, and their two adopted children to Boston; and within a year had those four individuals well adapted to a major change in their life. This adaptation reflected a major transformation of production patterns in the western United States.

Interestingly, the case workers and others who worked on that PG task receive a significant bonus in light of the dispatch and efficiency with which they solved the entire plant closing problem, the satisfaction of the Nielsens and the others helped, and the employment records of the displaced workers in their new locations. This bonus incentive, based on outcomes, had much to do with the efficiency and effectiveness of the intervention.

The Professional Governors use the resources they raise (a levy on payrolls) in proportion to the complexities of the problems they face. They receive rough annual indications and forecasts from the Professional Councils (see below) that tell them in which activities and geographical areas the governors can expect significant labor market disarticulation. They are able to allocate their budgets accordingly.

When the overall level of disarticulation is low, they are able to accumulate a reserve from year to year, which they use in the years when these disarticulations are high. To be sure, there could be years when the impact of major transformations would tax their resources to the limit. But this is where the Professional Councils must in some way become involved and play "innovation damping." There are still limits to the amount of change any society can sustain.

The Professional Governors carry on functions that were already well understood in the twentieth century. They bring together many services that already existed, such as unemployment insurance, workplace-based retraining programs, employment training and retraining programs, vocational education, career counseling, talent searching, and so on. The big difference is that the Professional Governors cover a much wider range of activities. They have access to planning data generated by thousands of institutions and organizations. They access these with a sophisticated information technology called the Informator, which I will describe later on. They also provide inputs to the Councils when they have to recommend steps to improve the competitiveness of sectors of the economy.

The PGs are highly decentralized. Since they have access to the best information available about the intentions of others in the economic system, case workers can readily and rapidly assist. There is hardly any need for bureaucratic controls because decisions are made on the spot. Case workers typically advise their clients on several options, determine with them their preferences, and allocate resources. To be sure, individual case workers sometimes have to make difficult choices if their resources are taxed. But with experience they have learned how to design help programs that tailor their resources to the demand. In other words, the level of assistance a PG provides also takes into account the need to ration scarce resources. For example, they often only pay a fraction of moving costs to deter individuals who might simply use their services to move around, travel, and constantly change job and scenery.

The PGs serve many different constituencies. They address not only the needs of workers but also those of managers and professionals. Moreover, they also serve to help self-employed workers, and they reach beyond recognized economic activities to assist children and adults who manage the household, including housewives, house husbands, and house companions. Thus, as I pointed out earlier, they are concerned not only in getting Joseph and Catherine retrained and settled but also in finding entree to the right schools for the Nielsens' two adopted children.

An Interview with Gala Dream Sheridan

G. D. Sheridan is a case worker with the Horse Racers Professional Governors in Tennessee. This interview takes place two years after the 2048 banning of horse races in North America.

G. D. SHERIDAN: Horse racing was phenomenally important early in the twenty-first century—just as bullfighting became so popular in Latin countries, including France, Italy, Romania—— It was a period when horse racing was even more popular than football and baseball. But you know, there was the lobby for the protection of the horse, and the issue was whether horses suffer too much in racing. I think they were wrong. It went too far, but the decision appealed to the electorate. Some five hundred thousand people were affected! You do not realize how popular horse racing had become, but there were all those scandals about doping and gambling. Oh well. Many other Professional Governors came into our networks of their own volition. We went to work two weeks before the legislation was passed. We used their planning to locate employment growth sectors. We were able to use a few incentives to motivate employees to take on new hires. But we had limited funds for necessary retraining.

158

QUESTION: After that it was routine?

G. D. SHERIDAN: Yes, pretty much. Your typical person in horse racing has many irons in the fire. They come from many diversified backgrounds, and each case worker could easily identify strengths and opportunities. A few people went into the circus, although, you know, there is the same pressure on circuses as on horse racing—but the Professional Governors in the circus field were helpful. Of course, circus people still expect some growth, so the horse and circus governors could see utility in conversions.

Most racers went into totally new careers. We handled most of that work force in about sixteen months, but as I said, we did not have as much to offer as we might. The legislature gave it a "low importance to economy" rating, which meant the Councils told us to limit assistance to minimum retraining and minimum employer incentives. I think that was a nasty way to handle a major dislocation. Why was it okay to go to horse races for years and years and then suddenly discover "intolerable suffering of animals"? We have this puritan attitude toward pleasure, so horse racing people are seen as "low importance." So we save the horses but do not help the lumpen proletariat of horse racing. About twelve percent were left unemployed. That was nasty. I should not talk that way. I'm sorry.

Professional Councils

The Professional Councils are a totally new institution. Their main functions are to advise legislative bodies on major plans and policies regarding the work activities each council supervises, to advise legislative bodies on necessary financial assistance for economic or geographical sectors in distress, to offer advice on and implement laws regulating work activities, to establish standards of good practice within the context of the regulations passed by legislative bodies and the courts, to provide guidance to the Professional Governors regarding the performance of their members, and to negotiate international agreements on good practice with their counterparts in other nations.

The Councils are the protectors of organizations —whereas the Governors protect individual workers. But more importantly, they protect the public and clients and they set the standards of "Good Practice" which also determine the ethical stance of the Governors and the work safety practices of the firms. They operate directly through their Professional Representatives who happen to be employed in each organization. They are therefore permanently linked to every organization and are the most influential new institution of the new century.

The Councils are a far departure from the professional associations of the twentieth century. They are funded by a set of special earmarked value added taxes which are spread differentially across all economic activities and which reflect overall levels of production of the economy. As a consequence, the Councils are centrally concerned in maintaining economic growth, competitiveness, and innovation. On the other hand, the rates of these value added taxes are voted anew every six years by state and federal legislatures, thus involving citizens, pressure groups, and others in the political process of supporting or downgrading specific councils.

New Social Institutions

An Interview with José Maria Uruzguatta

José Maria Uruzguatta is an engineer in the Mechanical Engineering Council. José Maria worked for ten years in high-speed railroad design in Monterrey, Mexico, for American Rail Builders (ARB), the big new North and South American transportation designer, builder, and operator. Eventually José Maria moved to the Council's Public Access Office in Portland, Oregon.

JOSÉ MARIA: The Councils are represented in every organization quite independently of any existing management structure in place. You therefore have within the regular managerial structures Councils made up of members selected jointly by management and professional bodies. The organizations share governance responsibility. At the plant, bureau, firm, or department level, the Councils participate with management in policy making. They are also responsible for the implementation of all the environmental, economic, public, and labor safety laws. As you know, we have abolished many of the old regulatory institutions. All this is simply done internally.

QUESTION: This is mind boggling. How do the Councils manage such a huge responsibility?

JOSÉ MARIA: They are trained and have all the necessary information. There is no problem.

QUESTION: I'd like to stop you right there. You have the fox in the chicken coop. What keeps the Councils from being foxes, eating chickens right and left?

JOSÉ MARIA: Today, what matters is overall results. My friends are not working in a vacuum. They are linked

161

to a Council Community Network that discusses and plans the operation of all the plants in their geographical areas. The Council Community Networks have access to the public, to educators, to community leaders—and they come to agreements. There is widespread discussion of big issues. Sometimes they take the decision to the legislatures or even to a public referendum. People are told the pluses and minuses. They often use the instantaneous preference recorders. Sometimes the public votes and the Council decide——

QUESTION: Slow down, please. Explain.

JOSÉ MARIA: In most cases the preference recorders are sufficient to give guidance. The public has learned to live with the instantaneous preference recorder. People realize the importance of their opinions. They therefore pay careful attention to the questions and to their answers when they happen to be sampled. They understand how important the samplers have become in our new political arena. Also, often the larger public is not involved because they do not need to be. Look, the big difference is that the people who serve on the Councils are concerned with the long-term effects of their actions. Keep in mind they serve their firms or agencies, but also their Councils. The Councils reward them in terms of career opportunities. Therefore the members of the Councils have nothing to hide.

QUESTION: Except their own idiosyncratic commitments! Suppose you are working, as you did, for American Rail Builders, and you are determined to place a thousand kilometer per hour high-speed track through

downtown Portland. What will stop you, since you are
deciding what is good and bad for all of us here
downtown? You create huge vibrations and noise. I'm
a hotel owner. I'm ruined. Please explain how you
resolve that simple conflict of interest.

JOSÉ MARIA: Okay, but American Rail Builders and the
Councils are directly concerned with results.
Ultimately, we pay the price. If I'm designing a
thousand kilo track, my very first concern is vibration
and noise. I cannot afford to ruin you and others
because my performance evaluations will, in due time,
show a down curve and——

QUESTION: Yes, yes, but suppose you have no idea how
bad the vibrations will be, and meanwhile there is a
huge profit to be made?

JOSÉ MARIA: Mistakes are made—not intentional mistakes,
to be sure. But first, I've modeled the one megakilo
track. We've had a pilot test. We wanted all the results
to be out because we wanted to get a sense of the
impact. I repeat, long-term results matter. In your
system, an enterprising organization could make a
huge profit, get out, and leave a wrecked community
behind. Today, we pay for long-term consequences.
We cannot afford not to want to know what the impact
will be. We are the first ones to push for further study.
Suppose your hotel were the only vibration spot. We
dig this track so it affects only one hotel in all of
Portland. We know this. We have the Council
Community Networks assess public reaction. We use
our instantaneous preference recorder. Suppose the
data shows general support. We go ahead, and
meanwhile, you get help from the Governors and your

Councils to rebuild, or turn the location into a magnetic vehicle park garage, or whatever. So the overall long-term satisfaction results are what matter.

QUESTION: But that must be a huge amount of work! How can the Councils carry all these tasks?

JOSÉ MARIA: Do you realize how much they save? Do you realize how expensive your controls and regulatory processes had become? Well, I forget—you are still there. Think of the paperwork you are still involved in. The endless forms you have to fill out. The millions of people who push papers and produce nothing. All the lobbying and court interventions that take place in your century? My question to you is exactly the same as yours to me. My mind boggles to think how unproductive your arrangements were! We are open because what matter to all of us are long-term results, long-term measures of satisfaction; yours was a hedonistic, short-term, slash-and-burn-and-run culture. We learned the hard way that if you wanted rapid change, progress, innovation, creativity, all these good things, you had to have a long-term view. We began to reward those who took such a view, and in due time taking a long-term view became part of our way of doing things. By then, our culture had changed. No one thinks like you today. You are history, my friend, history.

Professional Courts

Notwithstanding José Maria's assertions about how the long-term view helps harmonize the body politic, it turns out that conflict is still prevalent in the New System. But the court system has been revamped. New Professional Courts exist to adjudicate conflicts. These courts adjudicate conflicts between organizations, between members of organizations, and between organizations and groups of citizens, clients, and the like. In other words, as a hotel owner I may link with the Lovers of Silence Network, proceed to challenge the one megakilo track under my wine cellars in the basements of the hotel and try to save my aging wines from certain destruction. The Professional Courts are specialized. I would have to appear before the Transportation Communication Court (TCC).

The idea of specialized courts is not new. For example, Article I, Section 8 of the United States Constitution vests in Congress the authority to create tribunals inferior to the Supreme Court. Specialized courts were created, including the United States Tax Court, the United States Customs Court, the United States Court of Customs and Patent Appeals, and the United States Court of Claims (Benveniste, 1981, pp. 125–127).

The rapid expansion of specialized courts after 2010 had much to do with reforms aimed at sharply reducing the costs of litigation, a trend toward making the judicial branch more responsible for the economic and social consequences of their decisions, and the need to introduce a technical discourse in the judicial mind-set.

Each Court can investigate the cases that appear before it. In most instances, they take an active role in gathering data, hold expert hearings, have access to confidential information, and use and have access to their own experts. Judgments are often rendered by the bench on the advice of appointed expert panels. All the decisions of the Courts are available to anyone; and all the data, analysis, and arguments leading to decisions are published immediately. In important cases, the decision and documentation are transmitted for modest fees to interested subscribers.

The judges of the Professional Courts are appointed by an institution called the Professional Boards, which I will describe subsequently. Generally, they are appointed to limited terms. They tend not to be lawyers; in fact, very few of them are lawyers. Most are scientists, engineers, economists, sociologists, or psychologists. A fair number are philosophers and moralists, and quite a few are architects, designers, and artists. All judges receive short-term training in legal reasoning, and they are assisted on the Court staff by persons with legal training.

An Editorial

Here is a brief editorial from the *Unvanquished,* the daily publication-visual that appears at 7 A.M. in Portland, Oregon. It is dated August 27, 2050.

Editorial: Wine Versus Speed

Old Wines Hotel appeared before the West Coast Transportation Communication Court asking remedy against tunneling below their wine cellars by American Rail Builders (ARB). Old Wines Hotel argued that vibration from the new one kilo track would destroy their rare collection of Missouri wines. Old Wines Hotel claims the Councils are ideologues: "technospeed cultural types," they said. The Councils provided relief, suggesting Old Wines Hotel convert into a magnetic vehicles parking garage with a wine tasting room. Old Wines Hotel insisted that the Councils had a clear temperance bias, saying, "No wine can survive the vibrations of a one kilo track." Court ruled in half an hour against the hotel.

The *Unvanquished* deplores this hasty decision. The question remains: are our Professional Courts ideologically in tune with the body politic?

Having read this, I hastily called on José Maria to obtain his point of view.

JOSÉ MARIA: You must understand that the Court had all the evidence before them. They also have their sophisticated instantaneous preference recorders. They can obtain an instantaneous public opinion poll, which gives them a real-time measure of the current overall satisfaction gradient Old Wines Hotel has provided within and outside Portland. They matched this with an instantaneous public opinion poll/reaction of the one kilo track route alternatives and determined that there were insufficient positive gradients for Old Wines Hotel to stand in the way. They fed future data from models into their samples, and the data they obtained is a very close approximation of real preferences should the track be built. The Old Wines Hotel could have challenged their polls, but they did not. They knew those were the facts. The Court made a policy decision——

A Brief Summary

I will interrupt here and summarize what José Maria had to say:

• The Courts work with the Councils to determine the

costs of the remedies they propose before making decisions. In other words, the Courts are always fully informed about the known consequences of their decisions.

• Doctrines of "good professional practice" do not and cannot come out of thin air. The Courts cannot take arbitrary stances; they reinforce the Councils. They are continually obliged to operate in full view of their peers. In fact, they provide a visible forum where a widespread debate on the definition of "good professional practice" takes place.

• The Courts are efficient. They made the Old Wines Hotel decision in half an hour because that was the time it took to process the data, reproduce the visuals, and have the Court look at the results. The decision also reaffirmed the legitimacy of the analytical procedure. The Courts have legitimized the use of instantaneous opinion polls of measured satisfaction gradients to decide issues that have no complex long-term repercussions.

• In a democratic society dissent is important. The editor of the *Unvanquished* loved the Old Wines Hotel and is trying to build up public opinion against the Court decision. That is her right and privilege. Maybe in coming years wine appreciation will increase, and future Courts might make different decisions. But meanwhile, their decision will stand.

• Court procedures demystify organizations. The Courts have legitimate access to all data, records, and information. It is therefore very difficult and dangerous for any professional not to pay close attention to the high ethical standards set by the Councils and by the Courts.

• Lastly, the Courts provide an avenue to transform or "modernize" the standards set by the Councils. If the Councils get stuck and begin to impose good practice standards that are not generally acceptable to their members or to the public, this will tend to generate more conflicts and more Court interventions. When this happens, the Courts tend to pay closer attention to the way the Councils operate and at times question their performance.

Professional Boards

The Professional Boards are elected bodies whose dual functions are (1) to appoint members of Governors, Councils, and Courts and (2) to oversee the financing of these institutions. The Boards recommend to legislative bodies the various taxes and levies used to finance each of the three pillars of the new system. The Boards operate at local, regional, national, and international levels.

A Description of the Boards

Here is the text of a little pamphlet that describes the operations of the Transportation/Communication Boards in the United States.

The Transportation/Communication Boards of the United States of America

The T/C Boards include all local boards (populations 50,000 to 250,000), regional boards (27 in the continental United States), and the national organization in Washington, D.C. The National T/C Board represents the United States in the North and South America Free Trade Community and in the International T/C Board, located in Tokyo, Japan.

Appointments to local units of the Professional Governors, Councils, and Professional Courts are

carried out by local Boards. Appointments to
regional or national offices are carried out by
regional Boards or by the National Board.
International appointments are carried out by the
Tokyo center.

Elections for membership in the Boards are
held every five years. Members are usually elected
to five-year terms, which can be prolonged twice
for a fifteen-year term. After such service, members
can still serve in Councils or Courts.

The Boards not only recommend taxes and
levies but administer and channel the funding. In
our complex system, there are many unknowns.
The governors do not always predict correctly, and
neither do the Councils and the Courts. The T/C
Board operates an equalization scheme that
provides 50 percent of all revenues for unforeseen
contingencies. Monies are often transferred
regionally and locally, thus giving our system the
necessary flexibility and versatility.

Donations to the T/C Board are tax deductible.
Please donate generously. Our nation and our
communities need strong Boards.

The New System in Perspective

A synthesis of my future informants' views on what had been
accomplished by the New System follows. My interpretations
are included.

Many External Controls Abolished

The New System permits organizations to internalize many
regulatory controls. This saves scarce resources, in contrast

170

with the effort and time that went directly into control and regulation during the twentieth century. To be sure, the taxes and levies imposed by the Professional Boards are high; therefore, all that is saved by internalizing external control is not available for increased consumption or investment, but the net effect is that the New System costs less. More importantly, internalizing regulatory control has not only reduced paperwork, it has increased the response flexibility of all organizations and permitted far more innovation, in both public and private sector organizations.

They are also saying that placing regulatory control within the organization has demystified the organization. There is much more openness, much more access to internal information than before because the professional bodies charged with maintaining or defining standards of desirable professional practice happen to be both inside the organization and outside. The ethical discourse first takes place inside, where it should take place. The professionals inside are linked permanently with the Councils, who provide general guidelines for defining "good practice" and at the same time enforce the ethical standards of the profession with powerful incentives. Conflicts between regulator and regulatee, the us versus them, is greatly reduced, although conflicts are inevitable; but the professional courts resolve conflicts rapidly.

Increased Coordination and Reduced Fear of Change

The bureaucratic phenomenon of the twenty-first century can be explained in part in terms of fear. Of course, bureaucrats are not in constant fear; they are not so different from other citizens in that respect. But individuals in bureaucracies pursue cautious strategies. They want change, they want successful innovations, and they also want to reduce risks. They are well aware that large-scale errors can result in severe penalties. The New System reduces some of the potential risk of undertaking innovations by providing effective multifaceted assistance packages to individuals who are negatively affected by successful changes. Within the organization, incentives and the nature of work have been privatized. Individuals can become entrepreneurs. They have sufficient discretion and adequate resources to act. The support systems buffer individual innovators against failure, as private wealth could do in the past. The New System has democratized the capitalist organization. It has converted dull bureaucrats into Schumpeterian entrepreneurs.

Individuals work in organizations as they did in the 1990s, but they pursue careers in networks or spin-offs and often move. The New System, and more specifically, the Professional Governors, provide each individual with an alternative institutional support system, reducing the importance of the direct employers in the perception of all professional workers. It is difficult for those who are still in the twentieth century to comprehend this fundamental shift in perception. There is another important consequence of this shift.

In the 1990s, workers situated their work tasks within the narrow environment of the organizations with which they were affiliated. The immediate sources of rewards were within these organizations. Workers could pursue a career, change employers, seek to be seen and known in a larger work environment, attempt to please people who were not their current employers because they hoped these might become their future employers. But notwithstanding the ex-

172

panding nature of the relevant work environment, by and large, their current employers dominated their vision of who around them mattered.

My informants point out that they work in innovative milieus. The milieus are made of many organizations. They are able to identify with the milieu instead of the organization. Therefore, they have the ability to create protostructures to implement innovations. They do not fear change. In other words, the Professional Governors, the Councils, and the Courts not only help individuals adapt to errors, important as this may be, they also provide the fabric of linkages across organizational barriers which greatly facilitate networking. They reduce the fear of making errors; they also reduce the fear of acting outside the narrow context of one's organization because, in a new and more fundamental way, one belongs to all organizations.

One of my informants pointed out that in the twentieth century we worked that way when we were faced by disaster. The successful response of public and private organizations to major earthquakes, hurricanes, or manmade disasters requires the ability to create coordinated efforts and depends very much on the ability of individuals to link together as emergency needs emerge (Comfort, 1988). Individuals' marching orders may not give them the authority to do a necessary task, but they do it anyway. The reality of the disaster is sufficient to provide legitimacy for doing what no one, beforehand, has thought should be done. Yet, the response capability is enhanced if individuals already know who the others are, can identify with their counterparts, and share interests, languages, and linkages that permit rapid problem-solving. Thus disaster preparedness has much to do with the creation of adaptive structures that can be quickly activated when the earthquake, hurricane, or explosion has devastated the area. My informant points out that is what the new professional institutions accomplish.

More Opportunities for Ethical Discourse

The New System obliges everyone to take responsibility for their own actions. It places responsibility for the collective good inside the organization. Of course, human affairs are never conducted perfectly, and there are many different ways to interpret what is desirable or not. The Councils and the Courts provide overall guidance, and since responsibility is vested in every single individual—quite independently of position or status—there is much demand for guidance. Everyday practice—say in the schools, hospitals, and various industries—is always questionable. More questions are generated anytime changes are proposed. The twentieth-century organization was characterized by a very limited and circumscribed ethical discourse. By and large, management and the profit motive defined what was to be done, and external regulators were assumed to be capable of defending the public interest.

The elimination of external regulatory interventions has produced consequences opposite to what might have been expected. The profit motive is still there, but the elimination of external regulation has strengthened internal self-examination because it is no longer possible to place the blame elsewhere. It does not, as might have been expected, increase corrupt or dangerous behavior. When individuals are given direct responsibilities, they tend to act and meet these responsibilities. To be sure, one reason individuals within organizations take their responsibilities seriously has to do with the role of the Governors, Councils, and Courts.

This changes the nature of work in rather fundamental ways. It is a return toward the way the old crafts used to operate. Industry in the nineteenth and the twentieth centuries removed from ordinary workers any responsibility for what they were producing. They did not own the means of production, and their contributions were depersonalized. In contrast, the craftsmen of the previous centuries had always maintained complete responsibility for the quality of their work. If they built stone walls, they took pride in the walls they built. The New System obliges everyone to take complete responsibility for what they are doing. The new technology provides everyone with much more information about possible consequences of good or bad choices, but the important difference is the new ethics. The workers still do not own the means of production, but they are given responsibility for the consequences of their actions. The workers in the magnetic vehicle factory have to take responsibility for the designs they are promoting. They ask themselves if the consumer risks implied by higher speeds are "worth it"—to clients and to society at large—regardless of the profits or benefits the firm might make in the magnetic vehicle market.

The workers did not answer these questions in a vacuum. Management had much to say, since management shares this responsibility with the senior professional staff. Management had to think in terms of profits, financial statements, and their stockholders. Councils intervened, there were some Court cases, but in a rather short period of time most of these issues were resolved. What is striking is that they were resolved in favor of the public, and therefore also in favor of the owners of the factory. What is more striking still is that these issues were usually resolved internally, without extensive conflicts and delays.

Questions and Answers

A number of students of the future read a first draft of this book. After reading their comments, it seemed useful to simply incorporate a selected set of their suggestions and questions. These may illuminate issues that have not received sufficient attention in previous pages.

A Student of Corruption in High Places

"I find your model terribly naive and simplistic. To think that adding a new layer of so called 'professional' bureaucracy would somehow take care of the human propensity to take advantage when advantage can be taken seems at best misguided."

Several colleagues have also shaken their heads. They argue that people are motivated by their own ambition. Individuals in organizations pursue those strategies that appear to them to be to their advantage. What is to their advantage may not always be to the advantage of their firm or department. But in such instances, "little do they care about the public good when a profit can be made!"

My critics do not see any reason to expect a change in human self-interest in a short fifty years. They cannot believe that design issues at the magnetic vehicle plant would be resolved in favor of the public when the market was giving different signals. What happened to the profit motive, they ask? How could the workers know what is the public interest?

To summarize, they are perplexed when I suggest that organizations, and the individuals who work in them, could or would want to place self-interest and market mechanisms in second place. They are perplexed when I suggest that the magnetic vehicle factory would design safer and more expensive units when market demand and expected profits suggest faster and somewhat less safe designs.

Other critics argue that what I have really described as a New System is simply the legitimization of laissez faire. In other words, all government controls and restraints are abolished. These controls are replaced by the professional organizations—the Councils and Courts—whose real function is to give the appearance of restraint. Their real function is to lull consumers into believing they are protected when they are not. The New System becomes the "opium of the masses."

These critics argue that the designers at the magnetic vehicle plant are still competing for fame and money. Maybe they have to go through the motions of discussing what is "good practice." But "good practice" surely means that the designers come out with their pictures on the evening television and that they make a good income. My critics ask for a better explanation. They are convinced the designers went for the less safe vehicle, for which demand was high. Profits are profits, they argue; forget this nonsense about protecting a poorly defined and rarely understood public interest.

I called José Maria.

JOSÉ MARIA: Yes, human nature is quite unchanged, but there are important differences that your critics are not paying sufficient attention to.

For example, a rise in the level of education and information available to the consuming public. People today are far more educated and far better informed than they were in your time. They can use the Informator. These are information consoles. You can talk to them and ask questions. You might ask, "What are the pros and cons if I buy a one kilo magnetic vehicle?" You get a list of considerations. You want to know the expected accident rate. The console has the answer. It "speaks" back and gives it to you.

Keep in mind that the designers are focused on the long-term satisfaction of their consumers. They receive an annual prize when the aggregate happiness quotient of their consumers rises. There is a cumulative effect here. You and your critics are right: Everyone pursues strategies that are to his or her own advantage. But we have organized ourselves to seek consensus, and we have created a reward system that obliges the organization and all those in it to pay attention to long-term outcomes. You seem to underestimate the influence of the Councils, but we do not. They plan and act accordingly. The Councils wanted safer decisions. Although there were higher profits in the faster vehicles, the Councils were more interested in the real tangible costs of higher accident rates.

A Student of Welfare

"You describe very extensive internal controls that are de-signed to help individuals, groups, and organizations cope with the consequences of unforeseen or rapid changes. Your discussion assumes that errors have been made. Further-more, you assume some of these errors should, could, and would be corrected. So far, so good. I follow what you are saying. You seem to also assume that correcting errors after they happen is a pretty straightforward process. This is where we part company. In my view, you have oversimplified a very complex problem. It is unfortunate, but correcting errors after they happen cannot simply be a matter of making a claim and obtaining compensation. Errors are made all the time, but they are or can be made for many different reasons.

"Let me give you an example: my job is abolished because my plant is closed. You say, 'Here is an articulation error. These people were working, the company decided to shift to offshore production, plant closure followed, and now we ask the Professional Governors to retrain the workers and have them rehired elsewhere.' All appears straightforward, but it is more complex than this. The reason the plant was closed is that its operating costs were high, and the reason they were high is that the plant was mismanaged. Not only that, there was also extensive graft and corruption. Spare parts and assembly components were bought at artificially high prices, there were kickbacks, and much of this translated into high costs. But the managers did not care about high costs. They knew the Governors and the Councils would come to their rescue. They pocketed the illicit funds, drove the plant into the red, decided to shift to offshore production, and waited for the gracious help you describe in your book.

"To continue, what happens after corruption is unmasked? People become aware that one has to make judgments as to why errors occur. Some firms make errors because of events that are completely out of their control. But others make errors because management is stupid, inept, or simply crooked. Sooner or later your kind Governors and Councils find they have to make judgments: 'This fellow here is a good, hardworking architect, but it turns out that

179

we trained too many architects and many are out of work. Now, this other one is a known drunkard who could never complete a drawing even if you hired him.' To make these judgments your Governors and Councils are obliged to gather facts, process information, keep records, and document how they make decisions. Since they deny some applicants and support others, they are subject to scrutiny. Very soon, they begin to elaborate their own defensive strategies. To apply for remedies after a major error, one needs forms. These forms have to be processed. Bureaucracy takes shape as procedures are elaborated. Eventually, the Governors and the Councils are no longer a solution. They have become the problem. They are but one large-scale bureaucratic maze taking care to expand its influence and protect the pleasures of its members. I wish you well, but your little book has missed the mark."

This time I thought I would call Ms. Sheridan.

G. D. SHERIDAN: Of course there are lazy people, or bad people, or what have you. This does not alter one fact: when the error happens, some people are hurt. These people need intelligent help. This is what matters.

Now suppose you have lazy people, or suppose you have people who make dumb decisions. Our case workers will find out a good deal by just glancing at the available records. You underestimate how much access to information the new technology gives us. If we want to know what time an individual arrived at work each day during the last ten years, we know. We have the data. We do not need bureaucratic controls. We are problem solvers. We also have the right to access data banks once help is sought. If you drink too

much, we will know it, and we will give you the
address of the nearest twelve-step program. We are
not in the blame business, but we do make choices,
and we do have limited budgets. We decide to use our
resources according to their impact. If our clients are
dissatisfied with the remedies we provide or do not
provide, they can appeal our decision or go to Court.
The Court will review our procedure, priorities,
and reasoning and decide on the spot. I repeat, what
matters is the long-term impact of our decisions.

Gala Dream Sheridan is saying that it is not necessary to
blame people for failures. Once failures take place, what is
needed is to find ways to repair harm. She is not placing
any blame; she is looking for ways to repair damage. However, she did not really address the issue raised by my critic,
who was saying that once you knew you would get help,
you would not even try to help yourself. You would just wait
for the help to come. I put this point to Ms. Sheridan again.

G. D. SHERIDAN: Of course, your friend is right. Human
nature has not changed. But we do not guarantee
success to everyone. If they do not help themselves
the first or second time around, we stop. We know
them and they know us. Your critic gave the example
of a mismanaged firm. Their managers did not care if
they were in the red; there were kickbacks, and so on.
That can still happen, for sure, but it is much more
difficult now than it was in your day. There is so much
more exposure now than there was then.
Organizations are porous, much more transparent. It is
difficult to hide kickbacks, although I assume that still
goes on in high circles.

181

A Student of Discrimination and Prejudice

"My, my, so much wishful thinking. How quaint—and how utterly dangerous your scenario is. I mean, it is dangerous if one pays attention to it! You describe a set of mythical institutions that protect the narrow interests of narrow segments of our society: doctors, lawyers, accountants, bricklayers, conductors, painters. I fail to see why these institutions would have any wider interest than those of their members. The horse racing people are concerned with the careers and privileges of the people who work in horse racing: jockeys, attendants, veterinarians, and so on. What makes you think these Governors or their Councils are not going to reflect and reinforce the status quo? Who are they going to help? The 'safe' practitioners?

"Moreover, within each of these professions the politics of racial or gender discrimination and prejudice are bound to dominate the thinking and the decisions of these new institutions. They will protect the majority groups, the white males where the white males dominate. The white females in occupations where they dominate, the ethnic minorities where they are employed. The bricklayers' Governor will protect against recent immigrants, and the lawyers' Governor will——"

I call Antoine Olivier, a judge in the Laws Professional Court, which adjudicates conflicts between lawyers.

ANTOINE OLIVIER: Thank you for your brief message. Tell your respondent that he is partially correct and partially wrong. Some Governors and Councils reinforce the status quo, some reinforce innovative groups within the areas of responsibility. Some Governors and Councils are liberal, some are conservative. Discrimination still takes place, although in my opinion, which I base on considerable research, it has taken much more subtle forms that are not easily recognized. Overt, visible discrimination is made increasingly difficult because our organizations are open mirrors in this respect. Subtle forms of discrimination still take place. It is not a matter of helping or not helping someone of different linguistic or cultural background, as your critic suggests. It is what type of help, and where is it sent? Friends and family are so much more important, matter so much more today, that it is difficult to know how such influence is used. This is the price we have to pay for the informality of so many of our arrangements.

Tell your critic that the New System did not abolish human greed, anger, or anxiety. It altered the way politics take place. It did not alter the fact that people have values, commitments, desires, passions, and weaknesses. In those respects we have made little progress as time has passed. But the rules of engagement have been radically altered because our tasks and the environment in which we work have been completely altered. That is all I have to tell you.

My critic laughed. "Swept all of it under the carpet," he said. "A typical plot, that's what it is." He was agitated. I decided some people fear plots everywhere, even in imaginary scenarios about the future. Another friend pointed out that imaginary scenarios serve as utopias, later to become ideologies, and that is why they are dangerous.

Antoine Olivier, who followed our brief exchanges, added a few more words.

ANTOINE OLIVIER: As a judge in the Laws Court I have to emphasize the facts. Please tell your critic that he is

absolutely correct. Your book is fiction. I am a
fictional character in a book. But the idea is not
fiction. The idea is simply an idea. Will it become an
ideology? I doubt it very much! How could it? It is
much too complicated and obscure.

A Student of Planning

"I have read your scenario with interest," this thoughtful
questioner said, "but there seems to be much taken for
granted. For example, you describe how a family was moved
from one location to another, how help was provided, how
retraining and other services were brought together and
effective assistance granted. Your scenario simply assumes
the helpers knew something about employment opportunities. Furthermore, it also assumes there were employment
opportunities out there. All this sounds good on paper, but
it is not at all convincing. You do not say much about planning, nor do you suggest how jobs are created, how the
information is transmitted, how the system functions. Please
elaborate."

I called José Maria.

JOSÉ MARIA: Planning takes place, but it is highly
decentralized and partial. No one in 2050 would ever
dream of undertaking the kind of centralized planning
that was so fashionable, at least in some parts of the
world, nearly a hundred years ago.

L'économie dirigée, the notion of state control and
manipulation of the economy, was not replaced by
laissez-faire or total government relaxation of state
responsibility. As you know, it was replaced by a
blurring of private and public responsibilities, as

184

professional bodies began to play a much greater role. The professionalization of social life, as exemplified by the institutions you have described in this book, has provided a link between what is public and what is private. The professional institutions are outside government, although both the private sector and government help fund them, but their membership is based on private decisions. All these institutions "plan," in the sense that they study the future, project their role in the future, and determine what each of them should do to improve conditions. Organizations also plan, as do networks and probably every living individual except the very, very young. Planning means thinking about the future; it means deciding about preferable courses of action.

The big difference between now and the nineteen hundreds is that we know that planning has to be diffused, multifaceted, and decentralized.

It is diffused in the sense that it happens in many different locations. Let me give you an example: we have done much to reduce suicide among at-risk populations. Let us look at the planning to increase suicide prevention among teenagers. It is carried out by networks of organizations involved in different ways in the lives of teenagers: the health agencies, the schools, the media, the computing people, and the Professional Governors. All these are part of this specific yet diffuse planning effort.

It is multifaceted in the sense that problems are approached from many angles. The suicide prevention exercise brought in many diverse talents. Some people who had been studying how our youth spend their time opened a completely new vista on ways of conceptualizing suicide prevention. In fact, it shifted from "death prevention" into "life involvement." We simply began to pay attention to their need for involvement. We then involved our youth in the major activities of our institutions. But that would take too long to describe in detail.

Our planning is decentralized in the sense that it takes place at all levels. A tremendous amount of information is generated. This is where the new technology makes a huge difference. Take the couple and the children who were retrained and moved to new jobs, homes, and schools. That was possible because the case worker could access "intelligent" data processors on her computerized Informator. That case worker simply provided the Informator with all the information and parameters on that family, including tests on their work and life-style preferences. The Informator has access to all the plans elaborated at local, regional, national, and international levels. It can match the descriptions provided by the case worker with trillions of bits of information about probable futures. The Informator then selects ten or twenty possible solutions that match the parameters. The case worker is able to use these solutions—geographical areas where expansion is expected to take place, industries that are emerging, schools that are being expanded, and so on—to establish a plan for that family. The family participates in the process. In fact, they make the final choice. So, as you can see, the family and the case worker have access to a tremendous amount of information—facts and probabilities—about the future. In that sense, they plan, although at the same time, planning is taking place all over the world. Once their decision is made, it is a new plan and it is fed into the Informator so that the rest of the world can take it into account.

Let me explain. Once the family has decided to move, the Informator knows about their intention. It feeds this with the other trillions of bits of information, much of which has probabilities associated with it, so that it can attempt to answer questions. Now, keep in mind that most of the time the Informator is not able to provide final answers. The Informator rarely predicts events. But it is able to provide ranges, magnitudes, and types of possibilities. The Informator also provides some of the basic assumptions it has used in making each of its statements about possible futures. Moreover, it is well understood by everyone who uses it that the Informator only knows "declared intentions." It is no better than the information it is given, no better than the models and programs used. At times, it reads the future wrong. At times the Informator makes huge mistakes. We all know this; we make choices accordingly. Everyone knows that intentions are very different from actions, but the Informator makes informed decision making easier and quicker. More importantly, much of the input information fed into the Informator is policy oriented. Policy inputs describe desirable courses of action that reflect political preferences. For example, should we give more help to this or that group? The Councils continually assess public preferences and organize political participation in the policy process so as to reach a consensus on courses of action. They invent images of the future that rely on technical and political arguments. They organize political participation to create support.

A Student of Conflict and Secrecy

"You seem to suggest that with the Informator much information about 'intentions' is public knowledge. But that tells us nothing about conflicting intentions. Nor does it tell us anything about secrecy. Please clarify."

JOSÉ MARIA: Of course there is conflict. Take your example. One family intends to move, and they feed their plan into the Informator. The Informator will provide this information to others, but that may not alter the attractiveness of that location or of the employment opportunities that seem to be there. Others may also decide to move and they may want to move there. There is conflict, or at least excessive demand. The Informator does not adjudicate conflicts; at best it will describe high levels of intentional demand. Then prices come into play, and the Informator provides future price information. If many families want to move, future housing prices in the area will be estimated higher, thus deterring some people. To some extent, there will be a process of mutual accommodation, but that will not resolve everything. That's why we have legislatures, courts, a political and technical process of planning, and we have police and a national guard. Conflict is part of living, as you know too well.

You ask about secrecy. Obviously, many intentions

are kept secret. There are many reasons why secrecy is necessary, and I will not attempt to lecture you on that subject. But one cannot always tell the truth—sometimes it is not known and sometimes it is too painful. More importantly, secrecy is necessary to protect privacy, and privacy is often needed to innovate. Innovation implies criticism: what was done before was not right. Innovation is a precious, fragile flower; it means a lot to those who invent. We are still motivated by profit, although you have not stressed its importance in your book. The profit motive often requires secrecy. Secrecy is maintained, even when Councils intervene, and this inevitably distorts the quality of the information we use.

Privacy and secrecy have a very significant role to play when innovation takes place. You described the way groups and networks are empowered to have access to resources so that they can innovate. That is secrecy and privacy at work. They can act on their own and not clear with people above. They may threaten the existing power structure, but at the very beginning we allow them to get started—to initiate on their own, to do some preliminary work on their ideas. We want to nurture them until they are stronger, until they have a better chance to convince others if it turns out their idea has merit. Planning is a political and technical process. You demonstrated that in your book *Mastering the Politics of Planning*. Coalition formation requires secrecy, therefore secrecy is crucial to innovation. We accept this reality. Therefore, as you said previously, planning is incomplete, imperfect. The Informator knows only what it is told. That is why life is exciting! Why, even with planning, we still make mistakes! That's why we need Governors to correct errors after they happen!

A Student of Bureaucracy

"You leave so many unanswered questions! You casually indicate that these professional groups cover all types of activities. How many groups do you contemplate? It seems that you will involve a very large set of associations. Won't they become expensive bureaucracies themselves? The complex structure and division of responsibilities of Councils, Governors, Courts, and Boards will inevitably require some form of general governmental action and oversight. This would very likely lead to political pressures for government regulation of all these new institutions. You can expect considerable corruption; therefore government will have to police these institutions. It seems to me that you have created a monstrous bureaucracy which will probably defend the status quo tooth and nail."

This time, none of my friends seemed to want to call back, and I realized that they were beginning to tire. Then I began to fear that they might not have an answer. Then I realized that the chapter had ended.

My task, which consisted in presenting a plausible scenario, is complete. My description is plausible. Personally, I doubt very much that anything resembling this complex set of institutions will emerge—at least, not in the next fifty years. But your reactions are what matters. If this imaginary image has helped explain some of our current problems, so much the better. If you envision new and different images, and these prove useful, something will have been accomplished.

CHAPTER SIX

Inside the
Future Organization:
A Visit to The Firm

This chapter provides a second scenario to describe the organization of the future. We visit a typical firm to obtain a sense of the processes at work. Again, we are in a futuristic mode, and again, I use fictional interviews. At times, I provide extrapolations or assumptions based on the material presented earlier. I do not tell much about the firm we visit. My purpose is to illustrate how work might be changed, and I am doing this in broad general terms. The organization that I refer to as "The Firm" is a large American enterprise. It is engaged in manufacturing, and it is involved in international activities and transactions. The Firm is an important organization, one of several in its domain of activity.

It has been reorganized on many occasions, and many smaller firms have spun off as the result of several major new product developments. But The Firm has taken a novel role; it provides a physical infrastructure that other firms are able to access and use. The reader will be surprised to learn that The Firm runs schools, hospitals, hotels, restaurants, even a prison which is used by the complex of other organizations that also happen to be located in the same immense building structure I am about to visit. Although I do not describe them, The Firm also operates laboratories, conference facilities, libraries, and a host of other services that facilitate the intellectual and productive activities of the tens of thousands of workers and their families who spend considerable time in the facilities. We are not concerned here with details of what The Firm does. Suffice it to say that it is highly dependent on research and development, that it operates in a very competitive environment, and that it has a multicultural staff.

The Firm is organized in one of a multitude of different arrangements that are bound to exist fifty years from now. It is organized on the senior staff model, along the general lines described in Chapter Three. This professional structure happens to fit the needs of this particular organization. Obviously, not all organizations would be based on that model in 2050.

The reader needs to bear in mind that this is not a case study based on historical materials; it is a fictional narrative. Because it is fiction, I can confine the narrative to matters germane to this book. For example, I stress the importance of the technology because it allows the staff of The Firm to control others in ways still unknown today. I also focus on the new family dimensions of the workplace of the future. Within the limited parameters of this short fictional image, we can begin to glimpse arrangements different from the ones we know today—particularly the importance given to informal networks, how rewards orient the staff to collective action, how the senior staff uses artificial internal price mechanisms to allocate scarce resources, and how they guide the actions of their many individual entrepreneurs within The Firm without controlling them directly. We can see many workers take considerable discretion into their own hands.

There is an inescapably Orwellian quality to this account in that while The Firm appears to have merits, it also seems terribly constraining. I did not attempt to paint a pretty picture. Maybe the scenario is too pessimistic. The reader can assess whether it is plausible or desirable.

My Arrival at The Firm

I flew to Boston and took a magnetic vehicle to The Firm. These "mags," as they are known, are individualized public transportation cars. Once aboard, a passenger instructs the guidance system, the doors close, and the car goes off into the tunnel or onto elevated tracks. It stops at the station closest to the passenger's destination. Individual vehicles join others en route, forming larger cohorts, only to leave them to pursue their individual courses. The car I am in stops at a station directly in front of The Firm.

The building is some 150 stories high, with a solar collector facade, which, as I was to discover later on, still provides for well-lighted offices. Signs on the path leading to the main entrance directed one to three or four nursery schools, various restaurants, and a multitude of activity clubs. There were also electronic signs that listed the locations of a number of temporary work facilities. For example, from May 6 to July 2, the "model display group" would be located in wing five on the ninety-seventh floor.

At the entrance there was a clearance procedure. A guard checked my appointment and produced a yellow card with an electronic screen on it. This was an instruction map to the work area I was to visit. By then, a large flow of men, women, and children were coming into the building. Each had a pass that was recognized by large magnetic panels that the people passed. As they came in, one by one, each seemed intent on moving fast, although they seemed to smile a lot and there was much greeting and waving.

The elevator did not seem much different to me from the ones I am used to, although there was a screen flashing notices of meeting locations. It was crowded, and no one talked. At my destination, on the 101st floor, I entered a wide corridor opening on triangular work areas. I was on my way to the Relations Unit, R.U. My instruction map was activated and it flashed instructions: "Take the next left," then "Straight ahead," then "Enter R.U. double doors," then "Sit and wait."

I was in a large waiting room overlooking the R.U. work area, where a large number of men and women seemed to be milling around talking to each other. As I watched, I realized that they were talking to large screens on stands or to portable ones they were carrying in small bags. In a corner, what looked like a café—complete with tables, waiters, coffee urns, cups, and so on—was filled with men and women at tables talking, drinking, and—again—talking to screens on which I could see flickering images. In another corner I noticed sofas and easy chairs, and again the screens were present.

My instruction map flashed: "Ms. Hernandez, the R.U. staff person in charge of your visit, will be with you in six minutes. She is sorry to be slightly delayed." I noticed the six became a five, a four, a three, and on down to zero. A short woman appeared. Our conversation was very brief and to the point. She said I did not need to write this book. They would write it for me. As she left she gave me the following text, summarizing what she thought I would include in my book:

"You will visit a few people here. We will cover a series of topics. We have made references to the book literature of your time. We had to use your references and not our Informator since your readers would not be able to access our screens. You will be out of here after lunch."

No time is wasted at The Firm.

New Concept of the Organization

Ms. Hernandez left. My instruction map flashed: "Go to the café in front of you. Sit at table 5." I went to the café area, located table 5, and sat down.

"The CEO will come in two minutes to talk to you, have some coffee, have a croissant," said the little screen. A waiter had just left a cup of coffee marked "no sugar" and a croissant in front of me and another cup, covered by a lid, across from me. I took a sip of my coffee, then a bite of croissant. A tall woman came toward my table. My instructions flashed: "This is the CEO, Kate Fuller." She said nothing but handed me this text:

"The work literature on the future emphasizes the notion of self-employment. People will 'own' their work; they will be able to work anywhere and link with anyone to do anything (Robertson, 1985), but The Firm is a large organization linked to many smaller producers that provide components and services that The Firm uses or processes."

I asked the CEO why The Firm had persisted, why it had not broken down into thousands of "independents" articulating their work through the necessary technology. The following is her response:

195

"Our organization employs and pays its staff, it pays bills, builds or rents facilities, invests in equipment and plant, conducts research, organizes conferences, runs a small hotel, serves coffee, and so on. It is highly decentralized—much more so than you could imagine in your times. Contrary to what might have been expected, our organizations did not disappear. Toffler's (1980) concept of the electronic cottage was a romantic notion. He though people would work at home and be linked electronically. That was impractical! Yes, we do much more direct 'homework.' For example, most managers are tied to information and decision systems that provide them decision data and information on a constant basis (Forester, 1988; Robins and Hepworth, 1988), but the issue never became one of working at home or working in a plant, nor was it an issue of small versus big (Schumacher, 1973) because, today, the importance or the 'reality' of the organization is altered.

"In your century, the organization we now call The Firm was an employer. It was also the locus of power. Management was in charge, your stockholders mattered, the entire social order was centered on these individual, finite institutions. Each pursued their advantages, each attempted to survive, to grow, to control, and to gain.

"This concept of the organization began to change at the end of the century (Touraine, 1988; Itami, 1987). Unions changed their policies and linked with management to pursue collective interests (Heckscher, 1988). More importantly, informal networks began to matter much more because everyone finally understood that most tasks required getting many diverse efforts, resources, and workers together. Integration and the massing of resources became the most important dimension of work: interorganizational cooperation became central. The international dimension expanded this even more (Schermerhorn, 1984; Van de Ven, 1976; Oliver, 1990)."

Interorganizational Linkages

The CEO continued: "At first the emphasis was on enhancing organizational linkages to make organizations more competitive (Kilmann, Kilmann, and Associates, 1990). The emphasis was on enhancing teamwork, and through networking to increase the ability to act, flexibility would greatly increase as organizations linked, pooled resources and knowledge to invent, mass their resources, and implement (Wiewel and Hunter, 1985; Parker, 1990; Mueller, 1986). At that time, the organization was still the main umbrella, and networking was an activity involving individuals from many organizations.

"Gradually, the informal networks began to matter more than the formal organizations. This may seem surprising to you since the organizations provide the tools and facilities to perform, but the tools and facilities are less important than the work that is facilitated. The tools of production can always be brought together once the ideas and the possibility of action have emerged. When we decentralized organizations, we made the group and the network the important locus of action.

"We sit here in the café of R.U. in The Firm. But at the table next to us, you see six women and five men who have been meeting here every week for about half a day for the last six months. They are developing a new service in which five organizations, including The Firm, are involved. This informal network is far more important to their work, to solving problems, than their own organizations. When they need to sit down together, they use our Informator to communicate with their own organizations, but they could meet in any other organization and use any other Informator.

"I suppose you do not know about our Informator. It is accessed with these stands with screens. We also have portable ones. We talk to them. Typing disappeared decades ago. Our computers deal directly with voice instructions.

"Anyhow, the reason networks matter is simple: individuals in networks generate ideas and activities. Innovations matter very much. Our staff is rewarded in ways that encourage innovations. Therefore, networks matter to them. Of course, you are here in a problem-solving department; therefore networks matter. R.U. is problem solving. We will take you to a routine department. That is the next step on your program. There it is somewhat different."

The CEO had taken out a package of pink cigarettes. "Care for one?" she asked. I looked surprised. She laughed. "We smoke again, now that cancer has been eliminated. That is why your 1950s movies are still so popular. We find them natural because people smoked so much then. After the turn of the century, smoking was completely abolished until a cure was found for cancer and other smoke-induced diseases."

Routines

My card flashed, "Please walk through the door marked Coffee Detail." I rose, pushed the door open, and entered a room where several coffee urns were brewing and five or six waiters were preparing trays. Croissants were coming out of a large metal container, an automated oven. I could see containers with baking ingredients feeding pipes to the baking machinery. A strong baking smell permeated the room, and the ubiquitous screens stood in one corner. I could see one flashing: "Twenty coffees and croissants for bar of purchasing." One of the waiters turned toward me. I was not prepared for his long lecture, which he delivered like a schoolmaster in front of a class full of young students.

"This is Coffee Detail. We are showing you this operation because it is a typical routine department. At the time you are writing your book, much work is routinized and much is not. At the end of the twentieth century the production line had already changed. The rigid production conveyors of the beginning of the century, where workers performed highly routinized operations, were already history. Production went from rigid low-flexibility conveyor assembly, where you only produce one black Model T Ford automobile, to flexible assembly, where decisions are made along the line to alter production cycles so that you can produce different models in different colors. After that, automation gave increasing responsibility to work teams and created parallel production cycles. Later came the institution of on-time production so that you first sold the automobile and immediately produced it, as needed, with all the detailing the customer wanted. By then you were well along on the road to automation and decentralization. The large monolithic production organization was being replaced by disintegrated production, with a host of small interdependent firms feeding larger ones (Coriat, 1990; Cole, 1989; Scott and Storper, 1986).

"Today, the most routinized production workers are replaced by programmed robotics. Our few production workers are there to solve problems, maintain the equipment, or modify routines. But, I repeat, most routinized production is done by programmed machines. Therefore, our worker has become a problem solver, a 'worker manager' (Vallas, 1990; Hirschhorn, 1984; Morgan, 1988). He or she has to watch for glitches and adapt the routines to handle crises or unforeseen events or to reprogram the machine.

"Nevertheless, routinized work still exists. In-person servers, such as nurses, waiters, or receptionists, are employed in person-to-person activities. Some are routinized, like mine; others provide tremendous discretion and opportunities for creativity. But as you can see in this room, we have eight waiters, all males, who deliver coffee and croissant orders and do not do much more.

"Obviously, we could program and automate this operation. Coffee and croissant machines could be operated throughout the building. But we have found out through experience and research that creative work requires very supportive environments. For example, face-to-face intensive communication is always important (Walton, 1987), and communal drinking, eating, or bathing provides important opportunities. More importantly, service gives status to those served. It provides them with a sense of importance they would not have otherwise. This is why we employ so many in-person service personnel.

"Our waiters are expected to provide a supportive environment where others have the opportunity to think, talk, discuss ideas, and organize action. We use croissant machines because The Firm is not convinced that hand-baked croissants are really any different. But there are organizations that insist on hand-baked goods—they have more variety than we serve here, and they provide more restful environments. For example, some have 'cave rooms'—completely silent spaces with no consoles, no external communication networks—where random groups of managers meet for long periods every day. They have massage tables in the caves placed close enough together that the clients on the tables can talk to each other. These encounters are purposely unstructured. They use random meetings to foster accidental encounters. We are told this is to encourage serendipity.

"As routines were taken over by machines, the labor market split into a very large in-person servers sector; a much smaller operating, design, and maintenance technical sector; and a still smaller elite of symbolic analysts. The Firm employs thousands of in-person servers. For example, we have child care and educational facilities with one-to-one ratios or even two-to-one ratios! I mean two adults for every child. You cannot imagine how many services are now available within organizations. We have saunas with attendants. Managers, designers, and maintenance workers have access to the saunas, as do waiters, cooks, teachers, child care workers, nurses, masseurs, and so on. We have many in-person servers because that is what organizations like The Firm provide. They provide environments where ideas, networks, and spin-offs can be generated."

The waiter stopped. He had spoken nonstop, as if reading a lecture. It was a very odd encounter. I was not used to such monotone. The waiter was pointing to the flashing card in my hand. It said "End of interview. Please go back to your table at the café to meet Ms. Nielsen, a member of our senior staff. She will discuss symbols."

The waiter murmured, "She is well informed." He

opened the door. I asked him why he had decided to give me this lecture. He looked surprised, then, pointing to a screen behind me, he said, "I read the text, that's all."

Symbols

My yellow instruction map flashed the message "*Virgil possunt quia posse videntur*": "They can, because they think they can." Ms. Nielsen, a member of the senior staff, was waiting for me. She immediately began to talk.

"The Firm is not only a facilitating institution. Coffee and croissants do not provide ideas. The Firm provides one of the symbolic environments in which networks prosper. Meaning motivates action. The role of organizations in our century is to provide meaning so that we become motivated to act (Smirchich and Morgan, 1982; Feldman and March, 1981). The Firm is managed by the senior staff working with our CEO. The senior staff represent the major professional activities that matter here. They are scientists and engineers. The senior staff and our CEO set the script for our activities (Lord and Kernan, 1987; Eckblad, 1981; Gioia and Poole, 1984). They invent the languages that motivate our actions. They do the strategic planning. This is the way we keep some order in the disorder of creativity."

She waved for coffee, reaches for her bag, and takes out an elegant cigar container.

"To keep order, you need structure, and to create, you need order and structure. The senior staff set the long-term agenda. We have six-year plans that are constantly reexamined. Ours now is 'create happiness in the household.' We are focusing on the household. We have shifted focus. Our last agenda was 'early childhood.' We have pageants to affirm

202

the agenda, conferences to define the meaning of our language, ceremonies to glorify our successes, songs and uniforms to remind us of our purposes."

The coffee had come. Now she took out a large purple cigar and lit it. Soon she was in a cloud of smoke.

"We have these displays. They provide the background for action. We invent because there is structure. There is a shared understanding."

Trust

Ms. Nielsen continued: "We operate on the forgiveness factor. It is an old principle that goes like this: it is easier to obtain forgiveness for taking an action than to obtain permission to do it (Hagebak, 1982). Innovative organizations take risks. When you take risks, you make mistakes. I know, because they had me read your book, that you thought one could correct errors after they happen. That is much too simpleminded. There is always some damage that cannot be corrected. We take risks, and that means there is always some damage. Therefore, we also want to limit risk avoidance (Bohland and Gist, 1983; Nelkin, 1985; Barber, 1983). People have to be motivated to take risks, which is why I talked to you about the importance of the symbols we espouse. This is why we have this major campaign around a somewhat vague yet very significant theme, 'household happiness.' We emphasize our Latin dictum: *virgil possunt quia posse videntur*—they can, because they think they can. They have to believe to think they can. We know this today, and you and your generation did not.

"You had a destructive attitude toward creativity. Your generation was always ready to criticize, to place blame, to accuse, to find fault everywhere. Women, in particular, were too often criticized, rarely taken seriously. You had anticreative rituals. You only accepted what was safe and already recognized. You were very late in understanding that one had to believe in the possibility of success and that collaboration and support mattered (Hart, 1986; Majone, 1989; Johnson, 1985).

"I spoke about trust. It is not only trust about behavior, about mutual expectations. It is also trust that you are supported, that you have friends, that you are operating in a humane environment that approximates the way members of your family should treat you. Groups and networks are made of people who want to work together. They succeed because these people happen to work well together. The Firm provides a supportive environment where groups and networks flourish. We may have had more high-level women managers than men because women are often perceived to be more supportive.

"But your book is quite wrong. Women were not that different from men once they were accepted. They did not displace men at the top. We had similar purposes. Together we created environments for trust. Together we created the cafés and the saunas, and we were together when we removed criticism and blame. Once both men and women understood that trust matters, we knew we could not afford to blame. Rewards differ; that is enough in itself.

"You discuss outcome assessment in your book. Outcome assessment transformed the organization. We do not need to blame people because they blame themselves. Our reward structures take no pity. They go right through the rhetoric and the pretense. Outcomes, long-term outcomes, matter. The rest is left to the individual. Do what you want, we tell them, but you will need results, maybe not immediately, but soon enough.

"I cannot explain in detail how we allocate outcome rewards, although that is one of my responsibilities. We take long-, middle-, and short-term outcomes and weigh them. We allocate a large portion of our surplus directly to the annual bonus, and each of us receives an account of how our performance was allocated. The present determines the total surplus, but the allocation takes into account expected long-term consequences. In so doing, we have privatized the salary structure because everyone has a stake both in our immediate and long-term success. We have protected the future because the allocation of today's surplus is a reflection of expected future gain.

"Of course we can make mistakes and reward people today for future gains that never materialize. We surely make this kind of error, and we are continually on the lookout to correct for it. If you network and create an operating spin-off, you receive a portion of last year's surplus that takes into account probable future profits. Suppose the planning was wrong, the forecasts off. Your spin-off fails miserably. It will show in your bonus as soon as facts and forecasts shift. You are obliged to pay attention to both the present and the future. We usually operate on five- and ten-year futures. But there is also an institutional long-term future principle at work. If you contribute in some way to a client's happiness forever—say you write some beautiful Swedish fiddle music—you will receive a share of rewards for years to come, assuming, of course, there is a surplus.

"Now then, rhetoric, myths, ideologies, and symbols are needed, but we are at post-postdeconstruction today. Deconstruction philosophy helped us understand the importance of the underlying assumptions of our ideologies. Beyond that, what matters is the task. Therefore, deconstruction philosophy was helpful, but we have moved on (Baudrillard, 1975; Lyotard, 1988; Derrida, 1991). What matters is that we are aware that we do not need blame. We encourage creativity, and we give discretion to our designers and production operators. We let our symbolic analysts run with their ideas, and we set the situation so that they decide when and where to concentrate their efforts. We provide a structure in which they can perform. The mission of the CEO and the senior staff is to define the agenda to undertake long-range planning while our decentralized structure responds in real time to the changing environment."

Hierarchies

Ms. Nielsen went on, seemingly tireless: "We have flat hierarchies. We have a very thin top-management layer. I report directly to the CEO. I am part of the senior staff. About six thousand people work directly for me and report to me. This should cause you to pause and consider! I know what they are doing because we have monitors. They work in groups or in networks, but any one of them answers to me. Between each of them and me we have what we now call 'intermediary structures.' A group may have an informal leader chosen by the members. Several groups or networks may have coordinators or chairs. They are all intermediary informal structures. Some may be temporary, others more permanent, but the basic hierarchy of The Firm is very flat. We have about one hundred thousand workers and intermediary structure people, some two hundred senior staff, and one CEO. You understand, I hope, for one hundred thousand workers we only have two formal management levels: the senior staff and the top person.

"We are able to operate a decentralized innovative organization with a very flat hierarchical structure because much of our internal coordination is achieved through internal market mechanisms. We have internal prices and markets for our scarce organizational resources. Our groups and networks bid for most of the resources they need. We set the prices in light of overall priorities. As a result, management can focus on long-term issues because most of today's on-time decisions are made without our having to arbitrate.

"Our intermediary structures often have links outside The Firm. If we work in Europe or in the Pacific Rim, we usually tie in with others, but even here in the Americas we continually tie in with others. Moreover, we facilitate interorganizational arrangements by facilitating and financing informal networks. They often become incipient spin-offs.

"We place no blame, so my role with my six thousand friends is to provide an overall agenda. They are savvy enough to know which way the needs of our clients drive our innovations. In our activities, fundamental research plays a big role. Our informal networks include many university professors. We negotiate financial agreements to get innovations implemented jointly with government, universities, and other research institutions (Powers, Powers, Betz, and Aslanian, 1988; Johnston and Edwards, 1987; Stankiewicz, 1986). As you already suspected, American universities have changed. They have become entrepreneurs in their own right. They run huge enterprises that often tie in with government and the private sector. In a sense, they look more like us, and to some extent, we look more like them.

"The universities had to change their reward structures, and that was not always easy. In your days, the American university was increasingly in danger of narcissistic death, particularly in your social sciences. There was too much research intended for other academics. Too few paid attention to the long-term problems of the economy, and those who did were not always rewarded. But all this has changed."

Ms. Nielsen lit another cigar. I could see how a set of medical advances had translated into a new era for the tobacco industry.

"Intuition is what matters," she went on. "The Firm believes in intuition (Agor, 1990). In that way, we aim toward a zen of management. We do not blame; we ask, what is the meaning of what we do? We listen to the market. We collaborate because the task requires it, but we collaborate in a flat egalitarian structure (Kraus, 1980; Vaill, 1989). You see, our salary structures are very flat. Our CEO makes about twice what I make, and I make about twice what a worker makes at my age and experience. The total difference between our workers and our top managers is four times. But that is not the entire structure. Experience and achievement count within each ladder. Our CEO, the senior staff, and all the workers share many collective bonuses. They also obtain advancement within salary ladders. A young worker gets less than an older one, which is why I said I am compensated at about twice their rate.

"In your day, you thought that huge compensation differences were necessary to attract and motivate top talent. We quickly discovered that differences were necessary, but the size of the difference did not matter so much. On the contrary, the legitimacy of our CEO is directly related to the

208

fact that her lifestyle is not that different from ours. Her remuneration is not that different, but it is different. More importantly, we have a large stream of so called in-person service workers, some of whom do not exercise much discretion. They have far less access to resources than symbolic analysts. Yet, in terms of hierarchy and remuneration within The Firm, symbolic analysts do not make more than our waiters in this room. The difference is that they have access to more and larger bonus opportunities. Their work provides access to additional external sources of income outside The Firm—say bonuses for serving on interorganizational networks, bonuses for work done in organizations with which they are networking. This is the entrepreneurial dimension of work that is so important today. People are rewarded in terms of results. If you are very active and work hard, you can do quite well. As I said, we have privatized the salary structure.

"In terms of equality, the senior staff and CEO are one world, the workers another. I told you that if you want creativity, you need structure. We give tremendous discretion to our symbolic analysts and to some of our design, maintenance, and technical workers. You described how they have access to resources, how they can act on their own. All that is true. But the senior staff control the environment. We decide and provide the incentives. We define good practice. Basically we manage them, even if they still believe they are free to innovate. In fact, we want them to believe they are free to innovate, because belief matters."

Management

Now Ms. Nielsen seemed to take direct aim at my very own work: "Your book discusses *internal* incentives for innovation. As I remember, you discuss how incipient groups and networks have access to budgets and so on. That's fine, but your book does not discuss overall fiscal policy. Today, most governments provide direct incentives that greatly facilitate and accelerate the adoption of innovations. Your book is focused on groups and networks, and these innovators are interesting because they often become the next firm; they grown and ultimately replace us. They find capital because government works with the private sector to make capital available for innovators. In your day, the incentives worked backward, and some good ideas were picked up by foreign investors, but by and large there were insufficient government incentives for innovation. Your typical large corporate investors were pursuing takeovers because they could make a quick profit. They rarely paid any serious attention to new ideas because that was more difficult and took too long. All this changed, of course, and the changes have made our job much more difficult.

"Do we control everything? As you know, we have direct access to tremendous amounts of information. I can ask the screen over there what percentage of our work force were brushing their teeth between six and seven o'clock this morning and I will immediately obtain an estimate based on current data. I can ask sophisticated questions and get answers: How are we spending our budget? What are sales projections in this or that market? How do our cost trends compare with our estimates of our competition? What are long- and short-term client preferences telling us? We have a tremendous amount of information to digest and we have to make sense of it. But we still face uncertainties because our intelligence information and projections cannot keep pace with the accelerated rate of innovation.

"I said that we control our workers, even if they have the impression that they are in control. That is true, since we control our incentives, we control overall discretionary budgets, and we invent our myths of the future. On the other hand, we cannot be sure what any given group or network will decide to do. We have created the social environment in which they create. We can manipulate this social environment to some extent. Yet we do not always know what they will come up with. So, managing The Firm is a roller coaster ride. We, therefore, spend a lot of time on strategy because it is the long run that matters. In your day, the organization was not decentralized the way it is today. Therefore it could control directly.

"You talked constantly about strategic thinking, but that tended to be top-down strategy. Today, control is achieved by secondary means, through long-term incentives, through artificial internal price mechanisms, and through generalized ideological stances. That is why I mentioned our 'happiness in the household' agenda. We use language purposely to achieve desired ends, but we are well aware that most of our workers are educated, trained, and probably very capable. They have access to most if not all the sources of information I have access to. They can ask the screens questions just as I do. They can find out how their performance compares with that of their fellow workers and colleagues. They can find out at what time I brushed my teeth, what we are spending money on this afternoon. They are well aware of the problems we face; therefore, they attempt to solve problems. They know very well when we are in trouble, and they have learned to adjust themselves to the discipline required by collective action.

"There is complete openness. The only difference is their

access to people. We have easier screen access to individuals than they do. There is no way you can give open screen access to anyone when you are a CEO. We like to project the image of open access. So, outside the senior staff there has to be rationing. This is accomplished more or less effectively by randomizing direct access."

Environment of the Organization

Ms. Nielsen paused to cough briefly. Were these cigars really inoffensive? I did not have time to ask; she continued: "Keep in mind the large picture. In 1990 you had a world population of about 5.3 billion. It doubled to about 10.6 billion by 2035. After that there was no more nonsense about population policy and the world population stabilized. But while the United States had only 5 percent of the world population in 1990, it consumed about 25 percent of the world energy (Kaula, 1991). All that changed radically during the next sixty years.

"Yes, we solved the energy problem, or should I say we did not solve it? You saw our solar energy facade. Solar energy is far more important today than in your time, but as you know, we still depend heavily on atomic energy, and I do not mean fusion. We have not yet been able to achieve fusion, although much has been spent in that area. We depend more and more on very dangerous technologies. That is why management today is so much more difficult than it was in your day. We had to achieve international agreements to maintain high levels of world safety. And it is not only atomic energy that worries us. Even here in The Firm we use processes that are highly dangerous. For a while, the rich countries were able to export dangerous technologies

212

or to export and dump abroad the dangerous residues of industrial and commercial processes. But all this rapidly came to an end, and everyone was faced with difficult choices.

"The world situation that preoccupies us most is the maintenance of safe processes. This is the overriding responsibility of management. This is where we differ from our workers, who tend not to care as much, not to be as aware or as informed as we are of the consequences of their choices. We have to maintain a long-term view and we have to keep an eye on our competition.

"You correctly predict in your book that regulatory interventions would be internalized. I think your description is in the right direction, although again, it is not as simple as you make it sound.

"First, the world changed completely in the last fifty years. The Pacific Rim became the fastest growing economy of the world. China became the largest producer, and today China dominates most of world trade. There has been a substantial movement of world population, something we had certainly not foreseen. The poorer countries have exported labor to the centers of growth at such high rates that economic disparities have been attenuated through migration. You should notice, at lunchtime in the restaurant, the ethnic composition of the people in the dining room! We have people from everywhere. But the fast expansion of growth regions, the flows of population, and the rapidity of the transformation of the world economy internationalized most organizations. We were all in the same boat, and we had to be concerned with all the dangers surrounding us. Ever since the Rio Conference of 1992, the world has had to pay attention to its health. The Firm had to address the ecological agenda, and professional bodies had to take responsibility for addressing these issues.

"But the professional bodies did not do this spontaneously. Government had to intervene. This is a very long story, and it would take too long to explain. All I can tell you is that your description is incomplete. Government was not really able to completely abandon regulatory interventions because the professional bodies you describe needed government help to get started, particularly in the context of the world scene. It was more important to achieve a new synthesis of government and the private sector, a synthesis of the new capitalism and socialism (Halal and Nikitin, 1990). A synthesis based on the twin notions of accelerated change and security. We invented a third force between government and private interest. The Professional Governors and Councils you describe are a good approximation of this third force. They dampen the defects of the free market without some of the excessive costs of government intervention. This third force had consequences. It altered our own concept of the organization.

"The pragmatic virtues dominate our thinking today. Effectiveness replaced efficiency as the dominant paradigm. If you can do something that is wanted, that practical reality is more important to us than the details of how it affects the organization. The Firm is less important to us than what The Firm allows us to do. You and I are here today and we could be elsewhere tomorrow. It is what we produce, how we serve, what we invent that matters. We do not care about organizations the way you did. We do not pamper or protect them. They come and go.

"We are more centered on our clients—the people we serve—and on our workers, than you were. That is why I mention the happiness of both. When we discuss strategy, market transformations, or expansions, we always discuss long-term outcomes. They are the relevant measures of our contribution. But we ask about the happiness of both our clients and our workers (Quennell, 1988; Veenhoven, 1984).

"We had to agree to international ethical standards. I have mentioned over and over again that creativity requires structure. Once we removed centralized control, we had to depend on much more specific and shared ethical standards to protect against bad innovations, against unscrupulous behaviors, against corruption and falsification. Do not read me wrong. I am not suggesting that human nature was changed or that greed was eliminated. On the contrary! Greed is very much alive—and useful, since our incentive schemes depend on it. But we had to greatly improve the ethical performance of our private and public organizations, and we achieved this in a very pragmatic and effective manner: we created long-term outcome performance measures that evaluate ethical performance. It is as simple as that."

Ms. Nielsen said good-bye. My yellow instruction map was flashing again, the waiter reappeared, and we were off on a tour of the premises.

Physical and Other Facilities

We did not spend much time visiting the premises. The waiter assured me that once one had seen some of the facilities, the rest was more of the same. I asked why they only served coffee—a stimulant or a depressant, depending how one thought about it—when "happiness" was what they were about. "Nonsense," he answered, "there is no universal definition of happiness. That is typical of the senior staff.

They invent this rhetoric and imagine we believe them. We serve coffee because they tell us to. They ran an experiment some time ago. We began serving wine. Happiness and wine go together, they said. No siree. People were asleep at their stations as early as two in the afternoon. Therefore, we serve coffee." After that the waiter was silent except for very laconic instructions like "turn left," "this way," and brief, very brief explanations. But he had spoken without reading anything.

Privatization of Collective Space

What struck me most was the variety of working environments. People obviously had considerable discretion in designing their work spaces. Many private belongings had been brought to supplement a variety of standardized office supplies. There were desks or tables, chairs and sofas, many different lamps. Even the screens were varied. In some areas one would find birds, fish, and other small pets. In others, enormous green plants climbed all over the walls. Some areas had very fancy carpets, one had a billiard table in the middle of the room, another had a bathtub, and the waiter mumbled that "she liked to bathe often." He was not appreciative. I asked who the person was who occupied the space with the bathtub (in public view), and he explained that it was an area where teams spent days and nights working on intensive projects and that here, as in other similar spaces, there were bathtubs and other living facilities including bathrooms and beds. But that bathtub was special. One of the senior design staff members insisted on taking long baths "to clear her mind," and this apparently had been arranged. "Her happiness mattered." He seemed quite annoyed with this particular arrangement. Apparently they had staff meetings around the bathtub. The waiter did not approve.

One sensed two contradictory trends in the design of the facility. First, as I mentioned, they had these intensely personalized arrangements. Public spaces had become private. I asked the waiter and he mumbled that women were responsible for much of that. "They brought their kids, then they brought their pets and their furniture." It was obvious that he had left his pets at home. But I had seen many men in spaces that were no different. Some were decorated with paintings, one had hunting trophies, many were filled with golf or tennis memorabilia. A large space had a mini–bowling alley.

Second, one could see that work spaces were constantly being rearranged. During our short walk we had even bumped into a dozen or more people who were in the process of planning workplace arrangements for a project over the next two weeks.

I asked the waiter how they managed the privatization of public or collective space, including birds, plants, and large fish tanks, with the constant need for change and mobility. "You can bring your own stuff, but it is mounted on standardized tracks. All our equipment and furnishings are on these tracks." He pointed to the floor. One could easily move everything, the walls, the mirrors, the screens, the desks, even the bathtub, as long as each was disconnected. All you had to do was to instruct the screen: "Move large green plant behind me to office 32 down the hall and place it at location BC." Out went the plant and out would go tables with photographs of the family, walls with hunting trophies, and even fireplaces, with the fire still smoldering.

I thought to myself, technology permits the privatization of public space to facilitate creative work.

Family Facilities

The child care center had a high number of adults taking care of the children. The rooms were equipped with play areas and opened directly into gardens. The children had access to screens that allowed them to speak with their parents while they were at work. There was a nursery for infants, a toddler area, and a preschool group. There was also a small mini–magnetic track out in the garden for mag transport to other child care centers in the vicinity. This way the children could easily join organized activities, such as visits to museums, the circus, playgrounds, and gymnasiums.

We visited a primary school for the young children of the staff of The Firm. The waiter explained that it made no sense to transport children in one direction when parents went in another, so primary schools were now always attached to workplaces. Older children could go on their own to secondary schools, he pointed out. And no, he did not have any children. We visited a recreational area. There was a sauna and a large hot-water plunge. It was just before twelve noon, and the facility was filled with men, women, and children. "They are on a morning shift," he explained. "Twice a week they have a one-hour relaxation here. If they have children in the child care center, they can come too. After this they will have lunch, and we will also."

Women had joined the organization and, as a consequence, their families had also moved in.

Complaints and Prisons

We had entered the dining room. The waiters were in black and white uniforms. But the staff wore a wide variety of

218

garments. At one table they were wearing black togas and the waiter explained they were the ombudspersons, individuals who handle staff grievances. There were also people in jackets, ties, bows, pants, and skirts. I could see a huge variety of ethnic backgrounds, but by and large their clothes looked similar. There did not seem to be too much innovation in clothing. It all looked comfortable and simple, although women certainly wore feminine garments that looked highly fashionable, in many different colors and materials. Most looked attractive and many I should even say, very sexy (Hochswender, 1991).

I asked the waiter about the ombudspersons. Did they receive many complaints? The waiter shrugged his shoulders. He said that people were always complaining. Yes, there were difficulties. People complain about space, about moving, about the temperature, the food, the pets of others, the cleanliness of the bathtubs. "Who knows what they do not complain about!" Yes, they also complain about the coffee, about the waiters. "People are people," the waiter said, "and nothing is ever perfect."

What about sexual harassment? No, he did not think there was *much* sexual harassment. He thought that blaming others was less important today than in my time. When blaming is less important, people complain about their own fears, their own weaknesses. They turn inward. "The ombudsperson is usually a psychiatrist," he pointed out.

Ms. Nielsen was back. She introduced two Japanese staff members, and we all sat together. They were introduced as Jim and Lisa. I expressed some surprise because their names were not Japanese. Lisa explained that her real name was not easy to pronounce in English. It was normal to change names when one moved because "one became someone else when one went away."

Ms. Nielsen took over: "The way people think about the organization has changed. We needed a new ideology that could accommodate ambiguity. That is where our concern with outcomes made a difference. I do not know whether you can understand what I am saying—if you have not experienced it—if outcomes matter, the organization per se matters less. Places such as this one look impressive to you. You see all the services we provide."

A waiter had come with menus. He served some wine without being asked. "Punch in your order," he instructed me. There was a simple digital board in front of my seat. The menu looked splendid: bisque soup, duck legs, and mousse au chocolat, or oyster salad, leg of lamb, and tarte aux pommes, and several other dishes I did not recognize, as well as Peruvian spearfish, Greek dolmas, and caviar and champagne!

Ms. Nielsen pointed out that there was also a menu for children. Many of the working families eat both lunch and dinner at the restaurant so that they have more time at home, away from the automated kitchen and precooked dinners.

I punched in caviar and champagne. Ms. Nielsen spoke: "The Firm rents these services to many much smaller companies that do not have such facilities. Generally, they are offshoots, companies that were initiated by some people here—that grew out of successful networks—they pay a flat fee to remain here and use our restaurants, child care, schooling, hospital—even our prison."

"Your prison?" I was surprised.

"Yes, we run a prison for people who have committed serious infractions—people who are on the staff here or who work in similar enterprises. This is a white-collar prison. We are paid a flat fee by the state for taking people from other firms. There are not many people in the prison at present. Two or three. None are ours. The idea was to make prison life much more visible to deter corruption. Given our high level of decentralization, we had to make sure people understood that one could be caught and punished if one broke with the definitions of good practice. We have access to information, you know—and people can always send complaints to the ombudsperson.

"I'll give you an example. You asked your waiter about sexual harassment. There is very little inappropriate behavior these days. The reason is simple. If you complain to an ombudsperson that Jim here is constantly provoking women, asking for favors, or what have you, they will place him under total surveillance. We will know what he said and did on a twenty-four-hour basis—just as I know you asked your waiter about sexual harassment. I was not here, but I know when you asked, how you asked— We will continue the surveillance at very little cost and examine what he does. If there is any doubt, we will call him in, show him what is resented, and take care of it. Usually it stops there.

"On the other hand, we do not, nor could we have the time to, observe everything we record. If there is a complaint, nothing is easier than to call in the recorded sequence. The ombudspersons can call in sequences. Do you understand? Why there is very little trouble?

"What matters today is successful outcomes. Men and women work here together. We employ many married couples because it greatly facilitates everything if both work at the same site. We and they save—on transportation, on time lost away from each other. Their small children come here also. They often eat dinner after work, and even enjoy a movie before returning home."

I ate my food slowly. I could imagine the careful recording of my slow mastication. I became thoughtful.

Human Resources

Ms. Nielsen seemed not to notice my quiet mood. She went on: "I told you—or you already know—that women became very important to organizational success. I think your evaluation in your earlier chapters is pretty accurate. People are evaluated on outcome performance, and some women seem to do better than men. They intuit better. That is my opinion."

Suddenly Lisa was interrupting. She seemed slightly angry. "The organization has absorbed us! We have moved the family into the organization. We have two small children, born here. They are in toddler care, probably having nap time right now, and when I say born here, I mean not only in the United States, but here in this building. Jim is very successful. He started a spin-off group that worked out, but as a consequence, our work hours do not coincide any more. Also, he has to work in New York three days a week and in Tokyo once a month. It is exhausting. Yes, the food is good, but it is not our food, not our table, not our family. Do not believe it works well because it does not."

Problems with "Dead Wood"

Then Jim joined in. "We moved here because we wanted to live abroad and experience a different cultural environment. There were openings for several Japanese in the organization. We came and I never regretted it. In my opinion, our greatest achievement has been to find work for nearly everyone, men and women. I know we still have people in prison and people who have trouble finding work, although those are very few, since anyone can be trained or retrained. But there are many social problems we have not solved, not by any reasonable measures.

"We still have many who cannot work because of illness or defects. Many who—we must be frank—prefer not to work, are born to live contrary lives. You do not see them here, nor do you see them in the mags. The fact that we had huge migrations did not simplify social problems. On the contrary, it demonstrated how difficult it was to survive in many parts of the world.

"But this and many organizations became far more humane. They became homes away from home. They provided the sense of community that had disappeared in the large urban centers. The Firm is a community. It provides stability in a very unstable environment. But we had to find ways to deal with those who do not work, those who do not contribute: the dead wood."

Lisa spoke again. "We do not place blame, we just give facts. It is easy to find out whether someone is slacking off, not contributing. In your day you had too much respect for incompetence. How do you say this? You had a hang-up about people who do not pull their weight. There were many reasons historically, we are told. The unions had done so much to improve the economic position of their members; they had made a unique contribution to society. They had lifted the common people, greatly improved their economic circumstances, and in so doing they had created new markets and been instruments of economic growth. But the unions had not been so well suited to the new technologies, to a new world with differentiated, educated, and empowered workers (Kelley, 1990; Vallas, 1990; Thompson, 1989).

"The unions had protected their members, and at times they protected the status quo. But the unions were not the main difficulty. Much legislation had also been passed to protect workers from arbitrary dismissal. Without facts it was often much too difficult to prove incompetence, laziness, and plain free-rider enjoyment. There had also been a quest to balance ethnic and minority participation, which facilitated protective strategies. In short, in the 1990s, organizations tended to allow the dead wood too many opportunities, too many privileges. In due time, the unions failed and a new unionism and professionalism emerged suited to the needs of adaptive organizations (Moody, 1989; Heckscher, 1988).

"Our porous organizations rely on affinity groups. Our groups and networks are informal. Each of us in a group can assess who does what and who does not contribute. We drop the dead wood. We have no problem assessing performance because when in doubt we can always obtain the facts. As Ms. Nielsen told you earlier, we record everything. We all know that. This lunch is recorded. You would be astonished at the wealth of data that is recorded: your body temperature, your speech, your movements, and yes, how long it takes you to masticate, the chemical content of each bite, the flow of air, the light intensity. We have so much data that we are able to recreate past events and obtain data that was not recorded. The point is that we can always get the facts. If you do not contribute, others will know it. You will be dropped.

"What happens when you are dropped? You do not get bonuses. The entire incentive system is based on outcome measures mediated by performance evaluation. If you are dropped, you are out of the loop. We do not need to fire you, we do not need to assign you elsewhere. You will be asking for different assignments because your pay check has simply evaporated. The system is not cruel since every effort is made to help you find and train for new assignments, but there is no guaranteed sinecure. Dead wood cannot survive because performance is always assessed.'"

Performance

The waiter was shaking his head and saying, "Not really, not really." We all turned toward him and Lisa stopped. She smiled to him and asked, "You do not agree?" "Yes and no," he answered. "You are right. Everything is recorded. But as you know, there are ways of evading the recording technology. There are ways of masking or delaying the sensor, which will confuse the data. One cannot always accomplish this, but it is done. But that is not my point.

"You know and I know that competence and incompetence are all matters of judgment—they are value judgments. In the final analysis, the senior staff sets the expectations, and results matter. It is true that performance matters more today than it did in the past because work opportunities are highly differentiated. Most of the employment opportunities are in-person service work, the kind of work I perform. Some of my work is done by people who work part-time, half-time, or short-term, but most are permanent. We are not badly paid. As you know, pay is very egalitarian. But we have much less to say about the norms of good performance. Symbolic analysts and technical workers have a more direct role in defining performance.

"My point, the reason I kept saying 'no, no' to Lisa, is that performance is not assessed in a vacuum, or in some abstract absolute. Performance is assessed in terms of values set by the senior staff and confirmed by experience. At first, it is their values that count. They define the good and the bad. In the long run, what matter are outcomes."

Permanent Work Force

Ms. Nielsen had listened intently, leaning forward. Now she relaxed. She took a last puff from her cigar and then extinguished it. "The Firm is a community," she said. "Many spinoffs, many independent subunits or subcontractors are tied with us, some coexist with us for historical reasons. In this very complex environment, we need a very strongly devoted work force. As you know, most of our work is performed by symbolic analysts; by design, maintenance, or production workers; and by in-person service workers. Within these three broad categories, most of the core of our operations are carried on by permanent career people.

"It is not feasible to maintain high levels of devotion, commitment, I would say the passion, that make for today's success, without permanent career people. In your day there was much discussion about downsizing, hiring part-time workers, about de-skilling, about creating 'poor' jobs, about deindustrialization (Ginzberg, 1977; Bluestone and Bennett, 1986). To some extent those discussions were correct, but only partly correct. Manufacturing did matter, but as wages rose in every country and as automation replaced most routine production, manufacturing returned (Cohen and Zysman, 1987; Lawrence, 1984; Norwood, 1987). Manufacturing takes place where skilled labor, capital, resources, and markets emerge. In your book, you describe quite well how economic flows move from one region to another, but you

226

may be overstressing the relative importance of comparative wage scales. As routinized work was automated, wage scales mattered less than educational institutions, the research establishments, the availability of capital, the commitment of the work force. What matters, in turn, is the relative stability of the supporting institutions, which is why permanent career people matter.

"The big centers of innovation are in economic areas where there are sufficient institutions, such as The Firm, to provide networking seedbeds. As I tend to repeat over and over again, innovation requires structure.

"The Firm provides employment for many in-person service people. Most of the bulk of employment today is in in-person service jobs. But these jobs are extremely important. You are eating a gourmet meal here today. This is a gourmet meal by the standards of what can only be described as a gourmet food–deprived historical period. I mean that your world did not know gourmet food, except in rare instances. Nor did you know what child care meant or what nursing could become or what good social services look like. In-person service employment rose, and it also acquired far greater status as organizations began to realize that talented in-person service people were crucial to success. We pay great attention to who works at consumer windows. We are very careful to hire talent in all our in-person service functions because they are the underpinnings of our creative activities. You saw that our salary differentials are very flat. This tells you something. It tells you that in the last fifty years in-person service employment not only rose in numbers, it rose in importance. We became increasingly more dependent on in-person service.

"All of this brings me back to full-time versus part-time

or contract work. Some of our people are part-time, and in some cases it has to do with the phenomenon called the one-and-a-half-family unit. Two adults work at one and a half jobs so as to have a bit more time for household life. Of course many with access to places like The Firm—our Lisas and Jims—have two or even two and a half or three jobs. Single parents usually gravitate to places like this because we provide them much support. But it is not a one-way exchange. We receive from them the level of commitment that makes it possible to live with the high ambiguity of innovative centers. They know us and we know them. Trust matters, and the social pact matters."

The Social Contract

"In your day, part-time or short-term contracts were widely used to reduce costs. You practiced downsizing. You fired many middle-level managers. There was not much attention given to the work force because it was expendable. Since most of the work was highly routinized, management did not care much about the commitment of the workers. But when quality management emerged, you faced different issues. Routinization did not always guarantee success. You began to pay attention to teamwork, to empowerment, and to commitment (Walton, 1986, 1990). Those realities accelerated when routinized production was automated. One cannot expect people to innovate themselves out of their jobs. Teamwork, empowerment, and commitment are meaningless unless there is a social contract. This is what we provide.

"The Firm innovates all the time, and some of our people have moved around, many have left us, others have gone and returned. Many have acquired more responsibility, others have found worthwhile employment in a wide variety of assignments. Some members of the senior staff have returned to nonmanagerial functions because they preferred that life-style. There is much less emphasis today on fast-lane careers, power, wealth, and displays of importance. Not that human greed or ambition has lessened or that we are more at peace with ourselves. As Lisa pointed out, we blame less and we want to do more, but since so much of our work is creative, much more emphasis is given to performance, to the artisanship of work. The main incentive of work is work itself.

"You and your ancestors, during nearly two preceding centuries, lost the meaning of work. The artisan skills and pleasures were lost when work was depersonalized and routinized, when ownership of the tools of production was transferred to the owners of capital. But the artisan skills and pleasures were found again when routinized work was automated, when machines replaced people for the dull activities, and as a consequence, when people were given the latitude to invent their roles in a new social, economic, and technical workplace.

"There is far less anguish today than in your times, although, as I said, there is much ambiguity. Much is unknown, and we have difficult choices and options. Creativity and invention give much pleasure and result in many advances, but change also hurts and damages some people. Management today is the art of balancing pleasure and advance against pain and damage."

End of Visit; or, The Waiter Tells All

The waiter guided me outside through the restaurant garden. We walked toward the edge of the property. When we had gone some distance, he spoke at length. He did not hand me a text, as had been the practice inside the building, but spoke quickly. I will summarize, as best as I can remember, what he said, on the basis of notes I made later.

Secrecy

The reason he wanted to speak to me outside, near the path leading to the entrance, was that that area was out of the recording range. He explained that the recording was done through the electrical system, and could not take place where there were no electrical installations. The signals carried only about two hundred feet, he said.

Ms. Nielsen had been correct when she said that they recorded everything. But they could only record the signals they could capture. Moreover, it was possible to confuse the signal and even—if you had access to the code—to disconnect yourself or others from signal capture. Top management, including the senior staff, usually knew the code and could therefore disconnect. But then it would be known they had disconnected, so they needed a reason to do so.

He asked me to look around, and I noticed people walking around, talking to each other, sitting on benches, and generally avoiding signal capture. It was the way people avoided visibility, he said. He explained that much of the recording was defensive. It had to do with industrial counterespionage. The constant recording monitors were programmed to search for selected behaviors—for example, if you took a small camera out of your pocket and copied an internal document, the monitors would alert the counterespionage people, who would immediately seek you out. But espionage still took place since bright people could figure

230

out how the monitors are programmed. You had to be on your toes because you never knew exactly how they had programmed the monitors. He had once been arrested while serving dinner at a senior staff gathering because he apparently had come too close to an object that had been protected. He had no idea what it was.

"Secrecy prevails," he said, "although at the same time, there is tremendous access to information. In a decentralized system like The Firm, there has to be some political process that decides which way to go, what innovations are to be encouraged, which ones are to be ended. Since the senior staff shares decisions with top management, it boils down to the political economy of choices. Coalition building matters. The political process requires secrecy, at least in the formative stage." The people around us who were also out of range were not lovers seeking privacy or even conspirators, but people examining alternative policy options outside of the controls that are imposed on everyone.

Manipulation

I asked the waiter how he knew all this. He explained that any intelligent person would be able to figure out how manipulation takes place. "Obviously, choices have to be made, and these choices are good to some and hamper others. Given a central concern in maintaining strong commitment to and belief in the organization, there has to be a limited participatory process where the senior staff comes to defend the interests of their minions. They need secrecy for that, because they sometimes have to make unpopular choices."

He thought Ms. Nielsen was talented. But she was giving me the official rhetoric, as if all work was interesting or

231

providing the same kind of satisfaction. The imagery of a return to the artisan virtues was all very well and pretty, but Ms. Nielsen was not serving dinners night after night. He could tell her that he had done his repertoire of creative service, and as far as he could see, in-person service was 99 percent work and sweat and possibly 1 percent creativity.

"Ms. Nielsen glorifies the democratization of work. But it is a very limited democratization. There is a new flexibility: we can be democratic in the workplace—share decisions. I can decide with my colleagues how we will handle the tables or do the wines, but that's it. It is on-site democracy, not plain democracy. Our opinion matters little, and the senior staff likes to think that they represent our professional interests, but Ms. Nielsen never asks if my feet hurt.

"Some work is believed to be more important, and those who do what is more important benefit. Ms. Nielsen tells you that the salary structure is flat. Of course it is flat, because they have privatized salary structures. With outcome control and magnetic wave recording, it is bonuses that matter. Salary keeps waiters like me alive. But when they calculate my contribution to the overall outcome measure that triggers the bonus, I get a pittance compared to Ms. Nielsen. She said she earned only twice as much, but that is without the bonus, because the bonus is a private matter. The bonus comes to those who are visibly involved in the innovations and their implementations. They share in the profits. They do very well. Don't kid me. I have no idea why Ms. Nielsen was giving you this romantic stuff about flat wage structures."

A Surprise with the Instruction Map

Those were my notes on that brief encounter. The waiter said we should not stay there too long or he would be noticed. We returned to the main lobby, where I was asked to return my yellow instruction map. I had completely forgotten to use it. It had been in my pocket all that time. I took it out and it was still flashing a message: "You will have an interesting conversation with the waiter in the garden."

I gave the yellow instruction map to the guard, a young man with a smiling face. I asked if he liked to work there. He smiled and waved me along. I was in a crowd leaving the building. The Firm was memory, but I had my notes and the text provided by my hosts.

CONCLUSION

The Future
of the Organization

The New System and The Firm are heuristic scenarios. This last chapter returns to the present and reexamines the image of the future the scenarios depict. The scenarios provide insights, but they do not provide facts. Yet, both the analysis and the scenarios incorporate themes that can profitably be revisited.

There is the theme of decentralization and empowerment and the consequent need to still be able to bring efforts together, mass resources, and act purposefully. The Firm addresses this with an Orwellian, somewhat manipulative approach, where control, exhortations, and myths are combined with deliberate incentives to provide highly flexible yet coordinated action. This is only one way of organizing, and The Firm manifests obvious shortcomings in the way it motivates action. But the theme remains important.

A second theme is that of the third force. In both the analysis and the scenario, the idea recurs of new professional institutions that bridge the existing chasm between government and the private sector. Chapter Two discusses how rapid scientific and technological changes are bound to change the regulatory process, but the idea of a professional work force and of professional participation in the management structure combines many streams of thought, including the rising aspirations of a highly credentialed work force.

Third is the theme of correcting errors, of reducing some of the consequences of errors. The analysis presented the case for improving the overall societal capability to adapt to rapid change. Organizational ability to act flexibly, to innovate, to compete effectively, is not an independent property of organizational arrangements. Organizational capacity for change is embedded in the social structures in which organizations operate. The first scenario presents a novel set of social institutions that would facilitate organizational response to change.

Several other themes received less attention, although they deserve mention now. There was a discussion of the electronic cottage, namely the complete decentralization of work without the elimination of the physical organization: everyone might work by linking electronically to other work spaces and to vast robotic production installations. There was some discussion of the changing characteristics of the work force and of the growing importance of credentialing. There was the theme of women's new role in far more informal settings. There was the theme of human resources, becoming much more important, as capital, products, and people can move quite readily all over the planet.

Many other themes were not discussed. I have said very little about the overall environment in which organizations might operate. Very little was said about the social historical context in which these changes are taking place. This is necessary because it is not feasible to do justice to such vast issues and still focus primarily on organizational arrangements. Yet I have alluded to labor force migrations and suggested that cultural diversity would prevail in the organizations of the future. Several other themes were given far less importance, including how to make work more interesting or the vast ramifications of the new information technologies for organizational design. Moreover, I did not fully analyze the change process itself, in part because I have already addressed this in *Mastering the Politics of Planning* (1989).

In this last chapter, I briefly revisit eight themes that merit attention and that emerge from both the analysis and the scenarios: (1) the large organization lives on, (2) the adaptive organization, (3) human resource management, (4) decentralized discretion, (5) correcting errors after they happen, (6) internalizing regulatory practice, (7) the evolution of our understanding of the organization, and (8) the international culture of the organization.

The Large Organization Lives On

In this book there is a different portrayal of the electronic cottage. I believe that new technologies will not cause the organization to wither away. On the contrary, the creation of an international economic order based on competition is bound to vitalize the organization. In our scenarios, the creative individual—the one-person writer who works at home and communicates electronically with his or her publishers—is enmeshed with networks of organizations: with the printers, the people who maintain the technology, the suppliers of materials, the international marketing people, the finance advisors, the legal group, the advertising crowd, and on and on. The image of the electronic cottage masks the reality of complex interrelated sets of organizations composed of small or large firms or agencies working together, within which individuals and groups link together. If the portrait of The Firm were fully drawn, the reader would find that it comprises many operations and provides many services. In the scenario we are able only to glimpse one of its important functions: The Firm provides basic services, such as research facilities, restaurants, education, and child care facilities. These facilities are used by The Firm's staff and by the staffs of many other spin-off organizations that are still too small to maintain such basic services. The Firm provides a physical infrastructure in which people and families are able to work.

The important lesson here is that whereas organizations do not disappear, two major trends take place. First, organizations decentralize so that more and more what matter are the smaller subsets of organizations, the emerging new networks and spin-offs, and the creative milieus in which these organizations operate. Second, women's full participation in the organization implies radical changes in life-styles, and as both the analysis and the scenarios suggest, as women and men participate fully in the organization, they bring their families with them to the workplace.

The consequence of these two trends is the function played by The Firm. It is a "super" organization because it not only carries on its own activities but also provides a creative milieu in which many affiliated smaller organizations are able to emerge, prosper, and in some cases disappear.

The Adaptive Organization

This book discusses the new technologies, international competition, and the transformation of the world order as flows of resources and people move in new enlarged international markets. It discusses higher levels of uncertainty, how the world of work becomes more decentralized, therefore, more difficult to manage, how it becomes much easier to make errors. Given a turbulent environment, the organization has two major options. The organization can turn outward: it can adapt, it can learn, it can be responsive and even incite change in the environment. Or, in contrast, the organization can turn inward: it can manipulate and control its clients or the public. It can impose itself on its environment. A decade ago, I made the observation: "Some writers would argue that the modern organization is adapting and doing very well indeed. What appears as a malaise or as inefficiencies is really the vital sign of energetic adaptability. One could argue that much of the control and rigidity generated by giant corporations and government is as it should be. In an uncertain environment, organizations adapt by controlling their environment. There may be unpleasant consequences, but they are inevitable" (Benveniste, 1983, p. ix).

In the analysis I have introduced a typology of errors and suggested that defensive organizational strategies are dysfunctional to clients and to the larger public. In the international competition, those organizations or societies that can reduce the queuing time needed to translate ideas into action do better than others. There is a Darwinian principle at work. As a consequence, on-time production, rapid adaptation, and programmed robotic production translate into decentralized structures designed to maintain quality. But as rapidly changing technologies create organizational pressures to decentralize (so that the most common type of error—marginal errors—can be avoided), decentralization also tends to reduce the organization's ability to use defensive strategies based on centralization and routinization. The successful organization of the future will need to depend less on defensive strategies than firms do at present. The organization of the future will need to be a learning organization. It will need to look outward, not inward.

There are again two important lessons here. The first is that decentralization accelerates as organizations find it increasingly awkward not to adapt and compete. In other words, it is not rhetoric; the plain facts of international competition are that the organization has to be able to adapt and learn. The second lesson is that high levels of decentralization create very real problems of integration. As we saw in the scenario, The Firm provides the meta rules needed for collective creative work. It invents the myths and rewards that orient collective action. The myths are not fanciful, since the pragmatic realities of the external world dominate the decisions of the organization. Therefore, The Firm provides a structure where long-term coherent strategies are elaborated while rapid on-time decentralized responses are facilitated. One might have the impression that The Firm achieves integration through manipulation, and that it only appears to be decentralized. The senior staff keeps tight reins. This is not what the scenario shows. Ms. Nielsen managed in a novel way. She used incentives to direct action instead of issuing top-down commands. She used internal price mechanisms to determine resource allocations instead of arbitrating the allocation of these resources. She was far less in evidence, far more in the background. Therefore, the scenario shows that in the future the reins are looser, management lets go somewhat; this is why the organization matters less than the creative milieu in which it operates.

240

Human Resource Management

With the new information and production technologies, most routinized work will be replaced by programmed robotics except for in-person service. But, as we saw, even in-person service jobs will become professionalized.

Today electric utility companies still send a person to read home electric meters. Tomorrow this job will not exist. Meters will be read electronically; the charges will be posted daily on customers' bank accounts, so at least four or five additional routinized jobs will have evaporated. Utilities will no longer need a person to punch the meter readings into the computer that produced the billing. They will no longer need the operator of the mailing machine. The customer will no longer need to write a check. The bank will no longer need a person to punch the check information into the computer. The bank will no longer need the person who gathered and mailed checks to customers at the end of every month.

Routinized tasks, by definition, involve little discretion; therefore a machine or a system can be programmed to handle the routine and can be instructed to search for answers where alternative solutions are required. When the machine or the system cannot handle choices, a human operator can intervene. As routinized tasks are taken over by robotics, the labor force of the future will be completely transformed. At the same time, the labor force will be far more credentialed and possibly more educated. As education continues to serve as a social mobility valve, the demand for credentials will grow.

But the social demand for education will not be the only factor driving the transformation of the labor force. Technology will play a most significant role. Complementary social forces will operate simultaneously. The growing social demand for access to credentials will be matched by the transformation of work. Technology increasingly reduces routinized work that does not involve people contacts. The routinized work that persists will be in in-person services. The elimination of routinized tasks, except for in-person services, will result in three distinct labor forces: first, the highly educated and trained sophisticated symbolic analysts; second, the highly educated and trained technology operators, designers, and maintenance workers who exercise higher levels of discretion.

The symbolic analysts and the sophisticated technology operators will be the most important asset of the competitive organization of the future. Therefore, the organization that survives in the middle of the next century will have two central preoccupations: providing a working environment that attracts and motivates talented workers, and assuring itself that this talent is well trained and educated.

The third work force, providing in-person service, will also be highly trained to do work than can be very creative; this segment will provide the support infrastructure that facilitates and motivates the work of symbolic analysts and technology operators as well as the services that allow the family unit to fully participate in the workplace. Once women and men participate fully in the work force, the social arrangements will be transformed to efficiently provide services that were originally provided in the home. The quantity and quality of these services will become one of the incentives that attracts talent. Therefore, the training and importance of the in-person service work force will have to match that of the rest of the work force. The three work forces will be closely interrelated. The success of each will depend on the strength of the other two.

The important lesson is that the organization of the future will be far more dependent on its work force than organizations are today. Human resource management will take on new importance. I repeat: the organization will inevitably have to be concerned with the quality of the education and training its work force receives.

Given a new world economy where capital moves freely from country to country or from region to region, where new technologies make the dependence on the actual location of raw materials less important, either because substitutes can be used or because the raw materials can be moved relatively inexpensively across vast distances, and where instant communications permit organizations to coordinate the work of production facilities anywhere in the world, the factor that will increasingly dominate decisions to invest and build productive facilities will be the availability of an educated, skilled work force. Moreover, new transportation technologies will facilitate work force mobility. It will become increasingly easy to move workers to where jobs are. In our scenarios, as remedies for social errors are provided, flows of workers move to new job opportunities. Even international flows of skilled and educated labor increase as some economies grow faster than others.

Decisions to invest and build productive facilities will be guided by the availability of an educated and skilled labor force. Moreover, the infrastructure of educational and training institutions that creates this desirable work force will be an important guarantee that economic and social well-being can be maintained at high levels: High-quality educational infrastructures will produce the required talent. More importantly, migrations of talent will tend to locate where high-quality educational infrastructures are in place so that the children of these talented migrants may have the benefit of the same or better opportunities as their parents. Furthermore, lifelong education and retraining will become normative in many occupations and talent will have to remain in proximity to intellectual centers of research and training.

In other words, human resource management will become a central concern of all organizations. They will have a direct stake in assuring access to talent, and communities will have a much greater stake in their educational infrastructure. Community standard of living will be increasingly directly related to the quality, scope, and recognition achieved by the educational infrastructure.

The American public school system is perfectly well designed for a vast continental agricultural economy, but it is unsuited to the needs of the global economy of the coming century. A highly decentralized system guided by local school boards has become enmeshed in complex external bureaucratic controls as local levies to finance the schools have had to be bolstered by state monies. The few attempts at reform have failed to significantly address the deterioration of the professional standing of teachers. Most of these reforms have tended to be top-down, and many just increase the bureaucratization of the schools. As control of the purse evaporates, school boards lose significance and utility. State and federal reformers are just beginning to address the need to totally reconstruct the public school system.

One can only assume that it will become a national system, that school boards are bound to disappear, and that individual schools will be far more responsive to the needs of students and far more controlled by a well-trained profession of teachers. The American system of higher education fares better. It is still perceived as the largest and the best in the world. But it is also under attack, sometimes for good reason, more often in a dysfunctional manner. Paralleling the public schools, the public universities are also increasingly subject to external controls designed to ensure accountability and productivity. Unfortunately, these controls are ill-suited to guide a complex intellectual enterprise and often result in bureaucratic fads that have little to do with quality education and entrepreneurial research.

At the same time, the academy suffers from its own strength. The American research university is beautifully designed to resist external short-term pressures while responding to its own internal intellectual ferment. At times it can sink into narcissistic bathos as the academy pursues its own intellectual agenda. Higher education has slowly adapted to meet the needs of nineteenth- and twentieth-century industrial growth. It will adapt again to meet the needs of a new century, as the research universities are linked more directly to national and international transformation efforts. As the scenarios indicate, rewards, in the university of the future, are bound to be very different than current practice, and the universities of the future are bound to be linked directly into national and international development efforts.

There will be a return to preparation for skilled crafts as a large portion of the work force specializes to perform demanding jobs in the new and expanded in-person services. These trends are already evident in countries such as Germany, Sweden, and France, where apprenticeship, craft, and job training have much more importance than in the United States. The system of preparation for in-person ser-

245

vice jobs will also expand at higher levels of education as the demand for access to professional higher education expands. Similarly, the preparation and continued education of symbolic analysts and of technology operators will require new forms of higher education and training, designed not only for those graduating from school but also for workers with jobs and families.

Decentralized Discretion

The innovative organization of the future will have to depend on bottom-up innovation. The organization of the future will deal with a varied clientele, so information about the changing needs of the clientele will have to travel rapidly to those who provide services and products if the implementation of innovations is to take place in good time. The levels of discretion will increase—a major transformation of the organization.

The work force will change. Symbolic analysts and sophisticated technical workers will be more highly educated and trained. They will aspire to professional roles. They will be motivated by the challenges and responsibilities that come with higher levels of discretion. Even in-person service staff will exercise more discretion, play varied roles, and pursue excellence. Intrinsic motivators—namely motivation to work based on the satisfaction of work well done—will take on new importance. Our scenarios suggest far less extrinsic differentiation. Salaries are supposed to be more alike across hierarchical levels, although the scenarios were somewhat ambiguous in that they suggested that strong outcome rewards were also prevalent. The salaries have been "privatized" to encourage entrepreneurial behavior.

But the more important lesson, I repeat again, is that management will have to let go somewhat. In a sense, the management of the future will rely on the concept of optimal ignorance. The center cannot afford to control and review all decisions and innovations because the center does not always know best. Ms. Nielsen, in the scenario, refers to innovative management as the art of roller coasting. In a worldwide information society, there is too much information and not enough time to integrate. Rationality is based on optimal ignorance. What does optimal ignorance imply? It implies that management controls broad parameters but allows considerable ambiguity and even disorder while continually reexamining its long-term options. By increasing the level of decentralized discretion, the organization of the future also increases opportunities for success. The center knows less, controls less, because successful innovations are not always perceived to be successful ahead of time. Roller coasting and continued reexamination of long-term options also determine just how much discretion is given.

Groups or networks access resources directly; how much and how often determine the level of discretion. Conflict resolution, the ability of the periphery to arrange its affairs without recourse to the center's arbitration, also determines the permissible level of discretion.

You will recall that Ms. Nielsen emphasized the importance of ideological representations. She talked about "themes" that orient the actions of the staff. Obviously, The Firm seeks to channel the energy of its entrepreneurial staff in coherent directions. It invents myths that keep the organization together. It also plans, sets strategies, and controls inducements to maintain coherence. Ms. Nielsen seems to manipulate the situation, and I referred to the apparent Orwellian quality of the scenario. But we may be jumping to conclusions. It may well be that Ms. Nielsen is not that much in control.

As the periphery acquires new responsibilities, it also acquires new inducements and rewards. It links with others and creates networks. The organization becomes porous. It is no longer centralized. The right hand does not necessarily always know what the left hand is doing. Management accepts or tolerates higher levels of risk and ambiguity. Trust will be much more important in the twenty-first century than it is today.

When considerable discretion is granted, keeping tabs on progress takes on new importance. New technology will facilitate the oversight function. The Firm supposedly records every act. Of course this is fantasy, but one reason management is able to delegate is that it can still monitor. However, management learns to restrain itself. In the next century, guesses will matter more than they do today. Planning and strategic thinking will go hand in hand with hunches and intuitions. As we saw, internal organizational pricing mechanisms can be used to allocate scarce internal resources, thus relieving management of the responsibility of arbitrating internal conflicts and coordinating the work of its staff. In such ways, the organization of the future may depend much more on tightly knit communities that have worked together for long periods, communities familiar with each others' weaknesses and strengths. Personal friendships and kinship ties will take on new importance within the task situation. While this does not seem to be the case in The Firm, keep in mind that the waiter spoke very frankly and management knew he was doing so. There had to be strong ties keeping everyone together behind the more visible and apparent conflicts. One important lesson is that family ties or clan ties will be likely to play a more significant role in the future. There may well be a return to eighteenth- or nineteenth-century traditions, when friends and family were relevant in selecting co-workers. The concept in the modern organization of individuals being hired because they are trained and qualified will no longer be sufficient. Training and qualification matter, but familiarity, trust, and affiliation matter as well. The organization of the future will be marked by much more intense personal and humane relationships among individuals.

Correcting Errors After They Happen

The correction of errors after they occur is a central theme of this book. Considerable planning needs to take place—not the centralized planning that failed in the Soviet experiment—but partial, incomplete planning that serves as a technical discourse within which political accommodation is reached. Nevertheless, planners cannot foresee all the consequences of rapid change.

I have discussed planning at length in *Mastering the Politics of Planning* (1989). That book makes clear both the usefulness and sharp limitations of any planning exercise. More importantly, that book demonstrates why planning is inevitably incomplete, therefore imperfect: errors still take place.

To correct errors after they happen is a useful concept, but not a simple task. Providing remedies for the unforeseen and undesirable consequences of change inevitably incites more errors. And why worry about the undesirable consequences of innovations if government and tax payers will pick up the tab? However, if unforeseen undesirable consequences of innovations are not corrected after they happen, there will always be strong resistance to change.

Therefore, the society that is able to reduce the fear of innovations engendered by unforeseen undesirable consequences of change will be better able to reduce the queuing time needed for ideas to become action.

The New System is a futuristic scenario where a complex set of new institutions has been set up to carry out new and complex tasks. In it, Professional Governors, Councils, Courts, and Boards diligently pursue the common good, helping individuals, families, and communities adjust to major changes in the economy, defining what is acceptable or good professional practice, serving to police the compliance of organizations to environmental and other safety issues, arbitrating conflicts, and raising the necessary revenue for the New System to operate.

The presentation is idyllic and improbable, but it serves my purpose: I want to describe the task that has to be accomplished, even if I cannot really describe how it might be accomplished.

The New System scenario illustrates the role of a new professional institution distinct from government or from private or not-for-profit enterprise that carries on the complex tasks of correcting errors after they happen. It assumes that government cannot possibly undertake the difficult choices that have to be made, that the political process would inevitably result in payoffs that would encourage individuals and organizations to commit more errors.

The model I present assumes that American society has shifted its value priorities. The reader will note that the scenario eschews some fairness values. The notion of equity is altered. When horse racing is abolished and the relevant Professional Governor provides relief to affected jockeys, horse handlers, breeders, and so on, the Professional Council judges the affected economic sector to be of "low importance," thus reducing the level and scope of the remedies. In the scenario, decisions about correcting errors after they happen are made more in light of the ability of society to innovate and compete, less in terms of abstract concepts of justice or equity. The politics of economic competition matter more. Therefore, professional institutions provide a forum where political battles are fought in the technical language of the professions. In other words, equity is defined by the ability to compete, the rate of economic growth, and the willingness to innovate.

One might argue this to be a high price to pay for an elusive, competitive, societal advantage. The greater levels of willingness to innovate may not be worth the concept of equity needed to make the system work. Be it as it may, we need to be reminded that current attempts in the United States to correct major errors after they happen are not only expensive but often quite unproductive. Without planning, and with lowered regulations, the case of the savings and loan industry in the 1980s illustrates very high costs to tax payers, doubtful societal gains, and new avenues of political corruption (Fabritius, 1989; Mayer, 1990; Brintnall, 1991; Laughlin, 1991). The design of new institutions to correct errors after they happen cannot be left to chance. This task will require considerably more research and experimentation. The scenario is several steps ahead of our current experience and know-how. But it is clear that correcting errors after they happen has to be framed within overall strategies and plans that give it meaning and usefulness.

Internalizing Regulatory Practice

The argument for internalizing regulatory practice is no different than the argument for correcting errors after they happen.

Government regulatory interventions in the private or public sector, particularly interventions related to protecting the environment, the public, or enhancing workplace safety, are time-consuming, expensive to administer, and a deterrent to the rapid transformation of innovative ideas into new products or services. It is not so much the costs of remedies that matter, but the costs of reaching decisions about remedies.

Those societies that can achieve the benefits of regulatory interventions at lower administrative and time costs would be at an advantage. Again, a Darwinian principle emerges.

An effective way to reduce the costs of some regulatory interventions may be to internalize regulatory practice. It should be clear that not all regulation or government control can be internalized. But in the New System scenario, environmental protection, workplace safety, and consumer protection are internalized. This means that professional bodies both within and outside the firm or agency pass judgment on the characteristics, design, and risks of the products and services they provide. The Councils define "good practice."

Several arguments in the analysis lead to this line of reasoning. It may be useful to revisit these. There is the "know-how" argument: as technology becomes more complex, and in some areas more dangerous, the capability of the scientists and technical people working for the regulating agencies will most probably be far less up to date or sophisticated than the capabilities of the scientists and technicians working in the firms that do the actual research and are innovating. The regulators become increasingly diminished vis-à-vis the capability of those generating new ideas and approaches. There is the "rising costs" argument: as the costs of external regulatory intervention increase, namely the administrative and uncertainty costs of making decisions about regulatory interventions, there is more pressure to reduce regulatory interventions, although errors can be very costly.

There is the scientific knowledge argument. Since the basis for current regulatory choices is a combination of technical arguments, legal discourse, and plain political muscle, technical arguments are easily drowned by the complexities of the legal discourse or the less than subtle pressures of short-term political agendas. As the impact of science and technology increases, it will become necessary to strengthen the technical arguments and move the political agenda from short- to long-term considerations. As choices about conditions of life on the planet become increasingly near irreversible—for example, the deterioration of the ozone layer and the destruction of the rain forest—long-term considerations have to become part of the political discourse. This suggests the need for direct links between science, technology, and politics. The scenario suggests institutions centrally concerned with the long-term consequences of scientific and technological innovations.

The New System scenario suggests Professional Councils whose mission is to define "good professional practice." Presumably these Councils have access to sufficient resources to monitor the behavior and actions of their members. These new Councils regulate from inside, using their members inside organizations to obtain information and create a political forum to weigh the facts and reach decisions.

Would scientists and technicians within organizations pay attention to the guidelines provided by professional bodies? Judging by our current professions, one has to assume that far more than ethical standards would have to be used to motivate compliance. However, new professional bodies could establish strict disclosure requirements that might be enforced by severe penalties affecting the career prospects of noncompliants. My scenario is only a sketch. The important lesson is that it suggests that fundamental institutional changes are in the offing.

The Evolution of Our Understanding of Organizations

At the beginning of the twentieth century scientific management prevailed. The organization was conceived as a well-functioning machine. Time and motion studies dominated a scientific approach to management. A careful study of the best way to undertake a task resulted in efficient operations. The research sought to reduce fatigue and increase productivity. The organizational machine was carefully designed to achieve well-understood goals. The view of the organization was mechanistic. Labor responded to well-orchestrated economic incentive schemes. Work was allocated, supervision was limited to six or seven individuals, commands went down the hierarchy, information flowed upward.

Toward the end of the 1920s and the beginning of the 1930s, we became aware that the well-designed organizational machine was made of people, and that people are not motivated by economic incentives alone. We discovered the informal dimensions of the organization. This was the period when informal groups and human relations took center stage. Top-down directives needed to reflect bottom-up aspirations and motivations. We discovered that men and women are also motivated by intrinsic satisfactions related to work. We were beginning to pay attention to the voices below.

In the fifties and sixties we turned outward. We began to pay more attention to the environment in which organizations operate and we began to understand how different managerial structures are better suited to different technologies and different external conditions. If you produce electricity that is sold in a large urban center, you have a well-understood technology and a relatively predictable environment. The routines and structures for discretion take this into account. If you run a suicide prevention service, you know much less how to achieve results and your environment is highly variable and unpredictable. Here routines are less effective and the structures of discretion more important.

In the seventies, eighties, and nineties, the complexities and interrelatedness of tasks began to come to the forefront of preoccupations. People were increasingly aware that success is often tied to the articulation of the work of many organizations. Interorganizational coordination allows diverse resources to be massed on complex problems. In the late eighties and nineties the focus was on networking's implications and consequences (Savage, 1990; Kilmann, Kilmann, and Associates, 1990; Pennings and Marianto, 1992).

The concept of the porous organization follows logically from this progression. It emphasizes the role of informal groups, the impact of the task environment, and interorganizational networking to suggest that the future organization is far less well defined than the present one.

Accomplishment is what will matter in the future. How one arranges to perform work will become far less significant than achieving results. Accomplishments will be defined by markets and by political decisions, including planning. Envelope supervision will allow discretion within broad parameters. Once discretion and resources are given to informal groups coming from diverse parts of the organization or, as is more likely, from diverse organizations, new organizational arrangements will be created and recreated, with their own goals, human resources, financing, and capabilities to act. Moreover, as more collective incentive schemes are used, these reward schemes will propel new organizational arrangements in directions that may be quite diverse, no longer under the continued control of the organizations that provided the original seedbed for these initiatives, but still responsive to the needs of their consumers and clients.

This concept of the organization will be quite different from the current one. The organization per se will be less important, as flows of ideas, resources, and workers create and recreate new organizations, move to new organizations as they invent services and products, redefine tasks, create markets, and adapt to innovations. Therefore, trust will matter much more because the informal dimensions of the organization will be where the action is.

The scenarios in this book emphasize the importance of trust because decentralized discretion implies that management can no longer maintain the level of control our past concept of scientific management would call for. When management does not control and only monitors, it needs trust.

256

Management needs to know that those it empowers will act in directions it finds desirable. My scenarios address this issue in various ways.

First, the organization achieves greater trust because it incorporates the voices of clients and of the public. The scenario suggests that internalizing the regulatory processes results in a far more effective way of handling complex choices; more importantly, it also greatly increases trust between organization, clients, and public. Whether this is a realistic assessment is another matter. But preoccupation with trust is evident.

Second, the empowerment of informal groups at the periphery and the use of collective outcome rewards also increase trust. The organization reduces propensities to shunt blame up and down the hierarchy. At the same time, the center still maintains common interests with the empowered peripheries since they share a common interest in successful outcomes.

Third, careers take place in a much enlarged organizational environment. Whereas career paths now tend to take place within a single organization, by the middle of the next century, we can expect most careers to take place in many organizations simultaneously. Trust will have to increase because more diverse career path structures will reduce internal rivalries. More importantly, long-term ability in networking depends on maintaining strong long-term trust relationships as individuals link under different organizational settings.

Fourth, as new organizations grow, other organizations wither. The current bureaucratic malaise has much to do with organizational survival and with defensive strategies. As we reduce the fears associated with organizational demise, trust will increase because accomplishments will matter more than sustaining outgrown or useless organizational arrangements.

Thus trust and the creation of rapidly changing organizational arrangements are not necessarily as contradictory as it may appear. The organization of the future will lose importance. The formal organization will come down off its pedestal. What will matter in the next century are results, not protecting the organization for the sake of the organization. Organizations are easily established and just as easily discarded. What matters is the ability to act.

The International Culture of the Organization

In this book I have paid considerable attention to gender issues, but I have said little about culture. The time has come to revisit the concept of the international culture of the organization of the future.

As organizations become porous, I foresee the emergence of feminine management styles as an important development. Decentralized organizations facilitate innovation and change through empowerment. Therefore they require a management style that is people oriented. Current research indicates gender similarities in managerial style but also shows that women tend to be thought of as the ones who listen more, treat others as equals, share information, and maintain trust relations (Cann and Siegfried, 1990).

My scenarios highlight the resulting transformations within the workplace. As both men and women leave the household to work, they both bring their household into the workplace. The organization increasingly substitutes for or facilitates family life. At the same time, differences across gender tend to disappear as men and women are influenced by each other's style, work culture, and success. My analysis and scenarios alluded to increased flows of labor across national boundaries. I assume that as men and women from many cultures learn to work together, an international culture of the workplace will also emerge.

There is a growing literature on national culture and work (Lincoln and Kalleberg, 1990; Chao, 1990; Oreilly, Chatman, and Cadwell, 1991). We are well aware today that increased migratory flows of people and of management ideas and models across international boundaries are bound to transform all organizational cultures. This literature highlights existing differences. For example, Michel Crozier suggests that the French abhor face-to-face conflicts. Hence, he argues, French organizations tend to have higher formal hierarchical pyramids than American organizations. Hierarchical pyramids permit conflicts among peers to be arbitrated by superiors, thus eliminating face-to-face conflicts among peers (Crozier, 1964).

Other writers highlight the way family, status, power, individualism, and ability to deal with uncertainty vary across cultures and how these variations affect organizational life (Hofstede, 1984; Lammers and Hickson, 1979). But cultural differences do not explain how the multicultural international organization of the future will adapt to cultural variety.

Clues at what might happen may be found in today's multinational and therefore multicultural organizations —namely, the headquarters of multinational corporations or those of international agencies, such as the United Nations. The research in this area and my own six-year exposure to two United Nations agencies suggest that national cultural traits affect practice but that the resulting organizational climate quickly adapts to different cultural styles (Mansfield and Poole, 1981; Wilterdink, 1992). In other words, the task and other variables are more important than cultural traits in defining how work is carried out, although in the early stages of cross-cultural communication many misunderstandings take place.

When I served at UNESCO we rapidly learned that the French director general could have a dreadful temper and that his status gave him the right to speak to his staff in a demeaning manner often unacceptable to Americans. We learned that Latin Americans valued friendship ties and expected friendship to matter within the work situation. We learned that many cultures had a different sense of time, or of status, honor, or commitment. We learned that many valued the small exchange of courtesies that denote status, that attitudes toward women varied, and that attitudes to graft differed. We also learned that UNESCO was a terrible bureaucracy, a political football, and that 90 percent of the activity was wasted motion.

But we learned rapidly how to deal with the director general, how to communicate, why we had to wait for weeks before the representatives of the USSR could answer our questions, how the French perceived their role, why French civil servants who spoke fluent English insisted on speaking French in small meetings when no one else spoke their language, why a Russian colleague hated his English superior (who had forced him to hire a German secretary and had found out later on that those two had been involved in a tempestuous love relationship), why the old hands who had worked together in past years in the regional centers in Asia, Africa, or Latin America formed cohesive networks, how every action had to be negotiated, how fragile national egos had to be protected. We found out that the bureaucracy could still move. Ninety percent of the activity was wasted motion, but the 10 percent of productivity was well worth the effort.

International organizations differ among themselves, and UNESCO is not the model of the organization of the future. I use it to point out that the staffs of multicultural organizations learn about the cultural traits of their co-workers. Sooner or later, the structure and political arrangements of the organization—its history, membership, and tasks—define the language that bridges cultures. Trust is important in the organization of the future, and trust is readily established across cultural boundaries. In fact, stronger ties of affinity emerge when individuals learn to surmount cultural differences, when they learn each other's singular cultural traits, and when they create new patterns of work that reflect the symbols of different cultures. The task becomes that much more rewarding when attitudes and predispositions cannot be taken for granted. Multiculturalism provides a natural seedbed for the informal affinity groups that are the heart of the organization of the future.

Today, American, French, German, Korean, and Japanese organizations differ. The literature on national culture and organization suggests that an "Anglo Saxon" organizational culture exists that is more flexible, more inclined to decentralized structures and to less stratification, and that a "Latin" organizational culture exists that is more inclined to centralized decision making and less able to deal with uncertainty (Lammers and Hickson, 1979, pp. 420–434). If one studies other cultures, one finds that empowerment, delegation, risk taking, and problem solving take place in different manners. The evidence today is that many different national cultures

261

yield effective organizational structures. The organization of the future will be multicultural; many cultural traits will be submerged into a composite pattern that will acquire a universal characteristic of its own.

There are many implications. Americans, in contrast to Europeans or to the citizens of most other countries in the world, have considerable difficulty learning about and adapting to other cultures. The fact that the United States was fashioned out of a wide cultural mix has somewhat inoculated the average American against foreign cultures. In general, Americans know little about lands outside the borders of our vast continent. Few Americans speak foreign languages; few seek to understand how other cultures operate. Our failure in many foreign markets is attributed, in part, to our lack of ability or interest in the cultural dimension of organizational life.

An effective multicultural approach has to take into account the traits and characteristics of different national cultures. There is no formula, since the mix varies. It requires training and sensitivity. It is necessary to understand how different cultures handle uncertainty, risk, and innovation. Given these facts, we have to conclude that, obliged by circumstances to do so, Americans will adapt to the new organizational environment. They will learn languages, study the history and culture of other countries, and become as international and sophisticated as their competitors.

The lesson this book offers is that what we take for granted today may no longer be taken for granted tomorrow. Americans have made great contributions to management; they have created very efficient organizations. For a while, the American organization, and the American culture of the organization, dominated the world.

The Future of the Organization

Tomorrow will be different. Tomorrow will take place all over the world. The organization of the future is no longer an American organization, or a French, Japanese, Chinese, or Mexican organization. It is a new international organization. It behooves us to contribute to its invention.

Methodology

Writing about the distant future is fraught with danger since we are bound to miss so much, and if we attempt to imagine what might happen we begin to write science fiction. Given those handicaps, this book is an attempt to balance art and science.

Rational analysis can take various forms. We make predictions, namely, statements about the probability of expected occurrence of events at some vaguely defined future time. We make forecasts, namely, more precise calendar-bound predictions; or we make projections, namely, quantitative predictions (Bell and Olick, 1989).

Everyone makes predictions, forecasts, and projections in the course of daily life. I do just that when I feel confident that my Uncle Achilles will send me a birthday present. Or I do it more consciously, when I write an article predicting that attempts to regulate industry tend to be followed by attempts to deregulate it, and these reversals tend to continue over time. Both exercises have common characteristics. Let us briefly review these.

Common Characteristics of Predictions, Forecasts, and Projections

Domain and Theory Selectivity

In contrast to revelations, predictions deal with finite, discrete domains. I may write complex scenarios depicting various possible future events, and yet these attempts make no claim to encompass the totality of the future. When I write that government regulatory interventions tend to be followed by moves toward deregulation and that these alternations continue over time, this prediction is based on a theory that explains why regulatory bodies are created, how they function, their operations, and the political consequences of their interventions. Thus my predictions depend on a theory that does not attempt to account for all the factors that will impinge on regulatory practice in the future. To be sure, I can make several or many discrete predictions and integrate them in a composite image of the future. For example, my prediction about Uncle Achilles is based on a set of facts and theories: his affection for his nephews, the fact that I recently had a pleasant dinner with him where he even mentioned my upcoming birthday, and my sense that he respects and enjoys the traditions of exchanging gifts. But my prediction does not take into account other factors that could result in my not receiving a gift: Achilles's impaired health and memory, the death of his wife two days before my birthday, the collapse of his major source of income, his sudden revulsion at the burden of exchanging presents with so many nephews and nieces.

Continuity and Discontinuity Assumptions

All predictions assume domains of continuity and discontinuity. First, I assume that Achilles will continue to be alive.

266

I had also assumed his wife would be with us. I assume that gift giving and exchanging would continue as a valued practice between him and his nephews and nieces. Similarly, I assume that no earthquake will take place on the day of my birthday, no law forbidding exchanging gifts will be passed by a legislature imbued by some new unthought of Spartan ideology. I assume that no other major transformation of the social order will erase the image of a smiling Uncle Achilles with the wrapped package under his arm.

Similarly, in this book, I assume that our concept of organizational structure can change significantly, that technological innovations will continue at an accelerated pace, that new needs for regulatory interventions will emerge as the rate of invention accelerates, that the needs for external intervention conflict with the need for rapid innovation, and that this will lead to a major discontinuity in the ways we will conceive of regulation in 2050.

Imaginary and Intuitive Content

Rational predictions are not based on imaginary invention. Nonetheless, we do make assumptions and have intuitions about unknown events. For example, I may tentatively assume that Uncle Achilles will discover a new shop and find a present I never imagined receiving. But my analysis focuses on what I know or on what I know I can expect to know. I do not inject into my prediction material about Achilles finding a spacecraft and giving it to me, nor do I inject a fantasy about my uncle discovering the elixir of life, nor do I assume that human values will change so radically that regulatory practices will no longer be necessary as mankind espouses harmoniously shared collective goals. Yet, as mentioned above, intuition is used.

The literature on methodologies for studying the future is clear about the conservatism of predictions (Lanford, 1972; Miles, 1975; Schnaars, 1989); they are conservative because we cannot imagine everything that has not been invented yet and we cannot predict unforeseen events. But if predictions are to have any utility, they need to expand the scope of our awareness so that we can clarify in our own mind the coming shapes of emerging situations (Slaughter, 1990). There are many ways for us to expand the scope of our awareness of the future. In the last half century we have developed a number of useful methodologies to do so, and some of these methodologies provide opportunities to search for intuitive insights.

A distinction is to be made between careful analysis and sheer fantasy or science fiction. Take for example Wagar's *Short History of the Future* (1989). This is fantasy and science fiction. The hero, born in A.D. 2084, goes into a hibertube in A.D. 2200 for a long sleep of hibernation. We are told about the inevitability of progress, and Wagar's utopian description of the future includes nuclear fusion engines, antimatter propulsion, genetic improvement of the human race, and the colonization of the planet Mars. It is an entertaining tale, and it happens to contain useful insights. But it departs from what appears to be possible. It goes beyond what we know we might know. It leaves us in considerable doubt about what will in fact happen. It is not bounded by our current knowledge of our future knowledge. The reader of that tale may doubt hibertubes will be commonplace in 2084 and may also doubt that the planet Mars will ever be colonized. On the other hand, nuclear fusion, genetic engineering, and space travel are known scientific domains.

In this book I rely on a number of invented scenarios:

Methodology

A visit to a very large organization called The Firm circa 2050, interviews with staff members, and similar interviews with individuals familiar with the New System. These interviews provide an opportunity to explore how the organization in 2050 might cope with major technological, social, and economic dislocations. For example, the book describes a number of new social institutions called the Professional Governors, the Professional Councils, and the Professional Boards, which allow professions to play a new role in the management of organizations.

This material derives from what is known today. It is an intuitive response to a perceived discontinuity. It is nevertheless a fantasy. It is not a prediction.

The predictive content of the analysis takes place one step removed. The argument is that as the rate of invention accelerates, external governmental regulation will become too cumbersome, too slow, too imprecise. A new way has to be found to regulate if international economic competition is to remain important. Hence, the need to conceive of a new organization wherein professional bodies play an internal regulatory role. The New System is a fantasy. The problem is not.

Fantasies and science fiction have a heuristic function. They oblige us to consider mundane consequences. Suppose space travel became more common. What implications does this have on organizations? None, you might say—but, in fact, if space travel expands markedly it will be mostly for one reason: to serve as a means of high-speed travel from one side of this planet to the other. This, of course, could have repercussions on the way individuals in organizations maintain personal linkages across continents.

We have to be willing to inject a modicum of fiction in

the analysis if we are not going to be so bound by current events that our analysis has no futuristic content. We have to be able to ask "what if?" questions. We have to be willing to describe scenarios of the future. These questions do not imply that the "what if?" or the scenarios happen. But they lead to different ways of thinking about the future. This is where intuition and art join analysis. To discuss what we may know in the future requires us to be willing to take some risks, use intuition, and go beyond what can be strictly deduced from current facts and theories. If we go too far, we write science fiction. If we depart just slightly, we might have better insights and predictions.

Principal Methodologies

Most predictions are based on analysis using a wide variety of methodologies (Tydeman, 1988; Marino, 1972; Jantsch, 1967). I will not attempt to review all of them—but I will rapidly review the more important and useful methodologies so that we can better situate the nature of our task.

Methodologies differ in degree of sophistication. In some cases, simple extrapolations of past data into the future are used. In other cases, very sophisticated mathematical models are employed, using complex statistical techniques. The degree of sophistication of the methodology does not seem to contribute to the accuracy of predictions (Ascher and Overholt, 1983). Accuracy is influenced by other factors. The most important are time horizon and scope of the domain of the prediction (Benveniste, 1989). There is a greater likelihood that one may be able to predict what will happen in a specific domain next week or even next year than what will happen five, ten, or, obviously, fifty years hence. What

270

matter are the validity of the assumptions on which the predictions are based and the theories, knowledge, and understanding we may have about relevant processes. Moreover, as in other research fields, forecasting has its own fads. At one time, complex mathematical model building was very much in fashion; today these are more rarely used (Bright and Schoeman, 1973; Beck, 1991).

Trends and Extrapolations

If we have information about the past, we may be able to predict the future. For example, if we have good data on sales of refrigerators in the last ten years and plot these on a graph, we may feel confident they might continue, expand, or diminish in coming months and years because we know and relate the relationship between these sales and other social and economic factors that we can predict. Moreover, if we study past sales performance, we may infer that rapid growth in the past is reaching a saturation point and that future sales may grow more slowly or even reach a plateau. Level of sophistication depends on the complexity of our model of the relationships between refrigerator sales and other variables. For example, we may find that future disposable income is a good predictor of refrigerator sales, or we may find that rate of family formation or housing starts or housing sales are other useful indicators.

Trends and extrapolations provide relatively accurate predictions when future time horizons are short. For example, demographic predictions to estimate future births and deaths are relatively accurate over short time horizons. Good demographic data, including migratory flows, are then used to predict future enrollments in schools. These take into account other factors, including rate of student drop out, rate of class repetitions, flight to private education, and so on. Additional assumptions and additional extrapolations permit us to look a few years ahead, to estimate the numbers of teachers that need be hired and the number of school rooms that need to be built.

Morphological Analysis

Morphological analysis takes a broader view of the issues. We are no longer asking how refrigerator sales will evolve in the next few years, but instead, how people will live in the future, what their needs for refrigeration will be, and what all the ways are that refrigeration can be provided. Similarly, instead of projecting demand for automobiles, we ask how transportation needs will be met in the future. Morphological analysis takes a larger, more comprehensive approach to problems. For example, instead of simply extrapolating automobile demand as it relates to, say, income, fuel costs, highway expenditures, and so on, the analysis focuses on all known solutions, including high-speed rail, water and air transportation, underground travel, and so on. Predictions of automobile transportation are then derived from an analysis of the overall characteristics, needs, supply, and demand for all alternatives.

Morphological analysis requires our making assumptions about future policy: will very high speed rail corridors be created? Will highway subsidies be reduced? But morphological analysis is more useful in long-term studies of the future. Had we simply looked at past automobile demand trends and extrapolated these into the future, we would be less able to show the limits (population density, road congestion, and so forth) of automobile transportation, and we would not capture emerging long-term trends, such as increased population density and the return of rapid light rail and very high speed rail transportation.

Scenario Writing

Scenario writing is more holistic than the previous two. The technique consists in depicting how a logical set of events can, in time, create a new situation. The analysis relies on as many variables and events as can be handled and comprehended. For example, assume we are concerned with atomic proliferation and ask what might happen if a major atomic war were to take place between two underdeveloped countries—say between two large Asian countries. Scenario writing seeks to answer broad questions about possible future events that may or may not take place. There is less attention to exact time frames or to sequential analysis in selecting topics. Scenario writing permits the analysis to ask questions that might not come to the fore otherwise; it allows pursuit of different alternatives: suppose this happens? or suppose this happens instead? It allows us to eliminate unimportant contingencies and concentrate on more significant developments. Scenario writing is an important methodology in strategic planning, which departs from similar questions: What might we do if this and this happens? How should we react? What do we do next (Benveniste, 1989)?

Scenario writing is often used with other methodologies to achieve a more comprehensive overview of future events. It is also possible to write sets of scenarios covering different domains—say, for example, scenarios about changes in the economy, the politics, the consumer habits, the housing pat-

273

terns, the family, and so on—and combine these into an overall view. Similarly, scenarios within a single domain can start from differing assumptions, and sets of possible outcomes can be examined to determine the overall pattern of possible futures.

Modeling

Modeling requires a fairly complete understanding of the relationships between events. For example, we know much more about the relationship between energy consumption and economic growth than we do about family composition and motivation to work. It is therefore not surprising that modeling of the future was undertaken at first by economists. Models rely on well-understood relationships that can be represented by mathematical equations. Computers permit the construction of very complex models composed of hundreds of equations. Varying assumptions can be introduced, and the sensitivity of the outcomes in the model to these variations permit the analyst to study how these variations might affect the future. For example, models of world trade in energy sources are used to study the potential impact of fluctuations in energy supply and demand on future energy prices.

Some models permit gaming. They provide opportunities for analysts to "play" at making decisions in the context of changing information about future events. Gaming reveals how choices are made and the timing of important decision points. It also provides estimates of the consequences of alternative policies.

In contrast to scenario writing, modeling tends to be a more restricted methodology whose scope and quality depend on the quality of the data and the predictive ability of the set of equations used. It is a powerful methodology when the scope and quality of the equations describe the relevant empirical reality—in other words, when the analyst is able to capture in equations what matters most. A model attempting to capture the flow of goods through a production process is bound to be more powerful than a model depicting cultural trends.

Brainstorming and Delphi Technique

Brainstorming and the Delphi technique consist in collective guessing—or, more accurately, in a careful and supportive interrogation of panels of "experts" so as to allow their intuitions about the future to emerge. In brainstorming, the group works together, and every effort is made to allow all ideas to surface, however tentative these might be. The purpose of the exercise is to provide opportunities for experts to share intuitions and to build collectively on this shared experience. The Delphi technique differs from brainstorming in that members of the group are kept separate so as to avoid, or at least reduce, the group's psychological impact on the thinking of individual experts.

The interrogations take place separately (for example, through the use of questionnaires), but the principal results are then shared and subsequent iterations of the process take place during which diverse opinions may be confronted. Finally a consensus report is drafted, bringing together the main positions. These techniques are particularly useful in areas where intuition is more important than past knowledge of relationships. For example, they are used in predicting new trends in consumer demand and in attempting to predict important emerging areas of scientific advances.

Normative Methodologies

Normative methodologies seek to define desirable futures and work backward to spell out how such ends might be attained. All predictions contain assumptions about policies that will shape the future, so that in that respect they may contain normative elements, namely, assumptions about the way things should be instead of the way they might turn out to be. For example, once we assume that it is desirable that American policies toward children change markedly in the next five years, whatever choices we make determine the shape of our predictions about what benefits children may obtain in coming years.

Normative methodologies, sometimes labeled "backcasting," as contrasted to forecasting (Robinson, 1990), simply go a step further. They deliberately spell out desirable outcomes, work backward, describe the relevant processes at work, specify the relevant internal and external variables, and specify implementation requirements. For example, backcasting might spell out a set of desirable outcomes for young children in 2050—say, all children have access to health care, all children receive full-time attention from family or from child care services, all children attend educational programs at age three, and so on. A normative methodology would spell out the kind of legislation needed, the political actions that have to take place to pass the legislation, the modifications to existing education, health and other social services needed to implement the legislation, the probable costs, sources of financing, and other practical details of implementation.

It is important to keep in mind that while normative methodologies are more akin to planning or to policy implementation (Benveniste, 1989), it is also the case that all future work dealing with human intervention needs to include normative assumptions. For example, I argue in this book that by 2050 large organizations will continue to dominate the social landscape. There should be little doubt that there are normative value judgments imbedded in that statement. I attempted to justify the assumption, but it is clear that different assumptions could be made if different values were to dominate our choices.

Methodology of This Book

This work uses scenarios based on broad trends and organizational analysis. I deliberately avoid quantitative data and extrapolations. I also avoid forecasts. Mine is a general depiction of human arrangements based on an exploration of the impact of the six major trends described in the first chapter. I have used fiction because I want to present changing patterns of relationships that would not appear intuitively reasonable to readers without any attempt at invention. I have relied to a great extent on published futuristic materials, and to that extent, I have relied on the intuitions, models, and forecasts of others.

The central arguments I have used to fashion my scenarios start from understandings of specific relationships that have existed for long periods of time. For example, I place a heavy emphasis on the continued expansion of the levels of education of the population; this is based on popular aspirations to social mobility. As the labor force becomes more educated, independently of the technical requirements of their jobs, workers' attitudes and motivations change. This is one of the central transformations of the future work force. Similarly, I make intuitively reasonable assumptions about major technological changes, about future gender factors, and about the ways our understanding of organizations will change.

I use these factors to construct images of the future organization that do not rely on modeling or on any attempt at quantification. The principal reasons I avoid quantitative methodologies are twofold: the high level of inaccuracy inherent in long-term predictions and, more importantly, the potential distortions quantifiable projections create. Bad numbers drive good ideas away; or put another way, if we place too much faith in projections and forecasts, we may miss important but less precise changes that may turn out to be more interesting and significant.

References

Agor, W. (ed.). *Intuition in Organizations.* London: Sage, 1990.

Altshuler, A., and Zegans, M. "Innovation and Creativity: Comparisons Between Public Management and Private Enterprise." *Cities,* 1990, *7,* 16–24.

Andersson, A. E. "Creativity and Regional Development." *Papers of the Regional Association,* 1985, *56,* 5–20.

Ascher, W., and Overholt, W. H. *Strategic Planning and Forecasting: Political Risk and Economic Opportunity.* New York: Wiley, 1983.

Attewell, P. "The De-Skilling Controversy." *Journal of Work and Occupation,* 1987, *13,* 323–346.

Auletta, K. *Greed and Glory on Wall Street: The Fall of the House of Lehman.* New York: Random House, 1986.

Aydalot, P. (ed.). *Milieux Innovateurs en Europe* [Innovating milieus in Europe]. Paris: Gremi, 1986.

Aydalot, P., and Keeble, D. (eds.). *High Technology Industry and Innovative Environments: The European Experience.* London: Routledge & Kegan Paul, 1988.

Azrael, J. R. *Managerial Power and Soviet Politics.* Cambridge, Mass.: Harvard University Press, 1966.

Baird, J. E., and Bradley, P. H. "Styles of Management and Commu-

References

nication: A Comparative Study of Men and Women." *Communication Monographs*, 1979, *46*, 101–111.

Baldridge, J. V., Curtis, D. V., Ecker, G., and Riley, G. L. *Policy Making and Effective Leadership: A National Study of Academic Management*. San Francisco: Jossey-Bass, 1978.

Barber, B. *The Logic and Limit of Trust*. New Brunswick, N.J.: Rutgers University Press, 1983.

Barber, B. *Strong Democracy: Participatory Politics for a New Age*. Berkeley: University of California Press, 1984.

Barnet, R. J., and Muller, R. E. *Global Reach: The Power of the Multinational Corporations*. New York: Simon & Schuster, 1974.

Baudrillard, J. *The Miror of Production*. St. Louis: Telos, 1975.

Beck, M. B. "Forecasting Environmental Change." *Journal of Forecasting*, 1991, *10*, 3–19.

Becker, H. S. "The Teacher in the Authority System of the Public School." *Journal of Educational Sociology*, 1953, *27*(3), 129–141.

Bell, W., and Olick, J. "An Epistemology for the Future Field." *Futures*, 1989, *21*, 115–135.

Benedict, R. *The Chrysanthemum and the Sword*. Boston: Houghton Mifflin, 1946.

Bennett, A. *The Death of the Organization Man*. New York: William Morrow, 1990.

Benveniste, G. *Regulation and Planning: The Case of Environmental Politics*. San Francisco: Boyd & Fraser, 1981.

Benveniste, G. *Bureaucracy*. (2nd ed.) San Francisco: Boyd & Fraser, 1983.

Benveniste, G. *Professionalizing the Organization: Reducing Bureaucracy to Enhance Effectiveness*. San Francisco: Jossey-Bass, 1987.

Benveniste, G. *Mastering the Politics of Planning: Crafting Credible Plans and Policies That Make a Difference*. San Francisco: Jossey-Bass, 1989.

Berg, B. *The Crisis of the Working Mother: Resolving the Conflict Between Family and Work*. New York: Summit Books, 1986.

280

References

Berman, P. "From Compliance to Learning: Implementing Legally Induced Reform." In D. L. Kirp and D. N. Jensen (eds.), *School Days, Rules Days*. Philadelphia: Falmer Press, 1986.

Bezold, C., and Olson, R. *The Information Millennium: Alternative Futures*. Washington, D.C.: Information Industry Association, 1986.

Blau, F. D. *Equal Pay in the Office*. Lexington, Mass.: D. C. Heath, 1977.

Bledstein, B. J. *The Culture of Professionalism: The Middle Class and the Development of Higher Education in America*. New York: Norton, 1976.

Bluestone, B., and Bennett, H. *The Great American Job Machine: The Proliferation of Low-Wage Employment in the U.S. Economy*. Washington, D.C.: Joint Economic Committee, United States Congress, 1986.

Bohland, J. R., and Gist, J. "The Spatial Consequences of Bureaucratic Decision Making." *Environment and Planning*, 1983, *15*, 1489–1500.

Bowman, J. S. "Whistle-Blowing: Literature and Resource Materials." *Public Administration Review*, 1983, *43*, 271–276.

Brazelton, B. T. *Working and Caring*. Reading, Mass.: Addison-Wesley, 1985.

Bright, J. R., and Schoeman, M.E.F. *A Guide to Practical Technological Forecasting*. Englewood Cliffs, N.J.: Prentice-Hall, 1973.

Brintnall, M. "Political Science and the Savings and Loan Crisis." *Political Science and Politics*, 1991, *24*, 432–433.

Burke, E. M. "Citizen Participation Strategies." *Journal of the American Institute of Planners*, 1968, *34*, 287–294.

Burke, E. M. *A Participatory Approach to Urban Planning*. New York: Human Sciences Press, 1979.

Burns, T., and Stalker, G. M. *The Management of Innovation*. London: Tavistock, 1961.

Cann, A., and Siegfried, W. D. "Gender Stereotypes and Dimensions of Effective Leader Behavior." *Sex Roles*, 1990, *23*, 413–419.

Carrier, H. D. "Artificial Intelligence and Metaphor Making: Some

281

References

Philosophic Considerations." *Knowledge in Society,* 1990, *3,* 46–61.

Castells, M. (ed.). *High Technology, Space, and Society.* Newbury Park, Calif.: Sage, 1985.

Castells, M. *The Informational City: Information Technology, Economic Restructuring, and the Urban-Regional Process.* Oxford: Basil Blackwell, 1989.

Chao, Y. T. "Culture and Work Organization: The Chinese Case." *International Journal of Psychology,* 1990, *25,* 583–592.

Cleveland, H. "Information, Fairness, and the Status of Women." *Futures,* 1989, *21,* 33–37.

Coates, J. F., and Jarratt, J. "What Futurists Believe: Agreements and Disagreements." *The Futurist,* 1990, *24*(6), 22–28.

Coates, J. F., Jarratt, J., and Mahaffie, J. B. *Future Work: Seven Critical Forces Reshaping Work and the Work Force in North America.* San Francisco: Jossey-Bass, 1990.

Cohen, S. S., and Zysman, J. *Manufacturing Matters: The Myth of the Postindustrial Economy.* New York: Basic Books, 1987.

Cole, R. E. *Strategies for Learning: Small-Group Activities in American, Japanese, and Swedish Industries.* Berkeley: University of California Press, 1989.

Comfort, L. K. (ed.). *Managing Disaster: Strategies and Policy Perspectives.* Durham, N.C.: Duke University Press, 1988.

Coombs, P. H. *The World Educational Crisis: A Systems Analysis.* New York: Oxford University Press, 1968.

Coriat, B. *L'Atelier et le Robot* (The workshop and the robot). Paris: Christian Bourgois, 1990.

Crozier, M. *The Bureaucratic Phenomenon.* Chicago: University of Chicago Press, 1964.

Daft, R. L. *Organization Theory and Design.* St. Paul, Minn.: West, 1983.

Daft, R. L., and Lengel, R. H. "Organizational Information Requirements, Media Richness, and Structural Design." *Management Science,* 1986, *32,* 554–571.

Deaux, K., and Ullman, J. C. *Women of Steel: Female Blue-Collar Workers in the Basic Steel Industry.* New York: Praeger, 1983.

References

Denmark, F. L. "Styles of Leadership." *Psychology of Women Quarterly*, 1977, *2*, 99–113.

Derrida, J. *Derrida Reader: Between the Blinds*. London: Harvester Wheatsheaf, 1991.

Douglas, M., and Wildavsky, A. *Risk and Culture: An Essay on the Selection of Technical and Environmental Dangers*. Berkeley: University of California Press, 1982.

Drucker, P. F. "The Coming of the New Organization." *Harvard Business Review*, 1988, *88*, 45–53.

Drucker, P. F. *Managing the Future: The 1990s and Beyond*. New York: Dutton, 1992.

Duerst-Lahti, G. "But Women Play the Game Too: Communication, Control, and Influence in Administrative Decision Making." *Administration and Society*, 1990, *22*, 182–205.

Dunning, J. H. (ed.). *Multinational Enterprise*. New York: Praeger, 1972.

Durkheim, É. *The Division of Labor in Society*. New York: Macmillan, 1933. (First published in French in 1893.)

Eagly, A. H., Makhijani, M., and Klonsky, B. G. "Gender and the Evaluation of Leaders: A Meta-Analysis." *Psychological Bulletin*, 1992, *8*, 3–22.

Eckblad, G. *Scheme Theory*. New York: Academic Press, 1981.

Eells, R. *Global Corporations: The Emergent System of World Economic Power*. New York: Interbook, 1972.

Elliston, F., and others. *Whistle-Blowing: Managing Dissent in the Workplace*. New York: Praeger, 1985.

Fabritius, M. M. *Saving the Savings and Loan: The U.S. Thrift Industry and the Texas Experience 1950–1988*. New York: Praeger, 1989.

Fayol, H. *General and Industrial Management*. London: Pitman, 1949. (First published in 1919.)

Feldman, M. S., and March, J. G. "Information in Organizations as Signal and Symbol." *Administrative Science Quarterly*, 1981, *26*, 171–187.

Fenn, M. *In the Spotlight: Women Executives in a Changing Environment*. Englewood Cliffs, N.J.: Prentice-Hall, 1980.

Flaceliere, R. *Greek Oracles*. New York: Norton, 1965.

283

References

Fleishman, E. A., and Hunt, J. G. (eds.). *Current Developments in the Study of Leadership*. Carbondale: Southern Illinois University Press, 1973.

Forester, T. "The Myth of the Electronic Cottage." *Futures*, 1988, *20*, 227–240.

Friedan, B. *The Feminine Mystique*. New York: Dell, 1963.

Fuchs, V. *Women's Quest for Economic Equality*. Cambridge, Mass.: Harvard University Press, 1988.

Fulk, J., and Steinfield, C. (eds.). *Organizations and Communication Technology*. Newbury Park, Calif.: Sage, 1990.

Galbraith, J. *Organization Design*. Reading, Mass.: Addison-Wesley, 1977.

Ginzberg, E. "The Job Problem." *Scientific American*, 1977, *237*, 43–51.

Gioia, D. A., and Poole, P. P. "Scripts in Organizational Behavior." *Academy of Management Review*, 1984, *9*, 449–459.

Glazer, B. G. (ed.). *Organizational Careers*. Chicago: Aldine, 1968.

Goodman, P. S., Sproull, L. S., and Associates. *Technology and Organizations*. San Francisco: Jossey-Bass, 1990.

Googins, B., and Burden, D. S. *Managing Work and Family: Stress in Corporations*. Boston: Boston University School of Social Work, 1987.

Gordon, S. *Prisoners of Men's Dreams: Striking Out for a New Feminine Future*. Boston: Little, Brown, 1991.

Granick, D. *Management of the Industrial Firm in the USSR: A Study in Soviet Economic Planning*. New York: Columbia University Press, 1955.

Gutek, B. A. *Sex and the Workplace: The Impact of Sexual Behavior and Harassment on Women, Men, and Organizations*. San Francisco: Jossey-Bass, 1985.

Gutek, B. A., Cohen, A. G., and Konrad, A. M. "Predicting Social-Sexual Behavior at Work: A Contact Hypothesis." *Academy of Management Journal*, 1990, *33*, 560–577.

Hagebak, B. R. "Forgiveness Factor: Taking the Risk Out of Efforts to Integrate Human Services." *Public Administration Review*, 1982, *42*, 72–76.

Halaby, C. N. "Sexual Inequality in the Work Place: An Employer-

References

Specific Analysis of Pay Differences." *Social Science Research*, 1979, *8*, 79–104.

Halal, W. E., and Nikitin, A. I. "One World: The Coming Synthesis of a New Capitalism and a New Socialism." *The Futurist*, 1990, *24*(6), 8–14.

Hall, P. *The Generation of Innovative Milieux: An Essay in Theoretical Synthesis.* Berkeley: University of California, Institute of Urban and Regional Development, Mar. 1990.

Hanson, J. W., and Brembeck, C. S. (eds.). *Education and the Development of Nations.* New York: Holt, Rinehart & Winston, 1966.

Harris, P. R. *Management in Transition: Transforming Managerial Practices and Organizational Strategies for a New Work Culture.* San Francisco: Jossey-Bass, 1985.

Hart, S. "Managing Knowledge in Policy Making and Decision Making." *Knowledge: Creation, Diffusion, Utilization*, 1986, *8*, 94–108.

Hearn, J., and Parkin, W. *Sex at Work: The Power and Paradox of Organization Sexuality.* New York: St. Martin's Press, 1987.

Heckscher, C. *The New Unionism: Employee Involvement in the Changing Corporation.* New York: Basic Books, 1988.

Heimer, C. A. *Reactive Risk and Rational Action: Managing Moral Hazard in Insurance Contracts.* Berkeley: University of California Press, 1985.

Heithoff, K. A., and Lohr, K. N. (eds.). *Effectiveness and Outcomes in Health Care.* Washington, D.C.: National Academy, 1990.

Hertz, R. *More Equal Than Others: Women and Men in Dual Career Marriages.* Berkeley: University of California Press, 1986.

Higginson, M. V., and Quick, T. L. *The Ambitious Woman's Guide to a Successful Career.* (Rev. ed.) New York: AMACOM, 1980.

Hirschhorn, L. *Beyond Mechanization: Work and Technology in a Postindustrial Age.* Cambridge, Mass.: MIT Press, 1984.

Hochswender, W. "Is a Fashionable Image Empowering—or Does It Undermine Authority?" *Vogue*, Oct. 1991, pp. 230–236.

285

References

Hofstede, G. *Culture's Consequences: National Differences in Thinking and Organizing.* Newbury Park, Calif.: Sage, 1980.

Hofstede, G. *Culture's Consequences: International Differences in Work-Related Values.* Newbury Park, Calif.: Sage, 1984.

Holusha, J. "Layer by Layer to the Perfect Blend of Metals." *New York Times,* Dec. 1, 1991, p. F9.

Huber, G. P. "A Theory of the Effects of Advanced Information Technologies on Organizational Design, Intelligence, and Decision Making." *Academy of Management Review,* 1990, *15,* 47–91.

Huberman, M., and Miles, M. *Innovation Close Up.* New York: Plenum, 1984.

Huws, V., Korte, W. B., and Robinson, S. *Telework: Towards the Elusive Office.* New York: Wiley, 1989.

Illich, I. *Tools for Conviviality.* New York: Harper & Row, 1973.

Itami, H. *The Humanistic Enterprise System.* Tokyo: Chikuma-Shobo, 1987.

Jacoby, H. *The Bureaucratization of the World.* Berkeley: University of California Press, 1973.

Jantsch, E. *Technological Forecasting in Perspective.* Paris: OECD, 1967.

Jauch, L. R., and Kraft, K. L. "Strategic Management of Uncertainty." *Academy of Management Review,* 1986, *11,* 777–790.

Johnson, K. W. "Research Influence in Decision Making to Control and Prevent Violence." *Knowledge: Creation, Diffusion, Utilization,* 1985, *7,* 161–189.

Johnston, R. F., and Edwards, C. G. *Entrepreneurial Science: New Links Between Corporations, Universities, and Government.* New York: Quorum, 1987.

Jurma, W. E., and Wright, B.W.C. "Follower Reactions to Male and Female Leaders Who Maintain or Lose Reward Power." *Small Group Research,* 1990, *21,* 97–112.

Kanter, R. M. *Men and Women of the Corporation.* New York: Basic Books, 1977.

Kanter, R. M. *The Change Masters: Innovation for Productivity in*

References

the American Corporation. New York: Simon & Schuster, 1983.

Kaula, W. M. "Untrivial Pursuits." *New York Times,* Mar. 10, 1991, p. E15.

Kelley, M. "New Process Technology, Job Design, and Work Organization." *American Sociological Review,* 1990, *55,* 191–208.

Kemp, R. "Planning, Public Hearings, and the Politics of Discourse." In J. Forester (ed.), *Critical Theory and Public Life.* Cambridge, Mass.: MIT Press, 1985.

Kikuchi, M. *Japanese Electronics: A Worm's-Eye View of Its Evolution.* Tokyo: Simul, 1983.

Kilmann, R. H., Kilmann, I., and Associates. *Making Organizations Competitive: Enhancing Networks and Relationships Across Traditional Boundaries.* San Francisco: Jossey-Bass, 1990.

Korte, W. B., and Robinson, S. (eds.). *Telework: Present Situation and Future Development of a New Form of Work Organization.* Amsterdam: Elsevier, 1988.

Kraus, W. A. *Collaboration in Organization: Alternatives to Hierarchy.* New York: Human Sciences Press, 1980.

Kutscher, R., and Personick, V. "Deindustrialization and the Shift to Services." *Monthly Labor Review,* 1986, *109*(6), 3–13.

Lammers, C. J., and Hickson, D. J. (eds.). *Organizations Alike and Unlike: International and Interinstitutional Studies in the Sociology of Organizations.* London: Routledge & Kegan Paul, 1979.

Lanford, H. W. *Technological Forecasting Methodologies: A Synthesis.* Washington, D.C.: American Management Association, 1972.

Laughlin, R. J. "Causes of the Savings and Loan Debacle." *Fordham Law Review,* 1991, *59,* 301–321.

Lawrence, P. R., and Lorsch, J. W. *Organization and Environment.* Homewood, Ill.: Irwin, 1967.

Lawrence, R. *Can America Compete?* Washington, D.C.: Brookings Institution, 1984.

References

Lee, N. *Targeting the Top: Everything a Woman Needs to Know to Develop a Successful Career in Business, Year after Year.* Garden City, N.Y.: Doubleday, 1980.

Leventman, P. *Professionals Out of Work.* New York: Free Press, 1981.

Levy, F. S., Meltsner, A. J., and Wildavsky, A. *Urban Outcomes: Schools, Streets, and Libraries.* Berkeley: University of California Press, 1974.

Lincoln, J. R., and Kalleberg, A. L. *Culture, Control, and Commitment: A Study of Work Organization and Work Attitudes in the United States and Japan.* Cambridge, England: Cambridge University Press, 1990.

Lockwood, W. W. "Foundations of Japanese Industrialism." In B. E. Supple (ed.), *The Experience of Economic Growth: Case Studies in Economic History.* New York: Random House, 1963.

Lord, R. G., and Kernan, M. C. "Scripts as Determinants of Purposeful Behavior in Organizations." *Academy of Management Review,* 1987, *12,* 265–277.

Lundstedt, S. B., and Moss, H. (eds.). *Managing Innovation and Change.* Boston: Kluwer, 1989.

Lyotard, J. F. *Law, Form, Event.* New York: Columbia University Press, 1988.

Majone, G. *Evidence, Argument, and Persuasion in the Policy Process.* New Haven, Conn.: Yale University Press, 1989.

Mansfield, R., and Poole, M. (eds.). *International Perspectives on Management and Organization.* Aldershot, England: Gower, 1981.

Margolis, D. R. *The Managers: Corporate Life in America.* New York: William Morrow, 1979.

Marino, J. *Technological Forecasting for Decision Making.* New York: Elsevier, 1972.

Mayer, M. *The Greatest-Ever Bank Robbery: The Collapse of the Savings and Loan Industry.* New York: Scribners, 1990.

Miles, I. *The Poverty of Prediction.* Lexington, Mass.: Heath, 1975.

Miles, I., and others. *Information Horizons: The Long-Term Social*

References

Implications of New Information Technology. Aldershot, England: Edward Elgar, 1988.

Miller, D. B. *Managing Professionals in Research and Development.* San Francisco: Jossey-Bass, 1986.

Miller, R., and Côté, M. *Growing the Next Silicon Valley: A Guide to Successful Regional Planning.* Lexington, Mass.: D. C. Heath, 1985.

Miller, W. C. *The Creative Edge: Fostering Innovation Where You Work.* Reading, Mass.: Addison-Wesley, 1986.

Moody, K. *An Injury to All: The Decline of American Unionism.* New York: Verso, 1989.

Morgan, G. *Riding the Waves of Change: Developing Managerial Competencies for a Turbulent World.* San Francisco: Jossey-Bass, 1988.

Mueller, R. K. *The Innovation Ethic.* New York: American Management Association, 1971.

Mueller, R. K. *Corporate Networking: Building Channels of Information and Influence.* New York: Free Press, 1986.

Mumford, L. *The Pentagon of Power.* New York: Harcourt Brace Jovanovich, 1970.

Myers, C. A. (ed.). *The Impact of Computers on Management.* Cambridge, Mass.: MIT Press, 1967.

Nelkin, D. (ed.). *The Language of Risk: Conflicting Perspectives on Occupational Health.* Newbury Park, Calif.: Sage, 1985.

Newman, K. S. *Falling from Grace: The Experience of Downward Mobility in the American Middle Class.* New York: Free Press, 1988.

Nohria, N., and Eccle, R. G. (eds.). *Networks and Organizations: Structure, Form and Action.* Boston: Harvard Business School Press, 1992.

Norwood, J. "The Job Machine Has Not Broken Down." *New York Times,* Feb. 22, 1987, p. D5.

Oliver, C. "Determinants of Interorganizational Relationships: Integration and Future Direction." *Academy of Management Review,* 1990, *15,* 241–265.

Olson, J. E., Frieze, I. H., and Detlefsen, E. G. "Having It All? Com-

References

bining Work and Family in a Male and a Female Profession." *Sex Roles,* 1990, *23,* 515–533.

Oreilly, C. A., Chatman, J., and Cadwell, D. F. "People and Organizational Culture: A Profile Comparison to Assessing Person-Organization Fit." *Academy of Management Journal,* 1991, *34,* 487–516.

Orwell, G. *1984.* New York: New American Library, 1949.

Osborne, D. E., and Gaebler, T. *Reinventing Government: How the Entrepreneurial Spirit Is Transforming the Public Sector.* Reading, Mass.: Addison-Wesley, 1992.

Ouchi, W. G. *Theory Z.* Reading, Mass.: Addison-Wesley, 1981.

Parke, H. W. *Greek Oracles.* London: Hutchinson, 1967.

Parker, G. M. *Team Players and Teamwork: The New Competitive Business Strategy.* San Francisco: Jossey-Bass, 1990.

Pennings, J. M., and Marianto, F. "Technological Networking and Innovation Implementation." *Organization Science,* 1992, *3,* 356–382.

Perroux, F. *L'Economie du XXeme Siècle* (The economy of the twentieth century). Paris: Presse Universitaires de France, 1961.

Perrow, C. *Normal Accidents: Living with High-Risk Technologies.* New York: Basic Books, 1984.

Perrow, C. *Complex Organizations: A Critical Essay.* (3rd ed.) Glenview, Ill.: Scott, Foresman, 1986.

Perrucci, R., and Potter, H. R. (eds.). *Networks of Power: Organizational Actors at the National, Corporate, and Community Level.* New York: De Gruyter, 1989.

Peters, T. J. *Liberation Management: Necessary Disorganization for the Nanosecond Nineties.* New York: Knopf, 1992.

Pfeffer, J., and Ross, J. "Gender-Based Wage Differences." *Work and Occupations,* 1990, *17,* 55–78.

Porat, M. *The Information Economy.* Washington, D.C.: U.S. Department of Commerce, 1977.

Powers, D. R., Powers, M. F., Betz, F., and Aslanian, C. B. *Higher Education in Partnership with Industry.* San Francisco: Jossey-Bass, 1988.

Quennell, P. *The Pursuit of Happiness.* Boston: Little, Brown, 1988.

References

Reich, R. B. *The Work of Nations.* New York: Knopf, 1991.

Rice, R. E., and Associates. *The New Media: Communication Research and Technology.* Newbury Park, Calif: Sage, 1984.

Rice, R. E., and Shook, D. "Relations of Job Categories and Organizational Levels to Use of Communication Channels, Including Electronic Mail: A Meta-Analysis and Extension." *Journal of Management Studies,* 1990, *27,* 195–229.

Robertson, J. *Future Work: Jobs, Self-Employment, and Leisure after the Industrial Age.* Aldershot, England: Gower, 1985.

Robins, K., and Hepworth, M. "New Technologies and the Future of Cities." *Futures,* 1988, *20,* 155–176.

Robinson, J. B. "Futures Under Glass: A Recipe for People Who Hate to Predict." *Futures,* 1990, *22,* 820–842.

Rolfe, S. E., and Damm, W. (eds.). *Multinational Corporations in the World Economy.* New York: Praeger, 1970.

Rostow, W. W. *The Stages of Economic Growth: A Non-Communist Manifesto.* Cambridge, England: Cambridge University Press, 1963.

Rubin, L. J., and Borgers, S. B. "Sexual Harassment in Universities During the 1980s." *Sex Roles,* 1990, *23,* 397–411.

Ryavec, K. W. *Implementation of Soviet Economic Reforms: Political, Organizational, and Social Processes.* New York: Praeger, 1975.

Sabatier, P. "Knowledge, Policy-Oriented Learning, and Policy Change: An Advocacy Coalition Framework." *Knowledge: Creation, Diffusion, Innovation,* 1987, *8,* 649–692.

Savage, C. M. *Fifth Generation Management: Integrating Enterprises Through Human Networking.* Bedford, Mass.: Digital, 1990.

Saxenian, A. L. "Regional Networks and the Resurgence of Silicon Valley." Berkeley: University of California, Institute of Urban and Regional Planning, Dec. 1989.

Saxenian, A. L. "Contrasting Patterns of Business Organization in the Silicon Valley." Berkeley: University of California, Institute of Urban and Regional Planning, Apr. 1991.

Schermerhorn, J. R., Jr. "Determinants of Interorganizational Co-

References

operation." *Academy of Management Journal*, 1984, *27*, 811–829.

Schnaars, S. P. *Megamistakes: Forecasting and the Myth of Rapid Technological Change.* New York: Free Press, 1989.

Schumacher, E. F. *Small Is Beautiful: Economics as if People Mattered.* New York: Harper & Row, 1973.

Schumpeter, J. A. *Capitalism, Socialism, and Democracy.* (2nd ed.) New York: Harper & Row, 1947.

Schwartz, F. "Management, Women, and the New Facts of Life." *Harvard Business Review,* 1989, *89,* 65–76.

Scott, A. J., and Storper, M. (eds.). *Production Work, Territory: The Geographical Anatomy of Industrial Capitalism.* London: Allen & Unwin, 1986.

Scott, W. R. *Organizations: Rational, Natural, and Open Systems.* (3rd ed.) Englewood Cliffs, N.J.: Prentice-Hall, 1992.

Senge, P. *The Fifth Discipline: The Art and Practice of the Learning Organization.* New York: Doubleday, 1990.

Shaiken, H. *Work Transformed: Automation and Labor in the Computer Age.* New York: Holt, Rinehart & Winston, 1985.

Slaughter, R. A. "The Foresight Principle." *Futures,* 1990, *22,* 801–819.

Smirchich, L., and Morgan, G. "Leadership: The Management of Meaning." *Journal of Applied Behavioral Science,* 1982, *18,* 257–273.

Staley, E. *Small Industry Development.* Menlo Park, Calif.: Stanford Research Institute, 1958.

Stanford Research Institute. *Possible Nonmilitary Scientific Developments and Their Potential Impact on Foreign Policy Problems of the United States.* Washington, D.C.: Senate Committee on Foreign Relations, Sept. 1959.

Stankiewicz, R. *Academics and Entrepreneurs: Developing University-Industry Relations.* New York: St. Martin's Press, 1986.

Stepanek, J. E. *Small Industry Advisory Services: An International Study.* Glencoe, Ill.: The Free Press, 1960.

Susskind, L., and Elliott, M. (eds.). *Paternalism, Conflict, and Coproduction: Learning from Citizen Action and Citizen*

References

Participation in Western Europe. New York: Plenum, 1983.

Thompson, J. D. *Organizations in Action.* New York: McGraw Hill, 1967.

Thompson, P. *The Nature of Work: An Introduction to the Labour Process Debate.* (2nd ed.) London: Macmillan, 1989.

Toffler, A. *The Third Wave.* New York: Morrow, 1980.

Touraine, A. *Return of the Actor: Social Theory in Postindustrial Society.* Minneapolis: University of Minnesota Press, 1988.

Truxal, J. G. *The Age of Electronic Messages.* Cambridge, Mass.: MIT Press, 1990.

Tydeman, J. *The Futures Methodology Handbook.* Melbourne: Commission for the Future, 1988.

Vaill, P. B. *Managing as a Performing Art: New Ideas for a World of Chaotic Change.* San Francisco: Jossey-Bass, 1989.

Vallas, S. P. "The Concept of Skill: A Critical Review." *Work and Occupation,* 1990, *17,* 379–398.

Van de Ven, A. H. "On the Nature, Formation, and Maintenance of Relations Among Organizations." *Academy of Management Review,* 1976, *1,* 24–36.

Van de Ven, A. H., Angle, H., and Poole, M. S. (eds.). *Research on the Management of Innovation.* Cambridge, Mass.: Ballinger, 1988.

Veenhoven, R. *Conditions of Happiness.* Dordrecht, Holland: Reidel, 1984.

Vernon, R. *The Economic and Political Consequences of Multinational Enterprise: An Anthology.* Cambridge, Mass.: Harvard Business School, 1972.

Von Hippel, E. A. *The Sources of Innovation.* New York: Oxford University Press, 1988.

Wagar, W. W. *A Short History of the Future.* Chicago: University of Chicago Press, 1989.

Wallace, A.F.C. *The Social Context of Innovation.* Princeton, N.J.: Princeton University Press, 1982.

Walton, M. *The Deming Management Method.* New York: Putnam, 1986.

References

Walton, M. *Deming Management at Work.* New York: Putnam, 1990.

Walton, R. E. *Innovating to Compete: Lessons for Diffusing and Managing Change in the Workplace.* San Francisco: Jossey-Bass, 1987.

Weick, K. E. "Technology as Equivoque." In P. S. Goodman, L. S. Sproull, and Associates, *Technology and Organizations.* San Francisco: Jossey-Bass, 1990.

Weisman, S. R. "Japan and U.S. Struggle with Resentment." *New York Times,* Dec. 5, 1991, p. 5.

Weiss, C. H., and Bucavalas, M. J. *Social Science Research and Decision Making.* New York: Columbia University Press, 1980.

Wiewel, W., and Hunter, A. "The Interorganizational Network as a Resource: A Comparative Case Study of Organizational Genesis." *Administrative Science Quarterly,* 1985, *30,* 482–496.

Wilensky, H. *Organizational Intelligence: Knowledge and Policy in Government and Industry.* New York: Basic Books, 1967.

Wilterdink, N. "Images of National Character in an International Organization: Five European Nations Compared." *Netherland Journal of Social Sciences,* 1992, *28,* 31–49.

Index

Index

Index

Index

Index

change, 51–52, 55–56, 117,
118; and client participation,
120; and commitment,
102–103; and communications,
145; and continuity, 55, 103;
and control errors, 90; and co-
operation/communitarianism,
53; decentralization, 36–38,
238; and democratization/pro-
fessionalization, 55; and discretion, 111–112; and environment scanning/boundary
spanning, 54–55; and error
management, 138, 249–251;
and family, 192, 238, 242, 246,
258–259; feminization, 23–31,
238, 258; governance, 74, 102;
and groups, 127, 138, 247;
human resource management,
241–246; humanization, 249;
informality, 54, 88, 127; and interdependent organizations,
39–42; international culture,
258–263; and interorganizational teams, 128; and management, 247; and meta rules, 97;
and networks, 35, 54–55,
129–134, 247; and nonroutinized behavior, 113; and organizational demise, 258; participa-
tiveness, 143, 146; and
politicized language, 147; po-
rosity, 123, 258; and power,
130, 132; and process/output
controls, 102; and professions,
132–133; results orientation,
258; and rewards, 126, 137,
246, 248; risk management,
118; and rules, 98–99; senior
staff model, 111; and skilled
crafts, 245–246; smallness, 41;
and synergy factor, 136–137;
temporal qualities, 131–132;
themes, 235–237; trends shaping, 3–56, 238; and trust, 99,

257; and unions, 115, 152; and
work force, 241–242, 246;
worker types, 38, 115, 242; and
worker values, 102–103; workplace change, 152, 258–259.
See also Organizations
Future trends: competition for
ideas, 4–14; new organizational understanding, 52–56;
new technologies, 31–42; organizational culture feminization,
23–31; rapid change institutionalization, 42–52; research and
development, 6–8; work-force
education, 14–23
Futuristic scenarios/analysis
themes: adaptive organization,
238–240; decentralization/em-
powerment, 235; decentralized
discretion, 246–249; error correction, 236; human resource
management, 241–246; internalized regulatory practices,
252–254; large organization
continuation, 237–238; new
professional institutions,
235–236; postoccurrence error
correction, 249–251
Futuristic scenarios: The Firm,
191–233; Informator, 33–34,
186–189; magnetic vehicle factory, 36–37, 67–68, 106,
112–114; New System,
153–190
Futurists, 31–32

G

Gaebler, T., 103
Galbraith, J., 57, 86
Gender: equality, 25–27; and line-
age, 25; and management style,
29–31; and wages, 27–28
Ginzberg, E., 19, 226
Gioia, D. A., 202
Gist, J., 203

300

Index

Glazer, B. D., 4, 126
Goodman, P. S., 33
Googins, B., 28
Gordon, S., 30
Governance: dual, model, 110–112; participatory, 74, 102. *See also* Democratization
Government: decentralization, 120; and economic competition, 5–6, 11, 56; and international information, 9; and private sector relations, 6, 56; regulation of common errors, 69. *See also* Private-public sector relations; Public sector; Regulatory interventions
Granick, D., 77
Groups: affinity, 131, 140, 142; characteristics, 128–134; cohesion, 139–142; and communication, 147; defined, 127; efforts, 142–143; and future organizations, 127, 138, 247; invitational nature, 128–129; long-lasting quality, 131–132; management, 133; and organizational change, 146; and power, 129–131; professional linkages, 132–133; resources, 129, 247; and trust, 142, 257. *See also* Economic/trade groups; Networks; Spin-offs
Growth: and economic internationalization, 12; myths of, 12. *See also* Economic/social development
Gutek, B. A., 28

H

Hagebak, B. R., 137, 203
Halaby, C. N., 27
Halal, W. E., 214
Hall, P., 125
Hanson, J. W., 15
Harris, P. R., 109

Hart, S., 145, 204
Hearn, J., 28
Heckscher, C., 196, 224
Heimer, C. A., 62
Heithoff, K. A., 104
Hepworth, M., 196
Hertz, R., 28
Hickson, D. J., 259, 261
Higginson, M. V., 23
Higher education: access, 22; and careers, 15; deficiencies, 244–245; differentiation, 19, 22; quality issues, 20–21; and women, 27. *See also* Credentialing; Education; Universities
Hirschhorn, L., 200
Hochswender, W., 219
Hofstede, G., 48, 259
Holusha, J., 39
Huber, G. P., 32
Huberman, M., 134
Human resource management: in The Firm, 222; in future organizations, 241–246
Hunt, J. G., 133
Hunter, A., 196
Huws, V., 35

I

Ideas: development/translation of, 13; international competition for, 4–14; queuing of, and change, 43; world forum generation of, 39. *See also* Innovation
Incentives, for change, 11
Independent creativity, 50
Informal groups. *See* Groups
Information: leaks, 89; and public sector needs, 9; worldwide, channels, 9
Informator, 33–34
Innovation: and affinity groups, 142; and articulation errors, 81–82; bottom-up, 124, 130,

301

Index

Learning. *See* Organizational learning

Lee, N., 23

Lengel, R. H., 35

Leventman, P., 46

Levy, F. S., 104

Lincoln, J. R., 259

Linkages: automotive-financial industry, 120–121; and decentralization, 120; groups/networks–professions, 132–133; organization-environment, 119–120; public-private, 121

Lockwood, W. W., 47

Lohr, K. N., 104

Long-term thinking, 50, 52. *See also* Strategic planning

Lord, R. G., 202

Lorsch, J. W., 57, 86

Lyotard, J. F., 206

M

Mahaffie, J. B., 27

Majone, G., 118, 204

Makhijani, M., 133

Management: bureaucratic organization, 108; control, 247; and discretion, 256; gender-based, differences, 29–31, 133, 258; Japanese, structure, 46; and marginal errors, 63; and meta rules, 97; and process/output controls, 102; and professionals, 74; seniority rights, 45–46; and telematics, 32; worker agreements, 114; worker separation, 108

Managers, employment anxiety, 46–47

Mansfield, R., 260

March, J. G., 202

Marginal errors: and articulation errors, 75, 78; characteristics, 61–62; and clients, 63; and control, 63, 64; and decentralization, 65–68; defined, 61; future, 63–68; and human/ technological error, 62, 63–65; key issue, 68; and management, 63; and opaque technologies, 64–65; and quality, 65; and risk, 62–63; tolerance level, 62–64. *See also* Errors

Margolis, D. R., 27

Marianto, F., 255

Marino, J., 270

Market demand: and articulation, 76; and artistic creativity, 119

Markets: and governmental cooperation, 11; internationalization of, 4

Masculine management style, 29–30

Mayer, M., 251

Media richness, 35–36

Meltsner, A. J., 104

Merit: and privilege/aristocracy, 14, 26; and women's role, 24. *See also* Pay; Rewards

Meta rules: and continuity, 125; defined, 96; and management, 97; and rules, 95–96

Methodology: of book, 277–278; brainstorming/Delphi technique, 275–276; modeling, 274–275; morphological analysis, 272–273; normative, 276–277; review of, 270–277; scenario writing, 273–274; trends/extrapolations, 271–272

Miles, I., 34, 268

Miles, M., 134

Milieu: creative, 136, 238; defined, 125–126; importance of, 125; innovative, 173

Miller, D. B., 132, 134

Miller, R., 132

Miller, W. C., 109

Mobility: education and social,

303

Index

15–21; women's career, 26;
work-force, 243
Modeling, 274–275
Moody, K., 224
Morgan, G., 200
Morphological analysis, 272–273
Mueller, R. K., 132, 197
Muller, R. E., 89
Multinational corporations, 89,
259–260

N

Nation states, 10
Nelkin, D., 203
Networks: characteristics,
128–134; and communication,
147; defined, 128; and future
organizations, 129, 247; invitational nature, 128–129; long-
lasting quality, 131–132; management, 133; organizational,
35, 54–55; and politics, 72–73;
and power, 129–131; professional linkages, 132–133; resources, 129, 247; and secrecy,
89; and trust, 257. *See also*
Groups; Spin-offs
New professional institutions: and
adaptive creativity, 173–174;
and future trends, 152; and organizational continuity/stability,
127; organizational role, 74,
127; origins, 152–153; pur-
pose/mission, 116; theme,
235–236
New System: accomplishments,
170–175; and bureaucracy,
190; and change, 171–174; and
conflict, 188; and coordination,
171–174; and democratization,
172; and discrimination,
182–184; and error-correction
theme, 236; and ethical discourse, 174–175; and external
controls, 170–171; and human

laziness/ineptitude, 178–180;
and human self-interest,
176–178; and planning,
184–188; and Professional
Boards, 169–170; and Professional Councils, 159–164; and
Professional Courts, 164–169;
and Professional Governors,
154–159; and secrecy,
188–189; student comments
on, 176–190; third-force
theme, 235–236; workers, 175;
workplace milieu, 173
New technologies: and decentralization, 36–38, 239; and decision making, 113–114; and independent organizations,
39–42; and information leaks,
89; and international ex-
changes, 39; and management
hierarchy, 46; and media richness, 35–36; and nonroutinized labor, 242; and organizational structure, 32–35;
predicting, 31–32; pro-
grammed, 33; and regulatory
interventions, 71; and social/
economic transformations, 83;
telematic, 31–32; and whistle-
blowing, 72; and work-force
changes, 38–39, 241–243. *See
also* Robotics; Technology
Newman, K. S., 46
Nikitin, A. I., 214
Nineteenth-century organizations,
126
Nohria, N., 128
Normative methodologies,
276–277
Norwood, J., 226
Nurturing management. *See* Feminine management style

O

Olick, J., 265
Oliver, C., 197

304

Index

Olson, J. E., 28
Olson, R., 34
Oreilly, C. A., 259
Organic solidarity, 75
Organizational culture: feminization of, 23–31; and gender equality, 25–27; international, 258–263; Japanese, 47–51; and management style, 29–31; and pay inequalities, 27–28; and sexual harassment, 28–29; and work, 259
Organizational learning: and articulation errors, 79; and environmental adaptation, 86; Japanese, 47; and management, 102; and process/output controls, 101; and rapid change, 42. *See also* Education; Higher education
Organizational responsibilities: and bureaucratic model, 108; and dual governance model, 110–112; and partnership model, 109; and professional model, 108–109; and senior staff model, 109–110
Organizations: adaptability, 53–54, 84; American vs. Japanese, 50–51; bureaucratic model, 55, 108; and change, 42; and collective vs. individual advantages, 52–53; conceptual evolution, 254–258; continuation, 237–238; control methods, 99–107; cultural adaptations, 51; defensive strategies, 239–240; demise, 258; and environment, 41–42; environmental linkages, 119–121; and government–private sector relations, 56; and information leaks, 89; insularity, 9; and long- vs. short-term thinking, 52, 53; management/work-

force separation, 108; and merit, 14–15; and meta rules, 97; multinational, 89; new understanding of, 52–56; nineteenth-century, 126; open system theory, 85; outcomes selection, 106; paternalism, 45; politicization, 72–73; porous, 121–125; professional structure models, 55, 108–112; rule usage, 97–99; and social distancing, 50–51; structure, 32–35; survival/advantage, 52–53; and trust, 53; twentieth-century, 126, 174, 254–255; and uncertainty, 58, 86–87; and whistle-blowing, 72–73; worldwide, linkages, 40. *See also* Future organizations; New professional institutions; Organizational culture
Orwell, G., 35
Osborne, D. E., 103
Ouchi, W. G., 50
Outcome controls: and cohesion maintenance, 106–107; measurement, 103–104; and professional workers, 115; relevance, 104; usage, 100
Outcomes: characteristics, 105; defined, 104; and envelope supervision, 113; vs. outputs, 104–106; selection, 106–107
Output controls. *See* Process/output controls
Outputs, 104–106
Out-sourcing, 46
Overholt, W. H., 270

P

Painting, 119
Parker, G. M., 197
Parkin, W., 28
Partnership model, 109
Pay, 27–28. *See also* Rewards

305

Index

Pennings, J. M., 255
Perroux, F., 136
Perrow, C., 52, 62
Perrucci, R., 128
Personick, V., 19
Peters, T. J., 3, 120, 131
Pfeffer, J., 27
Pittsburgh, Pa., steel production example, 83
Planning: and articulation errors, 79; investment, 8; long-term, 8; and New System, 184–188; nonbureaucratic, 142. *See also* Strategic planning
Political action, 72–73
Poole, M., 260
Poole, M. S., 42
Poole, P. P., 202
Porat, M., 33
Potter, H. R., 128
Power: decentralization, 132; defined, 88; and groups/networks, 129–131; in Japanese firms, 48–49; male/female, balance, 26–27; and problem solving, 130; redistribution, 130
Powers, D. R., 207
Powers, M. F., 207
Predictions/forecasts/projections: characteristics, 266–270; and continuity/discontinuity assumptions, 266–267; and domain/theory selectivity, 266; and imaginary/intuitive content, 267–270
Private-public sector relations: barriers, 11; and change/innovation, 56; cooperative, 6, 56; and economic competition, 9; linkages, 121; and worldwide economic/trade groups, 10–11. *See also* Government; Public sector
Problem solving, 38, 130
Process/output controls: in educa-

tion, 100–101; and future organizations, 102; problems, 101; and rapid change, 101; and reform, 103; and routinized work, 115; usefulness, 103–104
Production/distribution: and innovations, 39; internationalization, 40–41
Professional Boards: description, 169–170; functions, 169
Professional Councils: functions, 159–160; futuristic interview, 161–164; resources, 160
Professional Courts: characteristics, 167–169; functions, 164–165; futuristic editorial, 166–167; judges, 166; origins, 165
Professional Governors (PGs): characteristics, 154–155; constituencies, 157–158; decentralization, 157; electronics plant example, 155–156; functions, 156–157; futuristic interview, 158–159; resources, 156
Professional models: defined, 108–109; dual governance, 110–112; partnership, 109; senior staff, 109–110; types, 109
Professional Representatives, 160
Professional structures, 107–116
Professional teams, 112
Professionalism, 14, 55
Professionals: conflict resolution, 111; and dual governance model, 110–112; elite, 14–15; and partnership model, 109; and senior staff model, 109–110
Professions, 132–133
Programmed technology, 33
Public sector: change incentives, 11; political economies, 9; private sector linkages, 121; and risk taking, 121. *See also* Gov-

Index

Index

T

Task teams, 112, 113
Teachers, 126, 139–140, 143
Teams: defined, 128; interorganizational, 128; professional, 112; and quality performance, 67; task, 112, 113; work-force, 67
Technical assistance, 134–137
Technology: and apathy, 65; and control, 63; and education/ training demand, 17–18; high-risk, 62; opaque, 63–65; transfers, 12. *See also* New technologies
Technology operators, 38, 115, 242, 246
Telematics: future advances, 31–32; Informator futuristic scenario, 33–34, 186–189; and management practices, 32; and problem solving, 38; and telework, 34–35
Telework, 34–35
Third force. *See* New professional institutions
Third World countries, 12, 43, 44, 136
Thompson, J. D., 36, 79, 85
Thompson, P., 223
Time: and articulation errors, 76–77; and external intervention, 71–72; and outcome measures, 105
Toffler, A., 196
Touraine, A., 196
Trade blocs. *See* Economic/trade groups
Training, 17–18. *See also* Education
Trends. *See* Future trends
Trust: and accountability, 53; and competition, 53; and future organizations, 99, 257; and groups/networks, 142, 257; and

informal organizational linkages, 88–89; and organizational demise, 258; and rapid change, 258
Truxal, J. G., 33
Twentieth-century organizations, 126, 174, 254–255
Twenty-first century organizations. *See* Future organizations
Tydeman, J., 270

U

Ullman, J. C., 29
Uncertainty: and adaptive behavior, 59; and articulation errors, 78–80; denial of, 86–87; and errors, 59–60; and open system theory, 85–86; organizational response to, 86–87; oyster worker example, 58–60, 66; reducing, 58; and regulatory interventions, 70; and rules/regulations, 58, 92; and social life, 58
Unemployment, 46–47
UNESCO, 260–261
Unions, 115, 152
United States: educational deficiencies, 18, 244; international competition, 18; organizational insularity, 9; protectionism, 44–45; as world power, 45
Universities: future, 245; public, 20; and research, 7–8, 20–21. *See also* Higher education
U.S. Department of State, 121–123

V

Vaill, P. B., 146, 208
Vallas, S. P., 200, 223
Van de Ven, A. H., 42, 197
Veenhoven, R., 215
Vernon, R., 89
Von Hippel, E. A., 42

309